The Guaranteed Goof-Proof Healthy Microwave Cookbook

The
GUARANTEED
Goof-Proof

Healthy
Microwave
Cookbook

Margie "The Microwhiz®" Kreschollek

in consultation with Beverly Bentivegna, R.D., M.Ed.

BANTAM BOOKS

NEW YORK · TORONTO · LONDON · SYDNEY · AUCKLAND

THE GUARANTEED GOOF-PROOF HEALTHY MICROWAVE COOKBOOK
A Bantam Book / January 1990

Fashions by Donnkenny, Inc.

Book design by Ann Gold.

Library of Congress Cataloging-in-Publication Data
Kreschollek, Margie.
   The guaranteed goof-proof healthy microwave cookbook / by
Margie Kreschollek with Beverly Bentivegna.
         p.   cm.
   Includes index.
   ISBN 0-553-34794-2
   1. Microwave cookery.   I. Bentivegna, Beverly.   II. Title.
TX832.K683   1990
641.5′882—dc20   89-6927
                                                                CIP

Published simultaneously in the United States and Canada

Bantam Books are published by Bantam Books, a division of Bantam
Doubleday Dell Publishing Group, Inc. Its trademark, consisting of the
words "Bantam Books" and the portrayal of a rooster, is Registered in
U.S. Patent and Trademark Office and in other countries. Marca
Registrada. Bantam Books, 666 Fifth Avenue, New York, New York 10103.

PRINTED IN THE UNITED STATES OF AMERICA

BG   0 9 8 7 6 5 4 3 2 1

To the memory of my dear uncle,
Eugene J. Wood,
and my special father-in-law,
William L. Kreschollek, Senior

Contents

Acknowledgments

Much love and many thanks to my mom, Ann Lorinsky, for all her help in testing and retesting my recipes. My dad, Mindy Lorinsky, and my sister Candi for all the taste-testing. Other very good tasters include Gaile Piatt and the staff at Baldwin Middle School in Guilford, Connecticut. A big thank-you goes to you all.

Waldbaums/Foodmart, Rubbermaid Inc., Corning Glass Works, Nordic Ware, E-Z-Por Corporation, McCormick & Company, Inc., Pet Inc. (manufacturers of Progresso products), and First Brands Corporation (manufacturers of Glad products) all gave me the opportunity to experiment with and use their products.

Donnkenny, Inc., has always believed in me, and for that I can't thank them enough. Clairol, Inc., also deserves my many thanks.

My new test kitchen would not be the wonderful work center it is today without the help of Ann Collins and Amana, Bunny Park and Wes-Pine Millwork, Inc., General Electric, Franke Inc., Sullivan Tile Distributors, Magic Chef, Black and Decker, Ray Coyle, Robert Manzi of Grossman's for the kitchen design, Premium Lighting Center, and Juno Lighting.

Fran McCullough, Coleen O'Shea, and Joan Shiel at Bantam, along with Doe Coover, my agent, have always been there for me, and I hope you all know how much I appreciate you.

Foreword

To a nutritionist there is no more welcome news than to hear that people are paying attention to what they eat. Today's emphasis on eating leaner, lighter foods is accompanied by a healthy interest in fresh, natural ingredients. And if you have a microwave oven, you're in a perfect position to take full advantage of the latest research on healthy cooking and eating.

The microwave was invented to help save time in the kitchen, it's true. And it does! But did you know it can also save calories? Food prepared in a microwave requires less fat and salt than food cooked conventionally. You also lose fewer vitamins and nutrients by cooking vegetables in your microwave, while meat prepared in a microwave is much leaner, because the microwaving process extracts more fat than frying, roasting, or broiling. We now know, for example, that fish is a healthful substitute for meat (especially red meat). As a source of protein it is lower in calories and cholesterol and high in certain oils that researchers feel may help prevent heart disease. And what could be easier than fresh fish sprinkled with a little lemon juice and paprika and then cooked for just a few minutes? (For fancier occasions, you can dress up the fish with a fresh sauce or topping—see "Fish".)

Because the microwave is such a time-saver, it encourages you to use more fresh ingredients and cook from scratch. In little more time than it takes to heat up a frozen TV dinner or "lean" entree, you can prepare an elegant Seafood Paella or Burgundy Beef or a hearty Lamb and Spinach Casserole or Triple-Cheese Lasagne Swirls. Not only does homemade food taste better than store-bought prepared foods; it can also be much healthier. Many frozen entrees have surprisingly high levels of sodium, which can be dangerous to many people. By using the recipes in this book, you'll know exactly what is in everything you make, and you'll be able to tailor your cooking to your own needs or those of your family.

Not all nutritional advice is as simple as "cut down on red meat" or "avoid preservatives and excess sodium," of course. It's a rare week that we don't pick up the newspaper or turn on the television and hear of some new problem with the food we eat or some new miracle food. Omega-3. Oat bran. Cholesterol. Calcium. Saturated fats . . . polyunsaturated fats . . . monounsaturated fats! It's hard to separate fact from fad. And harder still to keep up with current guidelines and specific recommendations, not to mention conflicting reports.

There are, however, some basic considerations that everyone should bear in mind these days, and we have designed the recipes in this book with these concerns in mind. The authorities we trust most are the surgeon general and the American Heart Association. In the section that follows we've outlined their dietary guidelines to help you cut down on three key components in food: cholesterol, fat, and sodium, the principal offenders. Take a moment to read through this section so you get the maximum benefit from the book. In addition, each recipe in the book lists the total calories as well as the amount of these specific elements. Each recipe also has a nutritional profile, identifying it as low, medium, or high in sodium, cholesterol, and calories. So if you cook for someone with a special need (e.g., someone under doctor's orders to reduce sodium intake or to cut back on cholesterol significantly), you'll find that information at your fingertips.

Researchers seem to agree on a few other general guidelines: One is that using a wide variety of foods is the best approach to healthy eating. Yet to many of us the number of new foods available in the supermarkets is overwhelming. My local grocery store, for example, now sells 12 kinds of lettuce greens, six varieties of mushrooms, and several fruits and vegetables whose names I can't even pronounce! You should make an effort to experiment with new foods, however; the greater the variety of foods in your daily diet, the less likely you'll be deficient in any nutrient, vitamin, or mineral.

Second, it's recommended we consume less refined sugar (as in table sugar) and foods containing sugar. Instead, eat fresh fruits, and if fresh isn't available, substitute frozen fruit or fruit canned in its own juices. Avoid those that are packed in heavy syrup. (Honey and molasses aren't necessarily better choices than cane sugar, but molasses does have more potassium.)

Fiber has been shown to have many beneficial properties. It can aid in the prevention of some cancers, varicose veins, gallbladder disease, and heart disease, as well as help people lose weight. Fiber is found in all fruits, vegetables, and whole grains. It's recommended we eat three to four servings per day of fruits and vegetables and two to three servings of whole-grain sources. Because so much of our food is refined, it may be difficult to achieve enough fiber in our everyday diet. A supplement can be purchased in any supermarket or drugstore. You can also add fiber to your diet by adding unprocessed bran to your foods.

Researchers also seem to agree now that alcohol represents only empty calories and offers few nutrients, and as a result it should be used in moderation. When you cook with wine or spirits, most of the alcohol evaporates, leaving only the flavor to enhance the taste of the dish. You'll notice in many of the recipes here that we have substituted wine for margarine to sauté vegetables; this adds flavor without excess fat.

Finally, if you eat a balanced diet from the four major food groups—fruits and vegetables; grains, such as breads, cereals, and pastas; dairy products; and protein (meats, fish, and poultry) —you probably don't need any vitamin supplements, especially if they cause you to exceed the recommended daily allowance (RDA) of any mineral or vitamin.

I have been a nutritionist for nearly 20 years now, and in that time I have observed and helped a great many people with their dietary concerns. Some were young single people; others were older or had families. Some just wanted to watch their calories in order to shed a few pounds; others were under strict medical advice to reduce their cholesterol or sodium intake. But all these individuals had something in common: They were all busy people who didn't want to give up good taste in food.

How often I wished I could find a book that combined sound health advice with interesting, easy-to-prepare recipes. When Margie Kreschollek asked me to help her create a goof-proof microwave cookbook for healthy eating, I couldn't resist. With her extensive knowledge of microwave cooking techniques and my background in nutrition research, we can promise you that the recipes here are both flavorful and healthy—and of course they're goof-proof! We spent literally hours testing and retesting each one until the results satisfied both of us. The baking chapter was the hardest to do. To be sure our finished products would appeal to even the most discriminating audience (kids!), we took several finished desserts to a local junior high school. We knew we had succeeded when several teachers asked us for our recipes!

Eating healthfully doesn't mean the end of good taste. Nor does it have to mean spending endless hours shopping for exotic ingredients or creating complicated dishes. It is my hope that this book will serve as a catalyst for you, to encourage healthy eating and living habits for both you and your family.

—Beverly Bentivegna

The Basics

CHOLESTEROL

Cholesterol is a form of fat that is found primarily in animal sources and their by-products, such as eggs and dairy products. These are our main sources of protein, a nutrient we need daily. Rather than avoid all meat and dairy products, however, experts recommend we simply cut back. The leaner the meat, the lower the cholesterol, so choose lean cuts of meat and remove the skin from poultry, as the skin is a major source of cholesterol and fat in all poultry. Substitute fish for meat frequently, three to four times a week if possible. Avoid butter, ice cream, and other rich dairy items.

The American Heart Association recommends a daily maximum intake of 300 milligrams of cholesterol. Your body produces some cholesterol, but only as much as it needs. The overabundance we consume in food is thought to be a major cause of atherosclerosis, clogging of the arteries.

How can you achieve a limit of 300 milligrams of cholesterol per day? You have to count the milligrams. Here is a list of foods in which cholesterol is found with the amount of cholesterol in each.

Food	Amount	Milligrams of Cholesterol
Lean Veal	3 ounces	90
Lean Beef	3 ounces	70
Lean Lamb	3 ounces	70
Lean Pork	3 ounces	70
Organ Meats	3 ounces	300
Eggs	1 whole	215–250
Whole-Milk Cheese	3 ounces	100
Poultry, skinned	3 ounces	60
Lobster	3 ounces	25
Oysters	3 ounces	50
Shrimp	3 ounces	125
Crabmeat	3 ounces	50
Fillet of Fish	3 ounces	70
Scallops	3 ounces	45
Clams	3 ounces	40
Tuna	6½ ounces	100
Ice Cream	3 ounces	45
Cottage Cheese (creamed)	3 ounces	15
Butter	1 teaspoon	11
Vegetables	any amount	0

Although tuna seems to be a high source of cholesterol, research has shown they have a special property that doesn't clog the arteries; therefore, it's not necessary to avoid its use. Shrimp is the one shellfish that does clog the arteries and should be avoided or used only occasionally and in small amounts.

Recent research has found a form of fat known as Omega-3 that seems to help prevent heart disease. It's found in all fish, especially salmon, sardines, and bluefish. Some medical experts caution against the overuse of Omega-3 fats, especially in pill form. It's too new to know the long-range side effects.

FAT

Not all fat is bad. We need fat in our diet to utilize vitamins A, D, E, and K, to provide energy, and to guard against colds and injury by acting as an insulator. However, most of us take in much more fat than we need, and we eat foods that are rich in the worst kinds of fat. It's understandable, as fat provides palatability and taste to our food. But in a healthy diet no more than 30 percent of your total daily calories should come from fat, and you should know the differences among the various types of fat. How do you know how much fat you're getting? A gram of fat contains 9 calories. If you consume 2,000 calories a day, keep the fat to 600 calories at the most and choose the more healthful polyunsaturated fats whenever possible.

Three kinds of fatty acids are found in foods: saturated, which should be reduced; monounsaturated, used only for ethnic dishes; and polyunsaturated, which should be your number one choice. It's believed that saturated fat molecules cling to the arteries, clogging the passageway so blood can't pass through freely. If an artery becomes closed by the formation of plaque (excess fat formations in the artery), a heart attack can result. All animal sources and some vegetable sources contain saturated fats. You should avoid beef fat, lard, butterfat, palm oil, and coconut oil.

The vegetable oils made from palms and coconuts are often used in convenient premade foods, such as frozen dinners and desserts. Some dairy products contain butterfat, such as cream, whole milk, and cheeses, so it is preferable to buy the nonfat forms, such as skim milk and low-fat cheeses. Even nondairy products usually contain palm or coconut oils, and should also be avoided, unless labeled "polyunsaturated fat." This is why it is so important to read the ingredients label of the foods you buy.

Olive and peanut oils, which give that distinctive taste to Italian and Chinese cooking, are monounsaturated fats. They don't clog the arteries, but they don't prevent clog formation from taking place, as polyunsaturated fat does. They should be saved for special ethnic recipes.

Polyunsaturated fats include safflower, sunflower, cottonseed, canola, and soybean oils, as well as margarine. Margarine can be purchased in stick, tub, or liquid form. The more liquid the form, the better, although the tub form of margarine is acceptable for use in baking, in some cooking, and as a spread on rolls and toast. There are many brands of margarine, and all are polyunsaturated fats. The choice is up to you. Safflower and corn oils are thought by some experts to be better than other oils because they have a higher polyunsaturated ratio.

It is impossible to avoid saturated fat completely, as it is often combined with the other forms of fat. The goal recommended by the American Heart Association is to reduce your fat intake, as stated above, to 30 percent of your total daily calories and to limit saturated fat to 10 percent of a day's total fat calories. For example, if you consume 2,000 calories a day, no more than 200 should come from saturated fat.

Also, avoid fats in which the percentage of saturated fat is higher than the percentage of polyunsaturated fat, as indicated in the table below.

ACCEPTABLE FATS	POLYUNSATURATED FAT	SATURATED FAT
Safflower Oil	74%	9%
Sunflower Oil	64%	10%
Corn Oil	58%	13%
Soybean and Cottonseed Oil	40%	13%
Peanut Oil	34%	18%
Canola Oil	26%	6%
Olive Oil	9%	14%
FATS TO AVOID		
Beef Fat	4%	48%
Butter	4%	61%
Coconut Oil	2%	86%
Palm Oil	2%	92%

SODIUM

Which do you think has more sodium: french fries, a cheeseburger, a milk shake, or apple pie? If you chose the cheeseburger, you're right. (Even the milk shake has more sodium than the french fries.) Most people think of sodium simply as table salt, but sodium occurs naturally as a mineral in the earth and is found in all foods except sugar.

Sodium has also long been used as an ingredient in a wide variety of foods, drinks, medicines, and as a preservative. It is necessary to sustain life, as it is involved in nerve impulses, the regulation of fluids, and muscle contraction. To maintain these functions we need only 200 milligrams of sodium a day, the equivalent of 1/10 of a teaspoon of salt. Yet the average American consumes from 6,000 to 12,000 milligrams per day! High sodium intake is one of several factors believed to contribute to high blood pressure (hypertension). As with heart disease, hypertension has a genetic (family) association. If a member of your family has a history of high blood pressure, your chances of developing it increase. Hypertension is often referred to as the "silent killer," as there often are no symptoms until there's a major event, such as a stroke. Hypertension is not only an older person's disease. More and more young people have developed high blood pressure, and many don't even know it. It is estimated by the National Institutes of Health that about 60 million Americans have some degree of high blood pressure and are at risk for a stroke or heart attack. Reducing your sodium level can help reduce this risk. If you don't have high blood pressure or a family history of heart disease, you probably don't need to worry about salt— check with your doctor. If you *do* need to worry about salt, the good news is that a taste for salt is really just a function of habit; once you get used to much less salt, you won't miss it at all.

To maintain a healthy eating style, the American Heart Association recommends we limit consumption to 1,000 milligrams of sodium per 1,000 calories. For example, if you consume 2,000 calories, you shouldn't take in more than 2,000 milligrams of sodium. Reducing sodium doesn't necessarily mean bland food, however. To "wake up" or add flavor to food, experiment with herbs. Be careful when buying mixed herbs and spices that aren't salt-free, however, as many contain more salt than any other ingredient. Flavor was the primary goal in designing the recipes in this book. When preparing a recipe, don't be afraid to personalize the taste by adding more salt-free herbs. Here are a few other tips for reducing sodium, followed by a list of sodium content in common foods.

1. Avoid canned meat, poultry, and fish (except tuna packed in spring water or less salt).

2. Avoid premade convenience foods. Rather, make your own over the weekend, preportion, and freeze. When needed during the week, remove from the freezer and heat in the microwave.

3. Avoid canned and dehydrated soups and broths. Low-salt versions are acceptable or, better still, make your own and freeze for busy days.

4. Avoid the saltshaker. Remember, sodium exists in all foods. Use more herbs for extra flavor.

5. Avoid processed, smoked, and luncheon meats.

6. Limit cheese to 2 ounces a day or select low-salt forms. Check the labels, as not all low-salt cheeses are really low in sodium.

7. Avoid salty forms of seasonings.

8. Be careful of instant products unless the label tells you they are salt-free.

SODIUM LEVEL IN SOME COMMON FOODS

Food	Milligrams of Sodium
8 ounces (1 cup) Skim Milk	126
1 ounce Processed Cheese	460
1 ounce Cheddar Cheese	176
8 ounces (1 cup) Cottage Cheese	850
8 ounces (1 cup) Plain Yogurt	100
1 ounce Parmesan Cheese	454
1 ounce Part-Skim Mozzarella	132
1 ounce Swiss Cheese	107
3 ounces Roast Beef	51
3 ounces Veal	68
3 ounces Ground Beef (10% fat)	41
3 slices Bacon	302
3 ounces Sausage	504
3 ounces Bologna	908
3 ounces Chicken	132
3 ounces Fish (fresh)	89
3 ounces Fish (frozen)	102
3 ounces regular canned Tuna	430
1 Egg	69
2 tablespoons Peanut Butter	176
1 slice Whole-Grain Bread	132
1 cup packaged Macaroni and Cheese	1,086
1 cup regular Oatmeal	374
1 cup Rice or Pasta	4
1 Potato	7
1 cup Vegetables (fresh, except for celery, red beets, and spinach)	2–20
1 cup Vegetables (frozen)	10–120
1 cup Vegetables (canned)	450–900
1 cup Fruit (fresh)	1–7
1 cup Fruit (canned)	10–20
1 cup regular Tomato Juice	882

Food	Milligrams of Sodium
1 cup low-salt Tomato Juice	20
1 tablespoon bottled Salad Dressing	214
1 tablespoon Salad Dressing (oil, vinegar, and herbs)	trace
1 teaspoon Margarine	44
1 Pickle	928
1 cup canned Soup	1,076
1 ounce Mixed Nuts	183
1 piece store-bought Apple Pie	476
Fast-Food Ready-Made Hamburger on a Bun	1,510
Frozen Chicken Dinner	1,152
1 teaspoon Garlic Salt	1,850
1 Bouillon Cube	910
1 teaspoon Baking Soda	821
1 teaspoon Baking Powder	329
1 teaspoon Worcestershire Sauce	206
1 teaspoon regular Soy Sauce	320
1 teaspoon low-salt Soy Sauce	200
1 teaspoon Herbs (examples: Paprika, Pepper, Basil, Thyme, and Rosemary)	trace

MAINTAINING IDEAL WEIGHT

It seems we are forever on a diet. Most of us follow a "yo-yo" approach to dieting—we lose five pounds before the swimsuit season only to regain the five pounds plus two more by winter. The very term *dieting* arouses a negative reaction, a feeling of having to do without something we like. Rather than dieting, the healthy approach to maintaining normal weight is a lifelong change in lifestyle. Once you make up your mind to be healthier, a change in eating is relatively easy. You don't do without; instead you find a style of eating with which you feel comfortable. Why do you dislike spinach while I love it? Our preconceptions about food are just habits, formed in early childhood. If your parents disliked spinach or never served it, chances are you will be a lifelong spinach avoider. Just as your dislike for spinach developed as a habit over the years, so you can, with change and patience, change some past eating habits. There is no quick fix to maintaining your weight; it takes knowledge of what put on the weight (excess calories for most of us), a commitment to change unhealthy eating habits, and a month or two of patience while our new eating style becomes our new "habit."

Research has shown that if you're told to avoid something that was very pleasurable and important to you without a reason and an acceptable substitute, you will eight times out of ten cheat and go back to the food you were told to avoid. To be successful, dieting must be approached as a contract with yourself, the active participant in decision making. And yes, of course there will be special occasions and treats; look under the Splurges section for some healthy ones that have just a few extra calories.

A nutrition expert can help you in determining what your maintenance weight should be and provide tips to help you achieve the proper weight. But you need to agree with the plan designed for you and feel you can live with it for a long time, not the "quick fix." Dieting needs to be approached as a lifetime change in poor eating habits. What is a healthy approach to the number of pounds you should set as a goal? One to two pounds a week is a realistic goal that you can accomplish without losing needed protein, vitamins, and minerals. Remember, your new eating style should be designed with variety, including fruits, vegetables, cereals, whole grains, low-fat dairy products, meat, fish, poultry, whole-grain breads, and pasta.

Exercise is the other essential needed to maintain a healthy body.

Some Tips to Help You
Make That Change in Eating Habits

1. The thicker the food, the higher the calories. To make it look like you haven't given up amounts, use a thinly sliced fish fillet instead of a thick one. A 4-ounce fish fillet can cover over half the dinner plate, whereas a thickly sliced 4-ounce fillet covers just a small area of the plate. Visual appearance means a lot in satisfying our cravings.

2. Use a smaller dinner plate; it looks like you're eating more.

3. Substitute wine for fat and oils for sautéing in the microwave. No, you won't be increasing your calorie consumption, since the alcohol and many of the calories will evaporate in the cooking process, leaving you only the flavoring and some liquid.

4. Always shop after a meal, not when you're hungry. You will buy less, especially of higher-calorie snack foods.

5. Use your microwave more frequently. Microwave cooking is one of the healthiest ways of cooking. You not only retain more vitamins and minerals but also use less fat and salt in the preparation.

How Many Calories?

For the adult who wishes to maintain present weight, men can consume 2,400 to 2,800 calories per day, while women need only 1,700 to 2,000 calories per day.

For the adult who is overweight and wishes to lose one to two pounds per week, men need to cut down to 1,200 to 1,500 calories per day, while women need to cut down to 1,000 to 1,200 calories per day. These figures are based on the "average adult" energy usage. Most of us would be classified as sedentary. If you are a construction worker, athlete, nursing mother, or mother with four or more children to care for daily, you are the exception, having higher caloric needs than those listed.

CRITERIA FOR NUTRITIONAL PROFILE OF RECIPES

APPETIZERS

Calories

Low	0–49
Moderate	50–100

Sodium

Low	0–49 mg
Moderate	50–100 mg

Cholesterol

Low	0–19 mg
Moderate	20–50 mg

SOUPS

Calories

Low	0–149
Moderate	150–250

Sodium

Low	0–149 mg
Moderate	150–250 mg

Cholesterol

Low	0–49 mg
Moderate	50–75 mg

VEGETABLES

Calories

Low	0–100
Moderate	101–200

Sodium

Low	0–200 mg
Moderate	201–325 mg

Cholesterol

Low	0–49 mg
Moderate	50–75 mg

ENTREES

Calories

Low	0–369
Moderate	370–500

Sodium

Low	0–374 mg
Moderate	375–500 mg

Cholesterol

Low	0–114 mg
Moderate	115–175 mg

BREADS AND DESSERTS

Calories

Low	0–200
Moderate	201–325

Sodium

Low	0–200 mg
Moderate	201–325 mg

Cholesterol

Low	0–49 mg
Moderate	50–75 mg

SPLURGES

Calories

High	325 and above

Sodium

Low	0–200 mg
Moderate	201–325 mg

Cholesterol

Low	0–49 mg
Moderate	50–75 mg

Introduction

There comes a time in most people's lives when they take stock and realize that their continued good health is really number one on their list of priorities. When I was a young girl, I lost the most important man in my life to a heart attack. Years later, just after my marriage, a heart attack took my father-in-law away from us. We didn't know much in those days about the relationship between health and diet, but now that we do, it's time to take action in our own lives. What I want to do in this book is to help those I love, and you, learn to protect ourselves and our family members from heart disease, cancer, and other health problems influenced by diet. Knowing as I do that the microwave is the best available cooking tool to cut many fats in food preparation, I consulted with Beverly Bentivegna, a registered dietitian. Beverly really opened my eyes to the many ways of converting my quick and easy microwave recipes to quick and easy *healthy* recipes, and I want to share the results with you.

People usually think that they have to diet to lower cholesterol, and the very word *diet* usually brings to mind visions of depriving ourselves of foods we enjoy and substituting tasteless, boring ones. If you're like me, you won't go out and buy all kinds of new foods; you're pretty set in your ways, and any change has to come about within the framework of the foods you use every day. How about a way to make lowering your cholesterol and your blood pressure interesting and tasty, using fewer preservatives while cutting calories, cholesterol, and your salt intake at the same time? I'm really talking about eating good, *real* (but healthy) food. My family wouldn't have it any other way.

My husband is a chef, trained at the Culinary Institute of America, and believe me, his is a hard palate to please. My two sons, 13 and 10, are both good hearty eaters, and the recipes I have worked out for you have had to pass some very high standards for taste and appearance. Children set their eating patterns for life quite early, and if you start them eating healthfully they will carry these habits with them throughout their lives. I am confident that if my household approves, so will yours. The most surprising thing I found while putting these recipes together is that they're so good you actually forget they're also healthy.

My dad was a real meat-and-potatoes guy with heart problems, and my mother was having a difficult time getting him to change his eating habits. So I thought my parents would make perfect critics. Mom was far more flexible, but I knew Dad would be a real challenge. To everyone's surprise, Dad's life on a low-salt, low-cholesterol regime was not the horror he expected—in fact, he found the food quite to his liking and looked forward to something new every day.

I'm not asking you to make dramatic changes, but with just a few little tricks—some very powerful salt-free spices, using egg whites in place of whole eggs—together we can make your meals healthy. The point is, you don't have to give up your favorite foods, including sweets; you just need to learn to prepare the recipe with healthier ingredients. *Healthy* is the key word for this book, not *dieting*, and the recipes are for the entire family, not just the person with a problem or concern.

Now, what have you got to lose? Maybe a few pounds? Your cholesterol level will definitely decline. It certainly can't hurt you to try, and if your heart could talk, it would probably say "Thank you."

The microwave is still a new—and strange—cooking appliance to many, who will be glad to hear that I've taken the fear of mistake out of my recipes. I look at it this way: If I've taken all the time and effort to experiment, why should you have to? You don't. You will find a troubleshooting piece after most recipes. Read this information *before* starting, and it will help to reinforce the important techniques needed to be sure you create a perfect dish, one that not only looks but tastes like it was made in your conventional oven.

COOKING TIMES

Up until now, the times given in my recipes have been geared to 600- to 700-watt microwaves. From all the wonderful letters I have received, I find that many of you have small ovens or low-wattage ovens with 400 to 500 watts of power. Usually the wattage isn't even indicated on the oven, so this can get confusing. It's very hard to know how long to cook a recipe in a low-wattage oven, and many of you are having problems. A new feature in this book is giving you, alongside the usual 600- to 700-watt timing, cooking times for those ovens with 400 to 500 watts of power (indicated by the abbreviation *LW*). Every oven operates differently, but these times will give you an idea of where to start and how to judge the cooking time.

To save time and worry when repeating a recipe, jot down, right on the recipe, how long it took to prepare in your oven. This way, when you try the recipe again, you won't have to wonder; you will know.

WHY GOOF-PROOF?

Readers of my first book will understand why my recipes are different from those in other books, but for those of you new to the goof-proof concept, let me explain what this book will do for you. Goof-proof means just what it implies: The recipes come out right the first time, and you don't have to take the time to flip back and forth from section to section of the book to find out what to do next. Everything you need to know is in every recipe. There are special microwaving and health tips throughout the book to give you more information on particular topics.

Most recipes also offer you suggestions for serving or garnishing. Don't forget, presentation is one of the keys to good taste. If it doesn't look good, it probably won't taste as good as it should.

Even if you have never microwaved anything but baked potatoes and leftovers, equipped with my recipes, hints, and tips, your first adventure into microwave cooking will be a success. I not only tell you what to do but also what *not* to do and what will happen if you don't follow my instructions. No one can guarantee you that learning something new won't take some practice, but relax and be confident that I am giving you healthy goof-proof recipes that will please the whole family.

Microwave Basics

If you use your microwave mainly to heat coffee and leftovers, and for defrosting, read on. Probably you don't know how to make this oversized bun warmer really cook. I think the statement I hear most is "I'm a good cook who has been cooking for years, but I just don't know how to make this machine work."

Before you can make this time- and energy-saving appliance really work for you, you need to understand how it operates. Inside the top of most ovens (or sometimes in the bottom) is a magnetron tube. This tube emits microwave energy that spreads throughout the inside cavity of the oven. When the microwaves come in contact with the metal walls of the oven and metal screening in the door, they bounce back into the center of the oven and concentrate on whatever is there.

The microwaves themselves act only as a catalyst for the cooking process. They penetrate the food to a depth of no more than 1 to 1½ inches and cause no chemical change in the food. At the point of penetration they cause the molecules of the food—fat, water, or sugar—to vibrate. This vibration causes heat, and this heat, not the microwaves, spreads throughout the food. Therefore, the food is actually cooking itself, with the microwaves acting only as a starting mechanism to get the whole operation going.

As the heat spreads throughout the food by conduction, the food begins to cook from the outside edges to the center, making the center of the food the last place to receive the heat. When the oven is shut off, the microwaves are gone; they are no longer in the food, and you can't ingest them. Even though the heat catalyst has been stopped, the food continues to cook for five to ten minutes after the microwave energy is shut off.

Why is the food still cooking? Because the molecules of fat, water, or sugar are still vibrating and heat is still being spread throughout the food. Therefore, you always slightly undercook your food during the actual time the microwaves are on and let it finish cooking, without the help of the microwaves, in what is called *standing time.* If you leave most foods in the oven for the entire time required to cook them, and don't allow for standing time, the finished product will be overcooked. Also, if you eat foods straight from the oven, you're likely to burn your mouth; you must allow standing time to be sure the heating process has stopped.

Today's microwaves are safe, energy-efficient, and clean-cooking appliances. Should you suspect your oven is not operating properly or for some reason it is leaking microwaves, call a qualified repair person. He or she can test for leakages with special meters and, should you have a problem, repair the oven. A microwave oven is not an appliance you can repair yourself. You may be able to change a blown-out light bulb, but for any other problems, consult a qualified technician. If your oven is portable, you will probably save on repair costs if you take the oven to the technician rather than requesting a house call.

Microwave Don'ts

You're always told what to do in the microwave, but I want you to be aware that there are also some very important things *not* to do:

1. Do not operate your oven when it's empty; the microwaves must have something to penetrate. If you feel you might forget, keep a box of baking soda in the oven when not in use; the baking soda will also absorb excess moisture and odor. If you prefer, keep a glass of water in the oven for safety.

2. Do not use metal cooking containers or leave metal spoons or forks in a container when microwaving.

3. Do not leave metal twist ties on plastic bags when microwaving. If you think someone in your household might forget to remove them, start using plastic bread closures or the plastic closure tabs found in many supermarket produce sections on your bags to eliminate the worry. I have actually watched a metal twist tie arc, causing the paper covering to catch fire, which ignited the plastic bag it held shut. All this happens in moments, and you could have a major fire on your hands.

4. Do not allow your oven to become encrusted with spills and spatters. If this advice comes too late, no problem. Mix 2 cups of water with the juice of a lemon in a glass container, and micro-

wave on HIGH power for 12 minutes; this trick will help lift crusted food and keep the oven sweet-smelling.

5. Do not use chemical oven cleaners, abrasives, table knives, or scouring powder to clean your oven. Several brands of microwave spray cleaners are available, if you prefer, that will not harm the finish.

6. Do not turn your oven on and walk away without first looking inside to make sure there is no arcing or that you didn't leave a fork or spoon in the container. Always watch the cooking process for several seconds after turning the oven on before leaving. Should you see arcing, immediately shut off the oven and eliminate the cause before turning it back on. I once spread some margarine on a slice of toast and watched the oven light up like the Fourth of July. I had accidentally scraped up some of the foil wrapper with the margarine. This one tip can save you from ruining your oven with a fire.

7. Do not put anything with a foil wrapper in the oven to cook or soften, such as cream cheese, margarine, or frozen vegetables. Wherever the foil wrapper is touching itself, it will arc and can cause a fire if there is any paper or plastic in the oven.

8. Do not try to dry fabrics, including clothing, stockings, or towels, in the microwave. They can and do start fires.

9. Do not hard-boil or reheat in the microwave a peeled or unpeeled hard-boiled egg that isn't cut open. The heat builds up in the casing around the yolk, and the egg will explode, causing severe damage to the oven, not to mention the possibility that it may blow up in your face when you remove it.

10. Do not try to deep-fry or heat large quantities of oil in the microwave. It may splatter and burn plastic-coated areas of the oven; the container will become extremely hot, and you can get severely burned. This practice is very dangerous and should not be attempted, regardless of what you read in other books. But you won't be deep-frying anything in this book, fortunately.

11. Do not substitute newspaper for paper towels, especially when cooking bacon. The ink may contain metal substances that can cause the paper to catch on fire.

12. Do not try to pop popcorn in a regular brown paper bag. Yes, my mail says it can be done, and you may have success on

several attempts, but the law of averages says you will get caught when you least expect it. If the paper bag you're using contains metal particles or certain chemicals, you will have a fire. Use the disposable bags made specifically for the microwave or a microwave popper and be safe.

13. Do not use a container that touches the sides or top of your oven. You must have at least 2 to 3 inches between the container and the walls and ceiling of your oven for proper cooking.

14. Do not allow children to operate the oven without carefully educating them about the dangers. Keep a kitchen fire extinguisher nearby and be sure the children know exactly how to use it.

15. Do not operate your microwave if the glass in the door is cracked, chipped, or broken or if the door isn't closing properly.

16. Do not try to repair your microwave yourself; no matter how handy you are, this is a job for a professional technician.

17. Do not try to microwave puff pastry or phyllo dough; neither works in the microwave.

18. Do not microwave two-crust pies. Use either a lattice top or cutout dough pieces and place over the filling—otherwise the bottom crust will not cook.

19. Do not attempt to sterilize canning jars in the microwave. It is advisable to melt paraffin on your conventional stove top, over a double boiler.

20. Do not use regular meat or candy thermometers in the microwave. Either use the oven probe, if one comes with your oven, or use a thermometer made for microwaving. If you have only a conventional oven thermometer, insert it in food that has been removed from the microwave. Be sure to remove the thermometer before placing food back into the oven for further cooking.

21. Do not try to cover a microwave browning dish with anything but the cover it comes with. Covering this utensil with a paper towel or wax paper can cause a fire.

22. Do not salt the exterior of any food exposed to the microwaves, such as a roast or corn on the cob; salting causes unappealing dehydration spots to form wherever the granules touch the food.

Coverings

O ne of the most constantly used—and least understood—phrases in microwave cooking is "cover the dish." Many recipes you read (not mine, of course) will give you those exact instructions. My first response is, cover it with what?

The way you cover your dish will either save you cooking time and help produce a better finished product or add moisture where it isn't needed. Interchangeable, whether stated or not, are the cover or lid that comes with a particular dish and plastic wrap.

I have not found a brand of plastic wrap, to date, that doesn't melt onto the food unless a corner is pulled back to allow the steam to escape. *Venting* is the term used to describe this procedure, and by venting the steam you also prevent being burned by the sudden escape of steam that has built up inside a tightly covered container. This will also happen when you use a casserole cover or lid, so be careful.

You may have heard that all you need to do is poke holes in the plastic wrap. Believe me, I have tried, and if you're microwaving a recipe for any length of time, the steam buildup in the dish melts the holes shut. Venting is not necessary when using the casserole cover or lid because if it's microwave safe, it will not melt. You must also vent plastic bags of frozen vegetables. By making a small slit or X in the bag you allow the steam to escape instead of building up and melting the plastic onto the vegetables.

When using plastic roasting bags, be sure not to secure the bag tightly closed. Use dental floss, string, or a rubber band when closing a roasting bag and tie it loosely so that the steam can escape.

There are three basic methods for covering food in the micro-wave. To accomplish steaming inside the dish and hold in the moisture, cover with the dish lid or plastic wrap, pulling back one corner to vent the steam. When you want steaming to take place inside the dish but you don't want to hold in any extra moisture, cover the dish with wax paper. When your only concern is keeping the food from spattering the inside of the microwave, cover the container with a layer of paper towel.

The right covering makes all the difference between success and disaster, as one of my students learned. Donna works all week and does most of her cooking on the weekends, making nightly meals only a quick heat-up in the microwave. One weekend she prepared a meat loaf and refrigerated it for later use. The night she wanted to use it, she wrapped it in paper towels and heated it in the microwave. She ended up with a solid brick of meat. Why? Because instead of being held in the meat by vented plastic wrap, all the moisture was absorbed into the paper toweling, leaving a dry, solid brick of meat.

Before microwaving, think about just what you want to have happen in the cooking container—steaming with additional mois-ture, plain steaming, or just keeping the contents of the dish from spattering. Taking a moment to assess how you want the food to microwave will help you produce the perfect finished product.

Microwave Equipment

If you're a new microwaver or just beginning to use your microwave for recipe preparation rather than reheating, you may wonder which utensils are safe for microwave cooking. A dish that is considered micro-safe, or safe for microwave use, is one that allows the microwaves to pass completely through the container and concentrate on the food inside.

Metal containers reflect the microwaves and don't let them pass through at all. If a dish has a metal edging or decoration on it, the metalwork has a beginning and ending point, which is where the arcing takes place. Check your utensils carefully to be sure there is no metal decoration, as the arcing, if allowed to go on too long, will ruin the appearance of the container. The only metal that can be used safely in the microwave, and only if your oven manufacturer allows it, is small, completely flat pieces of foil used to shield areas you do not want to cook.

Many pottery and ceramic containers *gather* microwave energy rather than letting it pass through, and spots can get hot. When a utensil gets hot spots, it is not safe for microwave use. There is no need to guess which utensils are safe and which aren't. Perform a simple test: place a glass with 1 cup of water either next to or in the questionable utensil. Microwave on HIGH power for 1 minute. If the test piece is warm or hot, it is not safe for microwave use—only the water should be warm.

Today there are many plastic, paper, and glass cooking containers made specifically for microwave use. However, your everyday glass cooking containers as well as some of your household plastic will work. It is far better and safer to test a questionable piece than to risk burning yourself or having it melt. It is handy to have custard cups, glass mixing bowls, pie plates, micro-safe casserole dishes, glass measures in various sizes, and glass bread pans on hand. You know these items will microwave with no problem, and that saves you time and guesswork.

Many paper products are also made specifically for the microwave, but watch out for Styrofoam containers. Unless they say "safe for microwave use," they may melt when microwaved. The very first time I put a Styrofoam cup in my microwave it contained some extra pizza sauce to top a calzone. I heated the cup on HIGH for 1 minute and watched the sides melt right down to the bottom of the cup. Even if the Styrofoam is safe for microwaving, as a rule the disposable tops that come on paper or Styrofoam cups will melt, so remove them before heating.

Some wooden cutting boards can't be used, especially those with metal handles, but wooden chopsticks, skewers, and toothpicks shouldn't give you any problem.

If you're starting from scratch and want to purchase cookware just for microwaving, lines of both plastic and glassware are available in assorted sizes and shapes. Plasticware may stain after constant use, so be sure to check the instructions for cleaning that come with the item. It might be a good idea to insert them in this part of the book so you will always have them handy to refer to. Cookware manufacturers are now rounding out the inside square corners of their glassware to help overcome the problem microwaves have of overcooking whatever they find in square corners. When buying new glass containers, run your finger into the corners to be sure the piece has rounded inside corners; even if these containers cost a few cents more, the money they will save in ruined food will be worth it.

You'll notice in the recipes a line about elevating flat-bottomed dishes. If you're using utensils made for microwaving you can ignore this line, since the manufacturers recess the bottom and place a rim around it to eliminate this problem.

If I were to suggest any specific equipment for you to buy, it would be a meat or bacon rack and, if you're going to do stir-frying, a covered browning dish. There is really no piece of conventional equipment that can double for a microwave meat rack, which produces the best finished product. The covered microwave browning dish is a deep dish with its own cover. It is the only piece of equipment made specifically for the microwave that is supposed to get hot. Instead of allowing the microwaves to pass through this dish, it is coated with a substance that actually gathers the microwaves and gets hot, like the surface of a frying pan. You may already be acquainted with this principle if you have purchased frozen microwave pizzas, french fries, or fish portions. You may notice that they are all microwaved on what appears to be a foil-covered piece of cardboard. Actually, it is not regular aluminum foil but special packaging that also gathers the microwaves, gets hot, and keeps whatever is touching it crisp.

Another very useful item for cooking healthier food is the microwave-safe plastic colander, which will help remove lots of fat from ground meats.

There are microwave coffeepots, special waffle and hamburger grills, and even a small microwave pressure cooker on the market, all designed to help you cook your food faster with better eye appeal. But remember, if you question the safety of a container, test it. It is always better to be safe than sorry; once you have ruined a utensil it is always costly to replace it.

How to Stock Your Pantry

One of my main goals in putting these recipes together is to use ingredients readily available at your local supermarket. I know from my own experience that it's unrealistic to expect you to go to a special store on a regular basis; I always wind up picking up a supermarket substitute for that special ingredient. You won't have to change your normal shopping routine; just change some of the items you put in your shopping cart. For today's market, manufacturers are required to furnish the consumer with the nutritional breakdown of their products. We as consumers need to take full advantage of this service and guarantee ourselves that we are buying the best foods for our health. First and foremost: begin reading the ingredient labels on the products you're buying if you're not doing that already.

If you're concerned about sodium, you should know that the United States government has developed standards for the numerous products with reduced sodium. For an item to carry the label "salt-free," each ounce of the product must have less than 5 milligrams of sodium. If the label states "very low sodium," 1 ounce of the product must contain less than 35 milligrams of salt. Products bearing the terms "low-sodium" or "low-salt" must contain less than 140 milligrams of sodium per ounce. When you see "reduced sodium" on the label, the product contains 25 percent less sodium than the standard version.

Check your meat purchases carefully to be sure they are as lean as possible. If you don't see what you want in the meat case, ask the butcher to cut your meat to order. When lean cuts of sirloin are on sale, buy several packages and freeze them so that you don't have to run out at the last minute and take whatever is available, regardless of fat content, when you're ready to prepare a recipe. Get into the habit of trimming any excess fat from your meat before you begin to cook. Organ meats contain a high level of cholesterol and should be avoided completely.

Examine your poultry carefully as the fat and cholesterol are found in the skin. When using chicken cutlets, remove any excess fat remaining on the meat before you start cooking.

Fresh fish and shellfish of all varieties—except for shrimp, which is high in a bad form of cholesterol—are fine, but if you want to avoid salt, stay away from the canned versions, since salt is used to preserve them. Check the ingredients on the imitation crabmeat you buy to be sure it contains only fish and no added sodium or sugar, which some brands do. Look for canned tuna packed in spring water; both its sodium and its calorie levels are lower.

Nothing beats fresh fruits and vegetables. Frozen and especially the canned varieties have more sodium than fresh, and as a general rule you are always better off with fresh. Some ingredients used in my recipes, however, must come from a can. The most frequently used is low-salt canned tomato products. By checking the labels on the products available in your area you may find cans not specifically marked "low-salt" that do not contain salt at all. For instance, Progresso tomato puree contains *only* tomatoes, with nothing else added. You will be amazed at how tasty these low-salt versions really are, and when you add lively herbs and spices to the recipes, as I have done, you won't notice the difference.

If you're still buying whole milk and milk products, switch to low-fat or skim milk and cheese products. Milk is labeled "low-fat" (1 percent is better than 2 percent) or "skim," but you will have to read the ingredients label on packaged cheeses to determine which milk was used in its preparation. I use Parmesan, low-fat ricotta, low-fat mozzarella, and Swiss. Soft-spread margarine is used in place of regular margarine only because of the calories; most margarines are as a rule cholesterol-free, but it wouldn't hurt to double-check the brand you buy. If you want to check the fat level of a given food, it's useful to know (since most manufacturers list it in grams) that a gram of fat has 9 calories.

To find out the percentage of fat, multiply the fat grams by 9 to get the total fat calories, which you can then compare with the total calories—if it's over 30 percent, pass it by. Cream cheese is out; even the low-fat versions contain some cholesterol, but low-fat cottage cheese whipped in a blender or with an electric mixer can easily substitute. Sour cream is another dairy product containing cholesterol; plain low-fat yogurt has been substituted in all the recipes where sour cream was originally called for. Don't be fooled into thinking you can substitute imitation sour cream, which usually contains saturated fat. Don't assume nondairy products are substitutes for regular milk and dairy products, since in many of them highly saturated coconut or palm oil is the main ingredient. Please don't be concerned—you're not giving up everything tasty, just making some healthy changes.

Mayonnaise doesn't appear in any of my recipes, which substitute plain low-fat yogurt for two reasons. Mayonnaise is higher in calories and also contains some cholesterol. You may be surprised to learn that reduced-calorie mayonnaise is simply regular mayonnaise with water added to it—use yogurt.

Instead of using salt, enhance the flavor of food with herbs. You will find that I have incorporated McCormick's new line of Salt Free Parsley Patch spices in many of the recipes. These blends are very powerful and really make the difference between bland and very tasty food. If you're not used to cooking with spices and herbs, you're in for quite a surprise. Several other manufacturers have salt-free spices on the market, but McCormick is producing the largest line of varied flavors that I could find. McCormick tells me they are available nationwide, but if you can't find them in your supermarket, write McCormick & Company, P.O. Box 208, Hunt Valley, MD 21030-0208, Attention: Customer Service Department, and they can tell you where to find them in your area.

If you want to substitute your own herb blends for the McCormick's variety I list, here's what's in them:

All-Purpose: onion, parsley, basil, paprika, oregano, thyme, garlic, lemon peel, celery, and Italian red pepper.
Lemon Pepper: lemon peel, sesame seed, black pepper, paprika, dill, cumin, thyme, oregano, poppy seed, garlic, dill, onion, cayenne pepper, and licorice root.

Garlicsaltless: garlic, sesame seed, oregano, parsley, rosemary, basil, celery, cumin, paprika, thyme, orange peel, onion, and cayenne pepper.

It's a Dilly: onion, garlic, sesame seed, dill, lemon peel, jalapeño pepper, and cayenne pepper.

Popcorn Blend: paprika, parsley, basil, celery, oregano, thyme, cumin, onion, chili pepper, tomato, garlic, cayenne pepper, lemon peel, and jalapeño pepper.

Sesame All-Purpose: sesame seed, onion, parsley, basil, celery, oregano, paprika, thyme, garlic, lemon peel, and cayenne pepper.

You will notice that I don't use flavored canned soups in any of the recipes, because regular canned soups are extremely high in sodium. I find the flavored reduced-sodium canned soups considerably lacking in flavor. However, I do use low-sodium chicken or beef bouillon in many recipes and enhance its flavor with extra herbs and spices. The low-sodium bouillon is usually available in both powdered and canned form, so check your supermarket shelves. For even more flavor, I suggest making your own chicken and beef stock and freezing it in various-sized containers for easy use later. By keeping all-purpose flour, skim milk, and margarine available, you can make sauces with substantially reduced levels of sodium; adding various herbs enhances the flavor and produces a tasty equivalent to the tasteless varieties of low-sodium canned soups.

Stir-fry cooking is a favorite for many of us, but most recipes call for regular soy sauce and often MSG, which are both very high in sodium. Instead, purchase low-salt soy sauce and increase the Oriental flavor by adding fresh or powdered ginger and garlic.

Be careful when buying instant ready-made products. If you check their labels, you will see that many of them have high levels of sodium. I use only plain bread crumbs and not the flavored variety, which contains added salt. You will notice I recommend using long-grain rice instead of instant rice. However, check labels carefully—new and improved products are coming into the market daily, and if you're an instant rice user you may be able to find instant rices that are sodium-free.

Avoid buying products containing palm oil, coconut oil, beef fat, or lard. Do stock soft-spread margarine and wine for sautéing vegetables. The right oils are safflower, sunflower, corn, and soybean oil for other cooking purposes. Peanut and olive oils add certain unmistakable flavors to both Chinese and Italian recipes and should be used only when this unique flavor is called for.

Pasta can play a large part in your diet as long as you are careful to select eggless macaroni products. Eggless pasta contains no cholesterol and tastes the same, so check the labels carefully before purchasing.

Be careful when purchasing dietetic products. By government standards they contain no cane sugar but may have other sugars that provide the same calories as cane sugar. I don't use any sugar substitutes or dietetic products in my recipes because I feel by doing so I sacrifice both taste and quality. In limited amounts, sugar isn't high in calories but produces a flavor the substitutes just can't duplicate—that's why you will find regular sugar used in small amounts throughout the book.

If you are what you eat, you want to be sure what you eat is what you want to be.

PANTRY CHECKLIST

You can use this list as a guide when stocking your pantry shelf:

Fresh lean meats (sirloin cuts, pork tenderloin)
Poultry, preferably skinless
Fresh fish and shellfish (If you have a cholesterol problem, use shrimp in moderation)
Springwater-packed tuna
Fresh fruits, when possible, or those frozen or canned in natural juices
Fresh vegetables, frozen, or low-salt canned varieties when fresh isn't available
Cheeses that are low-fat or part skim milk
Low-fat or skim-milk products
Soft-spread margarine
Safflower, sunflower, corn, or soybean oils for general cooking
Peanut and olive oils for special ethnic recipes
Red and white table wine
Herbs and salt-free spices
Plain unseasoned bread crumbs
Low-sodium bouillon and bouillon granules
Low-salt soy sauce
Low-salt ketchup
Low-salt canned tomato products
Long-grain rice
Eggless pasta and macaroni products
Eggs (for the whites)

Appetizers

Fiesta Hot Beans

SERVES 10

EQUIPMENT: 2- or 3-quart round casserole dish, 4-cup glass measure

COOKING TIME: 27 to 35 minutes (Low Wattage ovens 32 to 42 minutes)

STANDING TIME: none required

NUTRITIONAL PROFILE: moderate calories, low sodium, no cholesterol

- **1 10-ounce box frozen green beans**
- **1 10-ounce box frozen wax beans**
- **1 10-ounce box frozen lima beans**
- **¼ cup water**
- **1 medium onion, diced**
- **½ cup (about ½ large) diced green pepper**
- **¾ cup cider vinegar**
- **½ cup sugar**
- **1 tablespoon cornstarch**
- **⅛ teaspoon freshly ground pepper**

Remove frozen vegetables from boxes and place in casserole dish. Drizzle with water and **cover** with lid or plastic wrap, pulling back one corner to vent the steam. (If dish is flat-bottomed, **elevate** on an inverted saucer.) Place on turntable if available. Microwave on HIGH for 10 minutes (LW 12 minutes). **Stir** and cook on HIGH for 6 to 10 minutes (LW 7½ to 12 minutes) or until vegetables are tender-crisp. (**Rotate** dish ½ turn every 5 minutes if not using turntable.) **Drain** and keep covered.

In glass measure, combine onion, green pepper, and 2 table-spoons of the vinegar. **Cover** with plastic wrap, pulling back one corner to vent the steam. Cook on HIGH for 4 to 6 minutes (LW 4½ to 7½ minutes), **stirring** every 2 minutes until tender-crisp.

Stir in sugar, cornstarch, and pepper. Gradually stir in re-maining vinegar, blending well. Microwave, **uncovered,** on HIGH for 4 to 5 minutes (LW 4½ to 6 minutes) or until mixture thickens, stirring every 2 minutes. Pour mixture over cooked beans and stir. **Cover** again and cook on HIGH for 3 to 4 minutes (LW 3½ to 4½ minutes) or until mixture is hot and bubbly.

Suggestions: Prepare in advance, omitting last step. Heat to hot and bubbly just before serving.

Substitute cooked fresh beans for the frozen if they're available.

For individual appetizers, serve mounded on a Bibb lettuce leaf.

FOR EACH SERVING:
75 calories
22 mg sodium
0 mg cholesterol
0 g fat

Oriental Meatballs

MAKES 40 MEATBALLS

EQUIPMENT: medium bowl, 9 × 13-inch baking dish, 1½-
or 2-quart round casserole dish, small bowl

COOKING TIME: 18 to 24 minutes (Low Wattage ovens 22 to 29 minutes)

STANDING TIME: 5 minutes

NUTRITIONAL PROFILE: low calories, low sodium, low cholesterol

MEATBALLS

1½ **pounds lean ground sirloin**
½ **cup plain dry bread crumbs**
2 **egg whites**
1 **small onion, minced**
½ **teaspoon dry mustard**
¼ **teaspoon garlic powder**
½ **teaspoon freshly ground pepper**
½ **teaspoon ground ginger**

SAUCE

2 **tablespoons brown sugar**
¼ **teaspoon dry mustard**
½ **teaspoon ground ginger**
1 **8-ounce can low-salt tomato sauce**
1 **cup unsweetened crushed pineapple**

In medium bowl, combine all meatball ingredients, mixing well to blend. Shape meat into 40 uniformly sized meatballs and place in baking dish. (If dish is flat-bottomed, **elevate** on an inverted saucer.) Microwave, **uncovered,** on HIGH for 4 to 5 minutes (LW 5 to 6 minutes), turn and **rearrange** meatballs, being sure to bring the ones in the corners and outside edges of the dish to the center and the ones in the center to the outside edges. **Rotate** dish ½ turn and microwave on HIGH for 4 to 5 minutes (LW 5 to 6 minutes).

Drain meatballs well and place in round casserole dish. In a small bowl, whisk brown sugar, mustard, and ginger into tomato sauce. Fold in crushed pineapple and pour blended mixture over meatballs. **Cover** dish with lid or plastic wrap, pulling back one corner to vent the steam. (If dish is flat-bottomed, elevate on an inverted saucer.) Place on turntable if available. Cook for 10 to 14 minutes (LW 12 to 17 minutes) on 60 percent power or MEDIUM, until the flavors have combined, carefully **stirring** every 5 minutes. (If not using turntable, **rotate** dish ½ turn when stirring.) Let **stand, covered,** for 5 minutes and use decorative toothpicks for serving.

Troubleshooting: The microwave extracts about ⅓ more fat from meat than conventional frying would, so be sure to drain fat as it builds up while cooking meatballs.

Suggestions: This dish is particularly good when prepared in advance to allow the flavors to blend.

For less restricted diets: If you're not watching your salt intake, use regular tomato sauce, which adds 32 mg of sodium per meatball.

FOR EACH MEATBALL:
41 calories
16 mg sodium
11 mg cholesterol
2 g fat

DEALING WITH
SQUARE-CORNERED CONTAINERS

Microwaves are attracted to and overcook whatever they find in the square corners of cooking containers. That's why most cooking utensils made for microwave use along with most new glassware products are made with rounded corners. If you are using square ones, be sure to move the food out of these square corners often to prevent overcooking.

Sesame Meatballs

MAKES 48 MEATBALLS

EQUIPMENT:	medium bowl, flat dinner plate, 2-quart casserole or chafing dish, 4-cup glass measure
COOKING TIME:	10¾ to 14 minutes (Low Wattage ovens 12¾ to 16¾ minutes)
STANDING TIME:	none required
NUTRITIONAL PROFILE:	low calories, low sodium, low cholesterol

MEATBALLS

1½   **pounds lean ground sirloin**
⅔   **cup (about 1½ medium) minced onion**
½   **cup plain dry bread crumbs**
1   **egg white**
¼   **cup skim milk**
1   **teaspoon Parsley Patch Sesame All-Purpose herb blend**
⅛   **teaspoon freshly ground pepper**
⅛   **teaspoon ground ginger**

SAUCE

2   **tablespoons soft-spread margarine**
2   **tablespoons all-purpose flour**
½   **teaspoon ground ginger**
½   **cup low-sodium beef broth or homemade beef stock (page 52)**
1   **teaspoon low-salt soy sauce**
2   **tablespoons toasted sesame seeds (page 71)**
¾   **cup plain yogurt**

Mix all meatball ingredients well in medium bowl. Shape into 48 1-inch balls. Place meatballs in circles on a flat dinner plate **elevated** on an inverted saucer. Microwave, **uncovered,** on HIGH for 3 minutes (LW 3½ minutes), drain any fat, and **rearrange** meatballs, bringing the less cooked ones from the center of the dish to the outside edges and the ones along the edges to the center of the dish. Cook on HIGH for 4 to 6 minutes (LW 4¾ to 7½ minutes) or until meat is no longer pink. **Drain** and place in casserole or chafing dish and **cover** to keep hot.

Place margarine in glass measure and melt, **uncovered,** on HIGH for 40 to 50 seconds (LW 50 to 60 seconds). **Whisk** in flour, ginger, broth, and soy sauce. Microwave, **uncovered,** on HIGH for 3 to 4 minutes (LW 3½ to 4¾ minutes), **whisking** every minute until thickened. Whisk in 1½ tablespoons of the sesame seeds and the yogurt. Spoon hot sauce over hot meatballs and sprinkle sauce with remaining sesame seeds. Serve with toothpicks.

Troubleshooting: Shape meat into uniformly sized balls to ensure even cooking.

For less restricted diets: If you're not watching your salt intake, use regular beef broth, which adds 19 mg sodium per serving, and regular soy sauce, which adds 5 mg sodium per serving.

FOR EACH MEATBALL:
35 calories
20 mg sodium
7 mg cholesterol
2 g fat

Marinated Mushrooms

SERVES 6

EQUIPMENT:	deep 2-quart casserole dish
COOKING TIME:	7 to 10 minutes (Low Wattage ovens 8¼ to 12¼ minutes)
STANDING TIME:	none required
NUTRITIONAL PROFILE:	low calories, low sodium, no cholesterol

⅓ **cup red wine vinegar**
¼ **cup water**
1 **tablespoon olive oil**
¾ **teaspoon sugar**
1 **garlic clove, finely minced**
1 **tablespoon finely minced onion**
½ **teaspoon Parsley Patch Popcorn herb blend**
¼ **teaspoon dried basil**
¼ **teaspoon dried oregano**
1 **pound small, uniformly sized fresh mushrooms**

In casserole dish, combine all ingredients except mushrooms, stirring to blend. **Cover** dish with lid or plastic wrap, pulling back one corner to vent the steam. (If dish is flat-bottomed, **elevate** on an inverted saucer.) Place on turntable if available. Microwave on HIGH for 4 to 6 minutes (LW 4¾ to 7½ minutes) or until boiling.

Add mushrooms, stir, **reduce** power to 80 percent or MEDIUM-HIGH, and cook for 3 to 4 minutes (LW 3½ to 4¾ minutes) or until mushrooms are tender, **stirring** every 2 minutes. (**Rotate** dish ½ turn when stirring if not using turntable.) Allow dish to **cool,** then refrigerate for 6 to 8 hours. Drain mushrooms and serve with toothpicks.

FOR EACH SERVING:
34 calories
8 mg sodium
0 mg cholesterol
2 g fat

Vegetarian Stuffed Mushrooms

SERVES 6

EQUIPMENT:	6-cup glass measure, paper plate
COOKING TIME:	6 to 9 minutes (Low Wattage ovens 7 to 11 minutes)
STANDING TIME:	1 minute
NUTRITIONAL PROFILE:	low calories, moderate sodium, low cholesterol

- **6 large _or_ 12 medium fresh mushrooms, stems removed and reserved**
- **2 tablespoons white wine**
- **¼ cup (about ¼ large) chopped red onion**
- **¼ cup (about 1 large stalk) chopped celery**
- **2 tablespoons chopped pimiento**
- **1 teaspoon Parsley Patch Lemon Pepper herb blend**
- **1 10-ounce box frozen artichoke hearts, thawed and chopped**
- **2 teaspoons freshly grated Parmesan cheese**

Carefully separate mushroom caps from stems. Wipe each cap with a damp paper towel (see tip, page 83) and chop stems. Place wine, onions, celery, chopped stems, pimiento, herb blend, and artichoke hearts in glass measure. Microwave, **uncovered,** on HIGH for 4 to 6 minutes (LW 4¾ to 7½ minutes) or until vegetables are tender-crisp, **stirring** every 2 minutes.

Fill mushroom caps with vegetable mixture, mounding tops,

and sprinkle with Parmesan cheese. Place filled mushrooms, making 2 rings with larger caps in the outside ring and smaller caps in the center ring, on a paper plate **covered** with 2 layers of paper towels. **Elevate** plate on an inverted saucer and microwave, **uncovered,** on HIGH for 2 to 3 minutes (LW 2¼ to 3½ minutes).

Let **stand** for 1 minute before serving.

Troubleshooting: Mushrooms are microwaved on a paper plate covered with 2 layers of paper towels to absorb the liquid given off by the mushrooms. Failing to place them on paper will cause the mushrooms to be soft and squishy rather than firm.

Suggestions: Prepare mushrooms in advance and refrigerate in tightly covered container. Microwave when ready to serve.

FOR EACH SERVING:
46 calories
57 mg sodium
3 mg cholesterol
trace fat

Onion and Mushroom Appetizers

SERVES 6

EQUIPMENT:	2-quart round casserole dish
COOKING TIME:	10 to 14 minutes (Low Wattage ovens 11½ to 16 minutes)
STANDING TIME:	3 minutes
NUTRITIONAL PROFILE:	moderate calories, low sodium, no cholesterol

> 1 **16-ounce bag frozen tiny whole white onions**
> 1 **pound (about 4 cups) small fresh mushrooms**
> ½ **cup white wine vinegar**
> 3 **tablespoons tomato paste**
> 2 **tablespoons olive oil**
> 1 **bay leaf**

⅛ **teaspoon dried thyme**
¼ **teaspoon freshly ground pepper**
2 **tablespoons sugar**
3 **tablespoons minced Italian parsley**

Place plastic bag of onions on 2 **layers** of paper towels and make a slit or an X in the bag to allow steam to escape. Microwave on HIGH for 4 to 6 minutes (LW 4½ to 7 minutes) or until no longer frozen but not completely cooked.

Place onions, mushrooms, vinegar, tomato paste, olive oil, bay leaf, thyme, pepper, and sugar in casserole dish, mixing to combine. **Cover** with lid or plastic wrap, pulling back one corner to vent the steam. (If dish is flat-bottomed, **elevate** on an inverted saucer.) Microwave on 80 percent power or MEDIUM-HIGH for 6 to 8 minutes (LW 7 to 9 minutes) or until onions and mushrooms are just tender. Let **stand, covered,** for 3 minutes, sprinkle top with parsley, and serve with toothpicks.

Troubleshooting: Forgetting to vent the plastic bag may cause it to melt onto the onions. Placing the bag on paper towels will help absorb any excess moisture and keep any coloring on the bag from staining the oven floor.

FOR EACH SERVING:
100 calories
14 mg sodium
0 mg cholesterol
3 g fat

Hot Tuna-Crab Curry Dip

SERVES 12

EQUIPMENT:	4-cup glass measure, 1-quart round casserole dish
COOKING TIME:	10¾ to 15 minutes (Low Wattage ovens 13 to 18 minutes)
STANDING TIME:	none required
NUTRITIONAL PROFILE:	moderate calories, low sodium, low cholesterol

    2   tablespoons soft-spread margarine
    2   tablespoons all-purpose flour
    ½   teaspoon curry powder
    1   cup skim milk
    ¼   cup white wine
    1   6½-ounce can springwater-packed tuna, drained
        and flaked
    1   cup (about 5 ounces) flaked fresh crabmeat
    ¼   teaspoon onion powder
    1   teaspoon Parsley Patch All-Purpose herb blend

Place margarine in glass measure and melt, **uncovered,** on HIGH for 45 to 55 seconds (LW 50 to 60 seconds). **Whisk** in flour and curry powder until smooth. **Whisk** in milk until blended. Microwave on HIGH for 4 to 6 minutes (LW 4¾ to 7½ minutes) or until thickened and smooth, **whisking** every minute. **Whisk** in wine until blended.

Place tuna, crab, onion powder, and herb blend in casserole dish, **stirring** to combine. Pour sauce over fish, stirring gently. **Cover** with lid or plastic wrap, pulling back one corner to vent the steam. (If dish is flat-bottomed, **elevate** on an inverted saucer.) Microwave on 50 percent power or MEDIUM for 6 to 8 minutes (LW 7½ to 9½ minutes) or until hot and bubbly, **stirring** every 3 minutes.

Troubleshooting: Forgetting to whisk sauce may cause it to be lumpy.

Suggestions: Serve with 12 slices unsalted melba toast rounds, which add 15 calories per round, or serve with a tray of fresh celery, carrot, cucumber, zucchini, yellow squash sticks, and broccoli and cauliflower flowerets, which adds 15 calories per ⅓ cup of vegetables.

FOR EACH SERVING:
60 calories
29 mg sodium
17 mg cholesterol
1 g fat

POPCORN

Popcorn is such a microwave favorite that many oven manufacturers have started putting a special popcorn feature in their ovens. Ovens with a popcorn sensor have a small microphone inside the oven that automatically shuts the oven off when there is no popping sound for a certain period of time. This feature works wonderfully with the prepackaged micro-safe popcorn bags, but even if your microwave doesn't have this feature, you can produce great popcorn, as long as you follow some easy rules.

Don't try to pop popcorn in anything but a microwave popper or the prepackaged bags made for microwave use. Using a regular brown paper bag or a casserole dish with oil is very dangerous and can start a fire.

Microwaves are attracted to fat, sugar, or water in food to begin the cooking process, and the only one popcorn contains is a small amount of moisture. The kernels with a higher moisture content pop first, leaving the low-moisture kernels to pop last or not at all. One brand I have found to be very consistent in popping is Old Capital Popcorn. The manufacturer tells me the reason the percentage of popped kernels is so high (98 percent) is that the corn is grown in Indiana, where the growing season is longer. Most companies harvest their ears of corn and use a combine, right in the fields, to remove the kernels. Old Capital removes its kernels inside the plant to prevent damage to the kernels, which allows more of the kernels to pop. The company also air-dries its kernels to give them a more even moisture as opposed to the heat drying that most other companies do. In the old days, any brand of popcorn kernels would do, but microwave technology requires the plumper popping kernel.

Should you be a popcorn fanatic like me, and unable to find Old Capital on your shelves in the supermarket, you can write for mail-order instructions: Old Capital Popcorn, 835 Quarry Road, Corydon, IN 47112. The company has the prepackaged bags as well as the loose kernels to use in a microwave popper.

STIRRING

When you see the word *stir* in a conventional recipe, you know you're supposed to move the food around in a circular motion with a spoon or fork. However, stirring in the microwave is a bit different. For microwave cooking you need to stir the food from the center of the dish to the outside edges and bring the food along the edges into the center to ensure even cooking.

Popcorn Olé

Microwave poppers are very inexpensive and help you cut out the fat you would need to use on your stove top or in an electric popper. Popcorn is low-calorie, high-fiber, only 54 calories and a trace of sodium per 1-cup serving. It makes a great appetizer or snack that can help fill that need to munch. For an extra treat, try adding this easy topping to your popped kernels.

SERVES 10

EQUIPMENT:	microwave popper, small and large bowls
COOKING TIME:	40 to 50 seconds (Low Wattage ovens 50 to 60 seconds)
STANDING TIME:	none required
NUTRITIONAL PROFILE:	moderate calories, low sodium, no cholesterol

1   cup unpopped popcorn kernels
2   tablespoons soft-spread margarine
1   to 1½ tablespoons Parsley Patch Popcorn herb blend

Using microwave popper, pop corn according to manufacturer's instructions. Place popped corn in large bowl. In small bowl, melt margarine, uncovered, on HIGH for 40 to 50 seconds (LW 50 to 60 seconds). Blend in herb blend and drizzle over popcorn.

Troubleshooting: Do not overload the popper with kernels. Experiment with timings in your oven; overcooking the kernels will obviously result in a burned batch.

Suggestions: For added flavor, sprinkle additional herb blend over contents of bowl.

FOR EACH SERVING:
74 calories
11 mg sodium
0 mg cholesterol
2 g fat

Soups

Homemade Chicken Stock

When I was first married, my husband, William, the chef, taught me to buy whole chickens and cut them up myself. It was a great deal cheaper, and in those days every penny counted. When chickens were on sale, I bought several, cut them up, deboned the breasts for cutlets, and used the bones, backs, and wing tips to make stock. I used to boil the stock for hours, let it cool, refrigerate it, skim off the fat, and freeze in small containers to use in all my recipes. Today I still bone my own chickens, but the microwave has cut hours off the time I need to prepare my stock. Best of all, this homemade stock is low in calories, salt, and cholesterol and adds much more flavor to your recipes than the packaged low-sodium bouillon could ever do.

MAKES 8 CUPS

EQUIPMENT:	deep 3-quart casserole dish, strainer, large bowl
COOKING TIME:	50 to 57 minutes (Low Wattage ovens 60 to 68 minutes)
STANDING TIME:	10 minutes
NUTRITIONAL PROFILE:	low calories, low sodium, low cholesterol

Backs, necks, and wings from 2 chickens, fat and skin removed
2½ **quarts (10 cups) hot water**
1 **large carrot, cut into 2-inch chunks**
1 **large celery stalk, with leaves, cut into 2-inch chunks**
1 **large onion, quartered**
1 **large garlic clove, halved**
2 **teaspoons low-sodium chicken bouillon granules**
4 **sprigs fresh parsley**
8 **black peppercorns**
1 **large bay leaf**
  pinch dried thyme

Skin and remove excess fat from chicken parts. Combine all ingredients in deep casserole dish and **cover** with lid or plastic wrap, pulling back one corner to vent the steam. (If dish is flat-bottomed, **elevate** on an inverted saucer.) Place on turntable if available. Microwave on HIGH for 10 to 12 minutes (LW 12 to 14 minutes) or until boiling. **Stir, reduce** power to 70 percent or MEDIUM-HIGH, and cook for 40 to 45 minutes (LW 48 to 54 minutes), stirring every 15 minutes. (**Rotate** dish ½ turn when stirring if not using turntable.) Let **stand, covered,** for 10 minutes.

Strain stock and discard bones, vegetables, and seasonings. Place stock in bowl and allow to cool. Once cool, **cover** and chill. The fat in the stock will solidify in a layer across the top of the bowl. Carefully lift fat with a fork and discard.

Troubleshooting: Use or freeze immediately, as stock will sour if left refrigerated too long.

Suggestion: Freeze stock in ¼-, ½-, and 1-cup containers, marked with contents, or freeze in ice cube trays. Once cubes are frozen, remove from trays and store in tightly sealed plastic bags.

For less restricted diets: If you're not watching your salt intake, substitute regular chicken bouillon granules, which add 223 mg sodium per cup.

FOR EACH CUP:
43 calories
26 mg sodium
8 mg cholesterol
2 g fat

Chicken and Vegetable Soup

SERVES 6

EQUIPMENT: deep 3-quart casserole dish
COOKING TIME: 24 to 32 minutes (Low Wattage ovens 28 to 38 minutes)
STANDING TIME: 5 minutes
NUTRITIONAL PROFILE: moderate calories, low sodium, low cholesterol

1½   quarts (6 cups) low-sodium chicken broth or home-made chicken stock (page 44)
1½   cups hot water
1   pound chicken breasts, skin and fat removed
½   cup (about 1 medium) chopped onion
½   cup (about 2 large stalks) chopped celery
½   cup (about 2) chopped carrots
1   cup (about 6 ounces) sliced fresh mushrooms
1   cup frozen peas
1   cup uncooked medium eggless noodles
1   tablespoon Parsley Patch It's A Dilly herb blend
1   tablespoon snipped fresh parsley

Place broth, hot water, chicken, onion, celery, and carrots in casserole dish. **Cover** with lid or plastic wrap, pulling back one corner to vent the steam. (If dish is flat-bottomed, **elevate** on an inverted saucer.) Place on turntable if available. Microwave on HIGH for 15 to 20 minutes (LW 18 to 24 minutes) or until chicken is tender, **stirring** every 10 minutes.

Remove chicken, cut into small pieces, and return to soup. Add mushrooms, peas, noodles, herb blend, and parsley. **Stir, cover,** and cook on HIGH for 9 to 12 minutes (LW 10¾ to 14¼ minutes), until noodles are tender. Let **stand, covered,** for 5 minutes before serving.

For less restricted diets: If you're not watching your salt intake, substitute regular chicken broth, which adds 900 mg sodium per serving.

FOR EACH SERVING:
231 calories
65 mg sodium
42 mg cholesterol
10 g fat

Turkey Rice Soup

SERVES 6

EQUIPMENT:	deep 3-quart casserole dish
COOKING TIME:	36 to 43 minutes (Low Wattage ovens 43 to 50½ minutes)
STANDING TIME:	5 minutes
NUTRITION PROFILE:	moderate calories, low sodium, moderate cholesterol

2   **tablespoons white wine**
½   **cup (about 2) sliced carrots**
½   **cup (about 2 large stalks) chopped celery**
½   **pound (about 1½ cups) sliced fresh mushrooms**
½   **cup (about 1 medium) chopped onion**
2   **large garlic cloves, minced**
1½   **quarts (6 cups) low-sodium chicken broth or home-made chicken stock (page 44)**
1   **15-ounce can low-sodium stewed tomatoes, cut up, with their juice**
1   **tablespoon minced fresh parsley**
¼   **teaspoon dried thyme**
¼   **cup raw long-grain rice**
2   **cups diced cooked turkey, fat and skin removed**

Combine wine, carrots, celery, mushrooms, onion, and garlic in casserole dish. **Cover** with lid or plastic wrap, pulling back one corner to vent the steam. (If dish is flat-bottomed, **elevate** on an inverted saucer.) Place on turntable if available. Microwave on HIGH for 8 to 10 minutes (LW 9½ to 12 minutes) or until vegetables are tender, **stirring** after 5 minutes. (**Rotate** dish ½ turn when stirring if not using turntable.)

Stir in broth, tomatoes, parsley, thyme, and rice. **Cover** and cook on HIGH for 25 to 30 minutes (LW 30 to 35 minutes) or until rice is tender, **stirring** every 10 minutes. (**Rotate** dish ½ turn when stirring if not using turntable.) Add turkey, stir, **cover,** and cook on HIGH for 3 minutes (LW 3½ minutes) or until heated through. Let **stand, covered,** for 5 minutes before serving.

For less restricted diets: If you're not watching your salt intake, substitute regular chicken broth, which adds 900 mg sodium per serving, and regular stewed tomatoes, which add 115 mg sodium per serving.

FOR EACH SERVING:
198 calories
55 mg sodium
59 mg cholesterol
5 g fat

Tortellini Soup

You'll recognize a familiar taste here—wonton soup, Italian version.

SERVES 8

EQUIPMENT:	deep 3-quart casserole dish, strainer
COOKING TIME:	28 to 35 minutes (Low Wattage ovens 33½ to 42 minutes)
STANDING TIME:	3 minutes
NUTRITIONAL PROFILE:	moderate calories, low sodium, moderate cholesterol

1½ **pounds cut-up chicken fryer parts, skin and excess fat removed**
1½ **quarts (6 cups) water**
  1 **large carrot, cut into 1-inch slices**
  1 **large celery stalk with leaves, cut into 1-inch slices**
  1 **large onion, quartered**
  1 **large garlic clove, halved**
  2 **low-sodium chicken bouillon cubes**
  2 **sprigs fresh parsley**
  1 **tablespoon Parsley Patch Sesame All-Purpose herb blend**

½ teaspoon freshly ground pepper
½ pound fresh spinach, washed and torn into small pieces
½ pound frozen meat-filled tortellini

In casserole dish, place chicken parts, water, carrot, celery, onion, garlic, bouillon cubes, parsley, herb blend, and pepper. **Cover** dish with lid or plastic wrap, pulling back one corner to vent the steam. (If dish is flat-bottomed, **elevate** on an inverted saucer.) Place on turntable if available. Microwave on HIGH for 18 to 20 minutes (LW 21½ to 24 minutes), stirring and **rearranging** chicken parts several times during cooking, with the thickest parts toward the outside of the dish. (**Rotate** dish ½ turn when stirring if not using turntable.) Remove chicken parts, cool, and refrigerate for use in another recipe.

Strain broth and return to casserole dish. Add spinach and tortellini. **Cover** and cook on HIGH for 10 to 15 minutes (LW 12 to 18 minutes) or until tortellini are just tender.

Let **stand, covered,** for 3 minutes.

Suggestion: Use the leftover chicken for Chinese stew (page 129).

For less restricted diets: If you're not watching your salt intake, substitute regular chicken bouillon cubes, which add 223 mg sodium per serving.

FOR EACH SERVING:
202 calories
77 mg sodium
57 mg cholesterol
8 g fat

Meatball and Zucchini Soup

SERVES 6

EQUIPMENT: medium bowl, dinner plate, deep 3-quart casserole dish
COOKING TIME: meatballs—7 to 9 minutes (Low Wattage ovens 8½ to 10½ minutes); soup—29 to 35 minutes (Low Wattage ovens 35 to 42 minutes)

STANDING TIME: 2 to 3 minutes
NUTRITIONAL PROFILE: moderate calories, moderate sodium, moderate cholesterol

MEATBALLS
1 pound lean ground sirloin
2 egg whites, lightly beaten
¼ cup plain dry bread crumbs
¼ teaspoon dried oregano
¼ teaspoon dried basil
¼ cup freshly grated Parmesan cheese
2 tablespoons skim milk
¼ teaspoon freshly ground pepper

Mix all meatball ingredients together in medium bowl. Shape mixture into about 54 1-inch balls. Arrange balls in circles on plate and microwave, **uncovered,** on HIGH for 3 minutes (LW 3½ minutes). Drain any liquid and rearrange, bringing the less cooked ones from the center to the outside edges and the ones along the edges to the center of dish. Microwave, **uncovered,** on HIGH for 4 to 6 minutes (LW 5 to 7 minutes) or until no longer pink. Drain any liquid and set aside.

SOUP
1 cup (about 1 large) chopped onion
1 cup (about 4 large stalks) sliced celery
1 cup (about 4) chopped carrots
1 garlic clove, crushed
3 cups low-sodium chicken broth or homemade chicken stock (page 44)
1 15-ounce can low-salt whole tomatoes, cut up, with their juice
⅓ cup alphabet macaroni
1 cup hot water
1 tablespoon snipped fresh parsley
¼ teaspoon dried thyme
1 bay leaf
1 tablespoon Parsley Patch All-Purpose herb blend
1 cup (about 4 ounces) sliced fresh mushrooms
2 small zucchini, sliced

Combine onion, celery, carrots, garlic, and 2 tablespoons of the chicken broth in casserole dish. **Cover** with lid or plastic wrap, pulling back one corner to vent the steam. (If dish is flat-bottomed, **elevate** on an inverted saucer.) Place on turntable if available. Microwave on HIGH for 10 to 12 minutes (LW 12 to 14¼ minutes) or until vegetables begin to soften, **stirring** every 5 minutes. (**Rotate** dish ½ turn when stirring if not using turntable.)

Stir in remaining broth, tomatoes with juice, macaroni, water, parsley, thyme, bay leaf, and herb blend. **Cover** and cook on HIGH for 8 to 10 minutes (LW 9½ to 12 minutes).

Remove bay leaf and add mushrooms and zucchini. Stir well. **Cover** and cook on HIGH for 6 to 8 minutes (LW 7½ to 9½ minutes) or until zucchini is tender.

Add meatballs, **stir, cover,** and cook on HIGH for 5 minutes (LW 6 minutes) longer or until meatballs are thoroughly heated. Let **stand, covered,** for 2 to 3 minutes before serving.

For less restricted diets: If you're not watching your salt intake, substitute regular chicken broth, which adds 450 mg sodium per serving, and regular tomatoes, which add 115 mg sodium per serving.

> FOR EACH SERVING:
> 226 calories
> 179 mg sodium
> 70 mg cholesterol
> 13 g fat

EGGS

The egg is the number one villain for anyone with a family history of heart problems and a tendency toward high cholesterol. If one egg gives you ¾ of a day's supply of clog-forming cholesterol, just imagine what 2 or 3 eggs—the typical American breakfast—will do. The cholesterol is found only in the egg *yolk;* therefore, you can substitute 2 egg whites for 1 whole egg. While saving your heart you don't have to give up good nutrition, since the egg white is an excellent source of protein.

But you worry about having all those useless egg yolks left over? Did you know that plant food contains a protein similar to the one found in egg yolks? Instead of buying costly plant food, add shine to your plants by diluting leftover egg yolks with a little water and using the mixture as plant food. Animals don't seem to have the same problems with clogged arteries their masters do, so another option is to mix the leftover egg yolks into your pets' daily food, increasing their body-building protein while giving them a shiny coat.

Homemade Beef Stock

Years back, when you could buy a hindquarter of beef for about 69 cents a pound, my freezer was always full. The butcher used to break down the hind, cutting steaks and grinding hamburger, and my husband used to cut the top, bottom, and sirloin sections into roasts, swiss steaks, and stew beef. I always asked the butcher to include all the bones with the order and used them to make beef stock. Today meat prices have skyrocketed, but some habits never change. I still use beef soup bones, and the microwave saves me hours of work.

MAKES 8 CUPS

EQUIPMENT:	deep 3- or 4-quart casserole dish, strainer, large deep bowl
COOKING TIME:	64 to 73 minutes (Low Wattage ovens 76¾ to 87½ minutes)
STANDING TIME:	5 minutes
NUTRITIONAL PROFILE:	low calories, low sodium, no cholesterol

4 pounds beef soup bones, excess fat removed
1 large carrot, cut into 2-inch chunks
1 large celery stalk, with leaves, cut into 2-inch chunks
1 large onion, quartered
2 large garlic cloves, halved
2 teaspoons low-sodium beef bouillon granules
4 sprigs fresh parsley
8 black peppercorns
1 large bay leaf
pinch dried thyme
2½ quarts (10 cups) water

Place soup bones, carrot, celery, onion, and garlic in deep casserole dish. (If dish is flat-bottomed, **elevate** on an inverted saucer.) Place on turntable if available. Microwave on HIGH for 4 to 6 minutes (LW 4¾ to 7½ minutes) or until bones appear crispy. Add all remaining ingredients and **cover** with lid or plastic wrap, pulling back one corner to vent the steam. Microwave on HIGH for 10 to 12 minutes (LW 12 to 14 minutes) or until boiling. **Stir,**

reduce power to 70 percent or MEDIUM-HIGH, and cook, **uncovered,** for 50 to 55 minutes (LW 60 to 66 minutes), stirring every 15 minutes. (**Rotate** dish ½ turn with each stirring if not using turntable.) Let **stand** for 5 minutes.

Strain, discarding bones, vegetables, and seasonings. Place stock in bowl and allow to cool. Once cool, cover and chill. Once well chilled, fat will solidify in a layer across top of stock. Carefully lift fat out of stock with fork and discard.

Troubleshooting: Use or freeze immediately, as stock will sour if refrigerated too long.

Suggestions: Package in ¼-, ½-, or 1-cup containers in ice cube trays and freeze, marked with contents and date. If freezing in ice cube trays, once frozen, remove cubes and store in tightly sealed plastic bags.

For less restricted diets: If you're not watching your salt intake, substitute regular beef bouillon granules, which add 223 mg sodium per cup.

FOR EACH CUP:
22 calories
21 mg sodium
0 mg cholesterol
trace fat

PACKAGING SOUP
FOR FREEZING AND REHEATING

To make reheating leftover frozen soup easier, line the container to be used for reheating with a large plastic bag. Fill the bag with cooled soup, secure tightly, and freeze in the container. Once frozen, remove the container from freezer and label bag with contents and date. When you're ready to defrost and reheat it, the soup will come right out of the plastic bag and slip perfectly into the dish for defrosting and reheating.

Angelo's Italian Soup .

My friend Angelo comes from an old Italian family, and he remembers that in his boyhood there was always a pot of soup cooking on the back of his mother's stove. Each pot was different, depending on what was available that week. The art of cooking always fascinated Angelo, and he patterned his career around the kitchen, teaching and working in the hotel field. One of the old habits Angelo finds hard to break is simmering his mom's soup for his family. Because he loses track of time when he pursues his woodcarving hobby, microwaving the soup has saved him from scrubbing many a burned pot.

SERVES 8

EQUIPMENT:	medium bowl, deep 3-quart casserole dish
COOKING TIME:	82 to 95 minutes (Low Wattage ovens 98¼ to 113 minutes)
STANDING TIME:	5 minutes
NUTRITIONAL PROFILE:	moderate calories, low sodium, moderate cholesterol

1	**pound lean ground pork**
½	**teaspoon paprika**
1	**tablespoon fennel seed**
½	**teaspoon freshly ground pepper**
2	**quarts (8 cups) hot water**
1	**pound (2 cups) dried green split peas, washed and sorted**
1	**medium zucchini, diced**
2	**medium carrots, diced**
2	**medium onions, diced**
1	**cup (about 4 large stalks) diced celery**
1	**tablespoon Parsley Patch All-Purpose herb blend**
4	**teaspoons low-sodium chicken bouillon granules**

Combine pork, paprika, fennel seed, and pepper in medium bowl. Mix well and roll into 1-inch round, uniformly sized meatballs. In casserole dish, combine water, split peas, zucchini, carrots, onions, celery, herb blend, and bouillon. **Stir** and **cover** dish with lid or plastic wrap, pulling back one corner to vent the steam. (If dish is flat-bottomed, **elevate** on an inverted saucer.) Place on turntable if available. Microwave on HIGH for 12 to 15 minutes (LW 14¼ to 17 minutes), then **reduce** power to 50 percent or MEDIUM, **stir, cover,** and microwave for 45 to 50 minutes (LW 54 to 60 minutes).

Drop uncooked meatballs into soup, **cover,** and cook on 50 percent power or MEDIUM for 25 to 30 minutes (LW 30 to 36 minutes) or until meatballs are cooked, vegetables are tender, and flavors blend. Let **stand, covered,** for 5 minutes before serving.

For less restricted diets: If you're not watching your salt intake, substitute regular chicken bouillon granules, which add 450 mg sodium per serving.

FOR EACH SERVING:
200 calories
71 mg sodium
50 mg cholesterol
5 g fat

Beef Barley Soup

SERVES 8

EQUIPMENT:	deep 3-quart casserole dish
COOKING TIME:	80 to 90 minutes (Low Wattage ovens 95 to 111 minutes)
STANDING TIME:	5 minutes
NUTRITIONAL PROFILE:	low calories, low sodium, low cholesterol

1   pound boneless lean sirloin beef, cut into ½-inch pieces
5   cups hot water
2   cups low-sodium beef broth or homemade beef stock (page 52)
1   15-ounce can low-sodium stewed tomatoes, with their juice
2   large celery stalks, sliced

1 **large onion, chopped**
1 **large garlic clove, minced**
1 **cup (about 4) sliced carrots**
1 **tablespoon Parsley Patch All-Purpose herb blend**
1 **teaspoon paprika**
¼ **cup pearl barley**
1 **9-ounce package frozen cut green beans**

Place beef and water in casserole dish. **Cover** with lid or plastic wrap, pulling back one corner to vent the steam. (If dish is flat-bottomed, **elevate** dish on an inverted saucer.) Place on a turntable if available. Microwave on HIGH for 15 minutes (LW 18 minutes).

Add beef broth, stewed tomatoes, celery, onion, garlic, carrots, herb blend, paprika, and barley. **Stir** well, **cover,** and **rotate** dish ½ turn if not using turntable. Cook on HIGH for 55 to 60 minutes (LW 65 to 75 minutes) or until meat is tender, **stirring** every 20 minutes. (**Rotate** dish ½ turn with each stirring if not using turntable.)

Add green beans, **stir, cover,** and cook on HIGH for 10 to 15 minutes (LW 12 to 18 minutes) or until beans are tender. Let **stand, covered,** for 5 minutes before serving.

For less restricted diets: If you're not watching your salt intake, substitute regular beef broth, which adds 223 mg sodium per serving, and regular stewed tomatoes, which add 86 mg sodium per serving.

FOR EACH SERVING:
110 calories
67 mg sodium
40 mg cholesterol
12 g fat

Beef Minestrone

SERVES 8

EQUIPMENT: deep 3-quart casserole dish
COOKING TIME: 87 to 99 minutes (Low Wattage ovens 104¼ to 118¾ minutes)
STANDING TIME: 5 minutes
NUTRITIONAL PROFILE: low calories, low sodium, low cholesterol

   3   **cups hot water**
  ½   **pound lean sirloin beef, cut into ½-inch cubes**
   1   **cup (about 1 large) chopped onion**
   1   **garlic clove, crushed**
  ¾   **cup (about 3 stalks) sliced celery**
  ½   **cup (about ¼ pound) fresh green beans, cut into 1-inch pieces**
  ½   **cup (about 2) thinly sliced carrots**
   4   **cups low-sodium beef broth or homemade beef stock (page 52)**
   1   **15-ounce can low-salt tomatoes, cut up, with their liquid**
   1   **teaspoon Parsley Patch All-Purpose herb blend**
  ⅓   **cup macaroni (ditaline 40)**
  ½   **cup zucchini, sliced into thin half-moons**
  ½   **cup fresh or frozen okra**
  ½   **cup frozen corn kernels**

In casserole dish, place water, beef, onion, garlic, celery, beans, and carrots. **Cover** dish with lid or plastic wrap, pulling back one corner to vent the steam. (If dish is flat-bottomed, **elevate** on an inverted saucer.) Place on turntable if available. Microwave on HIGH for 15 minutes (LW 18 minutes), then stir.

Add broth, tomatoes with liquid, and herb blend, **stirring** well. **Cover** and cook on HIGH for 15 minutes (LW 18 minutes). Reduce power to 50 percent or MEDIUM, **stir, cover,** and cook for 50 to 60 minutes (LW 60 to 72 minutes) or until meat is tender, stirring every 20 minutes. (If not using turntable, **rotate** dish ½ turn with every stirring.)

Stir in macaroni, zucchini, okra, and corn. **Cover** and cook on HIGH for 7 to 9 minutes (LW 8¼ to 10¾ minutes) or until vegetables are tender and macaroni is cooked. Let **stand, covered,** for 5 minutes before serving.

For less restricted diets: If you're not watching your salt intake, substitute regular beef broth, which adds 450 mg sodium per serving, and regular tomatoes, which add 86 mg sodium per serving.

FOR EACH SERVING:
101 calories
60 mg sodium
20 mg cholesterol
2 g fat

Farmer's Vegetable Soup

SERVES 6

EQUIPMENT:	deep 3-quart casserole dish
COOKING TIME:	56 to 68 minutes (Low Wattage ovens 67½ to 81½ minutes)
STANDING TIME:	5 minutes
NUTRITIONAL PROFILE:	low calories, low sodium, no cholesterol

1   **cup (about 4 large stalks) celery**
1   **cup (about 4) sliced carrots**
1   **cup (about 1 large) chopped onion**
1   **cup fresh (about 2 ears) corn kernels or frozen corn kernels**
1   **cup (about 2 small) diced potatoes**
1   **cup (about ½ pound) diced fresh green beans**
1   **large garlic clove, crushed**
1   **28-ounce can low-salt whole peeled tomatoes, cut up, with their juice**
6   **cups low-salt beef broth or homemade beef stock (page 52)**
1   **tablespoon Parsley Patch All-Purpose herb blend**
¼   **teaspoon freshly ground pepper**
2   **tablespoons snipped fresh parsley**
1   **cup (about 1 small) sliced fresh zucchini**
1   **tablespoon freshly grated Parmesan cheese**

Combine all ingredients, except zucchini and Parmesan cheese, in casserole dish. **Cover** with lid or plastic wrap, pulling back one corner to vent the steam. (If dish is flat-bottomed, **elevate** on an inverted saucer.) Place dish on turntable if available.

Microwave on HIGH for 50 to 60 minutes (LW 60 to 72 minutes) or until vegetables are tender, **stirring** every 15 minutes. (**Rotate** dish ½ turn when stirring if not using turntable.)

Add zucchini, **stir, cover,** and cook on HIGH for 6 to 8 minutes (LW 7½ to 9½ minutes) or until zucchini is tender.

Let **stand, covered,** for 5 minutes and serve topped with Parmesan cheese.

For less restricted diets: If you're not watching your salt intake, substitute regular tomatoes, which add 209 mg sodium per serving, and regular beef broth, which adds 900 mg sodium per serving.

FOR EACH SERVING:
143 calories
94 mg sodium
0 mg cholesterol
5 g fat

Cream of Broccoli Soup

SERVES 8

EQUIPMENT: 2-quart and deep 3-quart casserole dishes, blender or food processor
COOKING TIME: 24 to 29 minutes (Low Wattage ovens 31 to 37 minutes)
STANDING TIME: none required
NUTRITIONAL PROFILE: low calories, low sodium, no cholesterol

1   cup (about 1 large) finely chopped potato
1   pound fresh broccoli, finely chopped
½   cup (about 1 medium) chopped onion
½   cup (about 2 large stalks) chopped celery
½   cup (about 2) grated carrots
2   cups water
3   tablespoons all-purpose flour
3   cups skim milk
2   tablespoons snipped fresh parsley
1   tablespoon Parsley Patch Sesame All-Purpose herb blend
⅛   teaspoon freshly grated nutmeg

Combine potato, broccoli, onion, celery, carrots, and ½ cup of the water in casserole dish. **Cover** with lid or plastic wrap, pulling back one corner to vent the steam. (If dish is flat-bottomed, **elevate** on an inverted saucer.) Place on turntable if available.

Microwave on HIGH for 12 to 14 minutes (LW 14¼ to 16¾ minutes) or until vegetables are tender-crisp, **stirring** every 6 minutes. (**Rotate** dish ½ turn when stirring if not using turntable.) **Drain.**

In deep casserole dish, whisk flour into remaining 1½ cups water. **Whisk** in milk, parsley, herb blend, and nutmeg. Stir in drained vegetables and cover. (If dish is flat-bottomed, **elevate** on an inverted saucer.) Cook on HIGH for 8 to 10 minutes (LW 12 to 14¼ minutes), **stirring** every 3 minutes, until hot. (**Rotate** dish ¼ turn when stirring if not using turntable.)

Remove 1¾ cups of hot soup and place in container of electric blender or food processor. **Puree** mixture until very smooth. Return pureed soup to casserole dish, **stir, cover,** and cook on HIGH for 4 to 5 minutes (LW 4¾ to 6 minutes) or until heated through.

Suggestion: Garnish with fresh parsley or broccoli flowerets.

FOR EACH SERVING:
89 calories
63 mg sodium
0 mg cholesterol
trace fat

Old-Fashioned Pea Soup

SERVES 8

EQUIPMENT: deep 4-quart casserole dish
COOKING TIME: 1 hour 50 minutes to 2½ hours (Low Wattage ovens 2 hours 24 minutes to 3 hours 6 minutes)
STANDING TIME: 10 minutes
NUTRITIONAL PROFILE: low calories, low sodium, no cholesterol

1 pound (2 cups) dried green split peas, washed and sorted
½ cup (about 1 medium) chopped onion
½ cup (about 2 large stalks) chopped celery
½ cup (about 2) chopped carrots

4 **marrow bones or 1 1-pound shank bone, excess meat and fat removed**
1½ **quarts (6 cups) water**
1 **tablespoon Parsley Patch All-Purpose herb blend**

Combine all ingredients in casserole dish. **Cover** dish with lid or plastic wrap, pulling back one corner to vent the steam. (If dish is flat-bottomed, **elevate** on an inverted saucer.) Place on turntable if available. Microwave on HIGH for 20 to 30 minutes (LW 24 to 36 minutes) or until boiling, **stirring** every 15 minutes. (**Rotate** dish ½ turn when stirring if not using turntable.)

Reduce power to 50 percent or MEDIUM, cover, and microwave for 1½ to 2 hours (LW 2 to 2½ hours), **stirring** 2 or 3 times during cooking. (**Rotate** dish ½ turn when stirring if not using turntable.) Cook until all vegetables are tender, the soup is thickened, and the peas have dissolved. Let **stand, covered,** for 10 minutes before serving.

Suggestion: If soup is thicker than you would like, add a small amount of water until it has the consistency you prefer. This recipe freezes and reheats perfectly.

FOR EACH SERVING:
65 calories
16 mg sodium
0 mg cholesterol
trace fat

Vegetables

ARTICHOKES

When selecting artichokes, be sure the leaves are tightly closed—those with loose-spreading leaves will be tough. To prepare the artichokes: Begin by slicing off the top third of the artichoke, then slice the stem end off as close to the bottom as possible, so it will stand up. Next, snap off any small leaves near the flat bottom. Using scissors, cut off the tips of the outer leaves. Rinse each artichoke under running water and shake off all excess moisture. Brush fresh lemon juice (see box, page 124) over the cuts so they won't turn dark.

Those of you who have only watched and never indulged may need a lesson in artichoke eating. To savor all the goodness the leaves hold, pull the leaf, upside down, through your teeth before discarding and going on to the next one. For everyone's convenience, be sure to serve small bowls to hold leaves as they are discarded. Once all the leaves are removed, cut the round bottom from the artichoke, cut it into pieces—and eat. If you miss a dipping sauce, try dipping the leaves into freshly squeezed lemon juice.

Artichokes alone are very low in calories. They are a lovely treat, and if you haven't tried them, maybe it's time you do.

Simple Artichokes

SERVES 1 PER PERSON

EQUIPMENT:	meat rack or round baking dish, grapefruit spoon or pointed spoon
COOKING TIME:	approximately 4 to 6 minutes per artichoke for all ovens
STANDING TIME:	3 minutes
NUTRITIONAL PROFILE:	low calories, low sodium, no cholesterol

1 to 4 fresh artichokes
¼ cup water for Method 2

Method 1. Wrap each artichoke individually in either plastic wrap or wax paper and place them in a circle on the outer edges of a meat rack if available, stem side up. If using wax paper, be sure to twist the ends closed.

Method 2. Place artichokes in a round baking dish, stem side up and toward the outside of the dish. Add ¼ cup water and **cover** with plastic wrap, pulling back one corner to vent steam. (If dish is flat-bottomed, **elevate** on an inverted saucer.)
    Microwave on HIGH as follows:

1 artichoke: 4 to 5 minutes (LW 4¾ to 6 minutes)
2 artichokes: 5 to 7 minutes (LW 6 to 8¼ minutes)
3 artichokes: 8 to 11 minutes (LW 9½ to 13¼ minutes)
4 artichokes: 12 to 15 minutes (LW 14¼ to 18 minutes)

Rearrange artichokes every 4 minutes. When cooking finishes, you should be able to pierce the bottom easily with a fork and the leaves should pull off with no trouble. Let **stand, covered,** for 3 minutes. Using a grapefruit spoon or pointed spoon, remove the fuzzy center.

FOR EACH SERVING:
53 calories
2 mg sodium
0 mg cholesterol
trace fat

GREEN BEANS

Green beans are available year-round and are a good source of vitamin A as well as potassium and calcium. To choose the freshest beans, be sure they are firm and snap when you bend them. Store unwashed beans in a plastic bag to keep them moist and rinse them before cooking.

Lemon-Dill Green Beans

SERVES 6

EQUIPMENT:	2-quart round casserole dish
COOKING TIME:	10 to 13 minutes (Low Wattage ovens 12 to 15½ minutes)
STANDING TIME:	5 minutes
NUTRITIONAL PROFILE:	low calories, trace sodium, no cholesterol

1 pound green beans, tops and tails removed
½ cup water
2 tablespoons fresh lemon juice (see box, page 124)
1 teaspoon Parsley Patch It's A Dilly herb blend

Rinse and cut beans into 1-inch uniformly sized pieces. Place beans and water in casserole dish and **cover** dish with lid or plastic wrap, pulling back one corner to vent the steam. (If dish is flat-bottomed, **elevate** on an inverted saucer.) Place on turntable if available.

Microwave on HIGH for 10 to 13 minutes (LW 12 to 15½ minutes) or until tender-crisp, **stirring** every 5 minutes. (**Rotate** dish ½ turn when stirring if not using turntable.) Let **stand, covered,** for 5 minutes. **Drain,** place beans in serving dish, and sprinkle with lemon juice and herb blend.

Troubleshooting: Be sure to cut beans into uniformly sized pieces so the entire batch will cook evenly.

Failing to use a round container may cause beans in the corners to overcook.

When stirring, be sure to bring the less cooked beans from the center of the dish to the outside edges and the ones along the edges into the center.

FOR EACH SERVING:
22 calories
trace sodium
0 mg cholesterol
0 g fat

FRESH VEGETABLES

Fresh vegetables may seem almost salt-free. Yes, there is some natural sodium in all foods. Fresh vegetables that have the highest amount of sodium are celery, red beets, peas, and dark greens, such as chard and kale. That doesn't mean you should never use them, because they're very good for you, but if you're watching your salt intake, use them sparingly (for example, once a week in quantities of ¼ cup only). Frozen vegetables, without added sauces and butter, are preferable to canned for your health, since they are lower in sodium and have more vitamins intact. Regular canned vegetables should be used only as the last resort.

Italian-Style Beans

SERVES 6

EQUIPMENT:	2-quart casserole dish, plastic dishwasher-safe colander and casserole dish to catch the drippings
COOKING TIME:	25 to 29 minutes (Low Wattage ovens 28¾ to 33½ minutes)
STANDING TIME:	none required
NUTRITIONAL PROFILE:	moderate calories, low sodium, low cholesterol

2 10-ounce paper-covered boxes frozen flat Italian green beans
¼ **teaspoon fennel seed**
½ **teaspoon Parsley Patch Garlicsaltless herb blend**
½ **pound lean ground pork**
¼ **cup (about ¼ large) chopped red bell pepper**
¼ **cup (about ¼ large) chopped red onion**
¼ **cup (about 1 ounce) sliced fresh mushrooms**
¼ **cup olive oil**
1 **teaspoon dried oregano**
¼ **teaspoon garlic powder**
¼ **teaspoon dried crushed basil**

Place both **paper-covered** boxes on 2 layers of paper towels on microwave floor. Microwave on HIGH for 7 minutes (LW 8 minutes). **Shake** packages, **turn over,** and cook on HIGH for 8 to 9 minutes (LW 9 to 10 minutes) or until tender-crisp. Place beans in casserole dish and set aside.

Combine fennel and herb blend with ground pork. **Crumble** pork mixture into colander set into a casserole dish. Microwave, uncovered, on HIGH for 3 minutes (LW 3½ minutes). **Stir,** breaking up meat chunks with a fork, and add red bell pepper, onion, and mushrooms. Cook, **uncovered,** on HIGH for 4 to 6 minutes (LW 4¾ to 7½ minutes) or until meat is no longer pink and vegetables are tender-crisp.

Add meat and vegetables to beans; sprinkle with oil, oregano, garlic powder, and basil. **Stir** and **cover** dish with lid or plastic wrap, pulling back one corner to vent the steam. (If dish is flat-bottomed, **elevate** on an inverted saucer.) Microwave on HIGH for 3 to 4 minutes (LW 3½ to 4½ minutes) or until heated through.

Troubleshooting: If frozen vegetable boxes are covered with an aluminum foil wrapper, remove it, or it will arc and set the paper box on fire. Microwave paper-covered boxes only.

Suggestion: If flat Italian green beans aren't available, substitute regular frozen or fresh green beans.

FOR EACH SERVING:
159 calories
19 mg sodium
25 mg cholesterol
10 g fat

BROCCOLI

Broccoli is not only a healthy source of calcium, potassium, vitamins A and C, and B vitamins, but it is also attractive to the eye. While low in calories, only 45 calories per stalk, broccoli has little sodium and no cholesterol. This versatile green vegetable has been recommended as a possible aid in preventing certain forms of cancer.

Select heads of broccoli that are firm with green stalks and dark green heads. Yellow buds or yellowing stalks indicate a lack of freshness and will lead to a tough finished product.

If you aren't going to use your broccoli the day you purchase it, store the head in a plastic bag and wash it just before using. Storing broccoli uncovered can aid in its wilting and will also send a strange odor throughout your refrigerator.

Broccoli Spears

SERVES 4

EQUIPMENT:	9- or 10-inch round glass dish or 12 × 8- or 13 × 9-inch baking dish
COOKING TIME:	8 to 12 minutes (Low Wattage ovens 9½ to 14¼ minutes)
STANDING TIME:	2 to 3 minutes
NUTRITIONAL PROFILE:	low calories, low sodium, no cholesterol

1 pound fresh broccoli
¼ cup water

Trim off hard bottom, divide broccoli bunch into spears as uniformly as you can, and rinse stalks well. The bud end cooks the fastest and must be placed in the center of the dish. Using a round dish works best, but if you have a large head, **distribute** the spears evenly in a flat baking dish, with the stalk end toward the outside of the dish and buds to the center.

Sprinkle water over spears and **cover** with plastic wrap, pulling back one corner to vent the steam. (If dish is flat-bottomed, **elevate** on an inverted saucer.) Microwave on HIGH for 8 to 12 minutes (LW 9½ to 14¼ minutes) or until the stalk can be pierced easily with a fork, **rotating** dish ½ turn every 3 minutes. Let **stand, covered,** for 2 to 3 minutes.

Troubleshooting: Sometimes the stalks have a hard outer layer; if this is the case, peel off a thin layer of skin the length of the stalk until you reach the bud.

Suggestion: Save yourself time and effort by jotting down the cooking time it took in your oven to achieve the degree of doneness you prefer. It will keep you from having to experiment again and again.

FOR EACH SERVING:
25 calories
10 mg sodium
0 mg cholesterol
trace fat

Broccoli Chunks

SERVES 4

EQUIPMENT:	2-quart round casserole dish
COOKING TIME:	8 to 10 minutes (Low Wattage ovens 9½ to 12 minutes)
STANDING TIME:	3 to 5 minutes
NUTRITIONAL PROFILE:	low calories, low sodium, no cholesterol

1 pound fresh broccoli
¼ cup water

Wash and trim off hard bottom. Divide into **uniformly** sized spears and cut each spear into uniformly sized 1-inch chunks. Place chunks in casserole dish and sprinkle with water. **Cover** with lid or plastic wrap, pulling back one corner to vent the steam. (If dish is flat-bottomed, **elevate** on an inverted saucer.) Place on turntable if available. Microwave on HIGH for 8 to 10 minutes (LW 9½ to 12 minutes), **stirring** and **rearranging** the chunks every 4 minutes until they can be pierced easily with a fork. (**Rotate** dish ½ turn when stirring if not using turntable.) Let **stand, covered,** for 3 to 5 minutes and drain before serving.

Troubleshooting: Sometimes the stalks have a hard outer layer; if this is the case, peel a thin layer of skin the length of the stalk until you reach the bud.

To ensure even cooking, when cutting chunks, be sure they are uniform in size, as things of the same size and shape microwave in the same length of time.

When stirring, bring the less cooked chunks from the center of the dish to the outside edges and the ones along the edges into the center of the dish.

FOR EACH SERVING:
25 calories
10 mg sodium
0 mg cholesterol
trace fat

Broccoli Polonaise

Instead of plain cooked spears, try zipping them up with one of the toppings in this and the following recipe.

SERVES 4

EQUIPMENT:	4-cup glass measure, serving platter
COOKING TIME:	broccoli—8 to 12 minutes (Low Wattage ovens 9½ to 14¼ minutes); topping—2 to 3 minutes (Low Wattage ovens 2½ to 3½ minutes)
STANDING TIME:	none required
NUTRITIONAL PROFILE:	low calories, low sodium, no cholesterol

1 pound cooked broccoli spears (page 67)
¼ cup white wine
2 scallions, diced
½ teaspoon garlic powder
1 tablespoon Parsley Patch Sesame Lemon Pepper herb blend
¼ cup plain dry bread crumbs
1 teaspoon capers
2 tablespoons chopped fresh parsley
4 lemon slices

While microwaved broccoli spears are standing, place wine, scallions, garlic powder, and herb blend in glass measure. Microwave, **uncovered,** on HIGH for 2 to 3 minutes (LW 2½ to 3½ minutes), until scallions are soft. **Stir** in bread crumbs until well blended. **Arrange** spears on a serving platter and spoon bread crumb mixture on top. Sprinkle dish with capers and chopped parsley and arrange lemon slices over spears.

FOR EACH SERVING:
61 calories
43 mg sodium
0 mg cholesterol
trace fat

Sesame Broccoli

SERVES 4

EQUIPMENT:	4-cup glass measure, serving platter
COOKING TIME:	broccoli—8 to 12 minutes (Low Wattage ovens 9½ to 14¼ minutes); topping—2 to 3 minutes (Low Wattage ovens 2½ to 3½ minutes)
STANDING TIME:	none required
NUTRITIONAL PROFILE:	low calories, low sodium, low cholesterol

1 pound cooked broccoli spears (page 67)
¾ cup plain yogurt

⅓ **cup skim milk**
1 **tablespoon Parsley Patch Sesame All-Purpose herb blend**
½ **teaspoon onion powder**
2 **tablespoons fresh lemon juice (see box, page 124)**
2 **tablespoons toasted sesame seeds (recipe follows)**

While microwaved broccoli spears are standing, **whisk** together yogurt, milk, herb blend, and onion powder in glass measure. Microwave, **uncovered,** on HIGH for 2 to 3 minutes (LW 2½ to 3½ minutes), whisking every minute, just until hot. **Do not boil.** Once hot, **whisk** in lemon juice. Arrange broccoli on serving platter and cover with sauce. Sprinkle sesame seeds over sauce.

Troubleshooting: Forgetting to whisk sauce may cause it to be lumpy.

FOR EACH SERVING:
76 calories
56 mg sodium
3 mg cholesterol
3 g fat

TOASTED SESAME SEEDS

MAKES 2 TABLESPOONS

EQUIPMENT:	1-cup glass measure
COOKING TIME:	3½ to 5¾ minutes (Low Wattage ovens 4¼ to 7 minutes)
STANDING TIME:	2 to 3 minutes
NUTRITIONAL PROFILE:	low calories, low sodium, no cholesterol

1 **tablespoon soft-spread margarine**
2 **tablespoons sesame seeds**

Place margarine in glass measure and melt on HIGH, **uncovered,** for 35 to 45 seconds (LW 45 to 55 seconds). **Stir** in sesame seeds, completely coating with melted margarine. Microwave, **uncovered,** on HIGH for 3 to 5 minutes (LW 3½ to 6 minutes),

stirring every minute, until light golden brown. Let **stand** for 2 to 3 minutes to finish browning. **Cool** and **drain** on paper plate covered with 2 layers of paper towels.

FOR EACH ½ TABLESPOON:
40 calories
27 mg sodium
0 mg cholesterol
4 g fat

Broccoli and Mushrooms

SERVES 6

EQUIPMENT: 2-quart flat baking dish, 1-quart round cas-
serole dish
COOKING TIME: 9 to 13 minutes (Low Wattage ovens 10½ to
15¾ minutes)
STANDING TIME: none required
NUTRITIONAL PROFILE: low calories, low sodium, low cholesterol

1 **pound broccoli, cut into uniformly sized chunks and cooked (page 68)**
2 **tablespoons white wine**
1 **cup (about 4 ounces) sliced mushrooms**
½ **teaspoon onion powder**
dash freshly ground pepper
½ **cup plain yogurt**
1 **teaspoon chopped fresh chives**

Place cooked broccoli in baking dish. Place wine and mushrooms in casserole dish. **Cover** with lid or plastic wrap, pulling back one corner to vent steam. (If dish is flat-bottomed, **elevate** on an inverted saucer.) Microwave on HIGH for 4 to 6 minutes (LW 4¾ to 7½ minutes) or until almost tender. **Stir** onion powder, pepper, yogurt, and chives into mushrooms.

Microwave, **uncovered,** on 50 percent power or MEDIUM for 3 to 4 minutes (LW 3½ to 4¾ minutes) or until heated through.

Pour sauce over broccoli, **cover** again, **elevate** on an inverted saucer, and heat on 50 percent or MEDIUM for 2 to 3 minutes (LW 2¼ to 3½ minutes) or until dish is bubbly hot.

Troubleshooting: Drain any excess liquid from yogurt container before adding to recipe.

Suggestion: For a change of taste, substitute cooked asparagus or green beans for broccoli.

FOR EACH SERVING:
50 calories
23 mg sodium
1 mg cholesterol
trace fat

CABBAGE

If you're using green cabbage only for coleslaw, you're really not enjoying this very versatile vegetable to its utmost. A rich source of vitamin C, this leafy green variety also contains vitamin A and B, potassium, and a small amount of calcium and phosphorous. It is also high in fiber and low in sodium and calories. And don't forget red cabbage and Chinese cabbage. When you boil vegetables on a conventional stove, many of the vitamins and nutrients are left in the cooking water. In the microwave, to preserve the high vitamin and nutrient count, cook just until tender.

Steamed Cabbage Wedges

SERVES 4

EQUIPMENT: 12 × 8 or 9 × 13-inch flat baking dish
COOKING TIME: 12 to 16 minutes (Low Wattage ovens 14¼ to 19½ minutes)
STANDING TIME: 3 to 4 minutes
NUTRITIONAL PROFILE: low calories, low sodium, no cholesterol

1 2-pound whole fresh green cabbage, cut into 4 uniformly sized wedges

¼ cup water

Place wedges in flat baking dish with the broader ends toward the outside of the dish and sprinkle with water. **Cover** dish with plastic wrap, pulling back one corner to vent the steam. (If dish is flat-bottomed, **elevate** on an inverted saucer.)

Microwave on HIGH for about 12 to 16 minutes (LW 14¼ to 19½ minutes). **Rearrange** the wedges and **rotate** dish ½ turn every 5 minutes. Once the cabbage is tender to your taste, let the dish **stand, covered,** for 3 to 4 minutes before serving.

FOR EACH SERVING:
25 calories
20 mg sodium
0 mg cholesterol
trace fat

Cabbage Casserole

If you'd like a change from just plain cabbage, try this summer cabbage casserole, which incorporates several native vegetables.

SERVES 4

EQUIPMENT:	12 × 8-inch baking dish
COOKING TIME:	11 to 14 minutes (Low Wattage ovens 13½ to 17 minutes)
STANDING TIME:	3 minutes
NUTRITIONAL PROFILE:	low calories, low sodium, no cholesterol

2 tablespoons white wine
1 small garlic clove, minced
1 green bell pepper, diced
2 fresh tomatoes, diced
1 medium onion, diced
1 teaspoon Parsley Patch All-Purpose herb blend

½ **teaspoon sugar**
⅛ **teaspoon celery seed**
 dash freshly ground pepper
4 **cups (about 1 medium) shredded cabbage**

Place wine, garlic, green bell pepper, tomatoes, and onion in baking dish. **Cover** dish with plastic wrap, pulling back one corner to vent the steam. (If dish is flat-bottomed, **elevate** on an inverted saucer.) Microwave on HIGH for 5 to 6 minutes (LW 6 to 7½ minutes) or until vegetables are tender-crisp.

Sprinkle herb blend, sugar, celery seed, and pepper over vegetables, mixing to combine. Add shredded cabbage to vegetables, **stirring** well. **Cover** and microwave on HIGH for 6 to 8 minutes (LW 7½ to 9½ minutes) or until cabbage is tender, stirring and **rotating** dish ½ turn every 3 minutes. Let **stand, covered,** for 3 minutes and serve as a side dish for meat or poultry.

FOR EACH SERVING:
54 calories
25 mg sodium
0 mg cholesterol
trace fat

CAULIFLOWER

Cauliflower is another vegetable thought to help reduce some forms of cancer. It is a good source of vitamin C, potassium, and phosphorus. One medium head of cauliflower contains 62 calories, a small amount of sodium, and no cholesterol. Mark Twain once said, "Cauliflower is nothing but cabbage with a college education." I don't think Twain had any idea, at the time, that the microwave could prepare this highly educated vegetable so quickly. But of course it's also delicious raw.

Cauliflower au Gratin

SERVES 4

EQUIPMENT: 2-quart round casserole dish, 4-cup glass measure, custard cup

COOKING TIME: 17½ to 22¾ minutes (Low Wattage ovens 21¼ to 27¼ minutes)

STANDING TIME: 4 minutes

NUTRITIONAL PROFILE: moderate calories, low sodium, low cholesterol

1   **medium head fresh cauliflower**
¼   **cup water**
1   **tablespoon white wine**
2   **tablespoons all-purpose flour**
1   **cup skim milk**
¼   **cup shredded Cheddar cheese**
1   **tablespoon soft-spread margarine**
¼   **cup plain dry bread crumbs**
1   **teaspoon Parsley Patch Sesame All-Purpose herb blend**
    paprika

Separate head of cauliflower into uniformly sized flowerets. Wash in cool water, shake off excess water, and place in casserole dish. Add ¼ cup water and **cover** with lid or plastic wrap, pulling back one corner to vent the steam. (If dish is flat-bottomed, **elevate** on an inverted saucer.) Place on turntable if available. Microwave on HIGH for 4 minutes (LW 4¾ minutes). **Stir,** bringing the pieces from the center to the outside edges and the ones along the edges to the center of the dish. **Cover** and cook on HIGH for 4 to 5 minutes (LW 4¾ to 6 minutes) or until tender-crisp. Let **stand, covered,** for 2 minutes and drain.

In glass measure, **whisk** wine and flour together. Whisk in milk until completely blended. Microwave, **uncovered,** on HIGH for 4 to 6 minutes (LW 4¾ to 7½ minutes), whisking every minute until thickened. **Whisk** in cheese until melted. Pour over drained cauliflower.

Melt margarine in custard cup on HIGH for 30 to 40 seconds (LW 50 to 60 seconds) or until melted. Add crumbs and herb blend, tossing to combine. Sprinkle crumb mixture over cauliflower and sprinkle top with paprika. **Cover** dish with wax paper and microwave on HIGH for 5 to 7 minutes (LW 6 to 8 minutes) or until dish is heated through and cauliflower is tender. Let **stand, covered,** for 2 minutes before serving.

Troubleshooting: Failing to whisk sauce may cause it to be lumpy.

If cheese doesn't melt completely while whisking, microwave on HIGH for 1 minute and whisk again.

To prevent margarine from spattering oven, cover custard cup with paper towel.

FOR EACH SERVING:
144 calories
173 mg sodium
13 mg cholesterol
6 g fat

Marinated Cauliflower

SERVES 4

EQUIPMENT:	medium bowl, 2-quart flat casserole dish
COOKING TIME:	6¾ to 10 minutes (Low Wattage ovens 8 to 11 minutes)
STANDING TIME:	5 minutes
NUTRITIONAL PROFILE:	moderate calories, low sodium, no cholesterol

1   teaspoon low-salt soy sauce
2   tablespoons white wine
½   teaspoon Parsley Patch Sesame All-Purpose herb blend
½   teaspoon dark sesame oil
2   teaspoons cornstarch
½   teaspoon minced fresh ginger
½   teaspoon sugar
4   cups fresh cauliflower flowerets, thinly sliced
1   cup (about 4 ounces) sliced fresh mushrooms
⅓   cup (about 3) chopped scallions
¼   cup slivered almonds
2   tablespoons soft-spread margarine

Combine soy sauce, white wine, herb blend, sesame oil, corn-starch, ginger, and sugar in bowl, **stirring** until smooth. Add cauliflower, mushrooms, scallions, and almonds, **stirring** to combine with marinade. **Marinate** for 1 to 1½ hours at room temperature or all day in refrigerator.

Microwave margarine in casserole dish, **uncovered,** on HIGH for 45 to 50 seconds (LW 50 to 60 seconds) or until melted. **Stir** in marinated vegetables and marinade. **Cover** with lid or plastic wrap, pulling back one corner to vent the steam. (If dish is flat-bottomed, **elevate** on an inverted saucer.)

Microwave on HIGH for 6 to 9 minutes (LW 7 to 10 minutes) or until vegetables are tender-crisp, **stirring** and **rotating** dish ½ turn every 3 minutes. Let **stand, covered,** for 5 minutes before serving.

Suggestion: The longer the vegetables marinate, the more flavor they will absorb. For more flavor, allow the vegetables to sit in marinade for several hours at room temperature.

For less restricted diets: If you're not watching your salt intake, substitute regular soy sauce, which adds 30 mg sodium per serving.

FOR EACH SERVING:
147 calories
154 mg sodium
0 mg cholesterol
8 g fat

EGGPLANT

Eggplant is plentiful in the summer but also available year-round. Prior to the eggplant's culinary use, it was used as a dye, a tooth polish, and an ingredient in love potions, as it was mysteriously called "the love apple." The versatility of the eggplant has yet to be discovered by many cooks even though it is low in sodium, provides dietary fiber, and a ½-cup serving of cooked eggplant has just 13 calories.

Select a firm, heavy eggplant free of scars or cuts. Be sure the skin is shiny smooth and not soft or shriveled, with a nice green top. Handle carefully and refrigerate, uncovered, for as short a period as possible, as eggplants will begin to develop soft brown spots and become bitter within a few days of refrigeration. To prepare eggplant for cooking, wash carefully; don't peel but cut off the top, rinse well, and pat dry before beginning the cooking process.

Eggplant Creole

SERVES 6

EQUIPMENT:	deep 2- or 3-quart casserole dish, 6-cup glass measure
COOKING TIME:	17¾ to 24 minutes (Low Wattage ovens 21 to 28¼ minutes)
STANDING TIME:	3 minutes
NUTRITIONAL PROFILE:	moderate calories, low sodium, low cholesterol

2 **medium eggplants, cut uniformly into 1-inch cubes**
2 **tablespoons water**
2 **tablespoons soft-spread margarine**
1 **tablespoon all-purpose flour**
2 **cups chopped low-salt whole canned tomatoes, liquid reserved**
1 **medium onion, diced**
1 **celery stalk, diced**
2 **to 3 scallions, diced**
1 **small green bell pepper, diced**
1 **teaspoon Parsley Patch All-Purpose herb blend**
1 **tablespoon light brown sugar**
½ **cup shredded Monterey Jack cheese**

Place towel-dried eggplant cubes in casserole dish and sprinkle with water. **Cover** dish with lid or plastic wrap, pulling back one corner to vent the steam. (If dish is flat-bottomed, **elevate** on an inverted saucer.) Place on a turntable if available.

Microwave on HIGH for 7 to 9 minutes (LW 8¼ to 10¾ minutes), **stirring** every 4 minutes, until tender. (**Rotate** dish ½ turn when stirring if not using turntable.) Let **stand, covered,** for 3 minutes; drain and reserve liquid.

Place margarine in glass measure and melt, **uncovered,** on HIGH for 45 to 55 seconds (LW 55 to 60 seconds). **Whisk** in flour until smooth. **Whisk** in liquid from chopped tomatoes and eggplant. Add tomato chunks, onion, celery, scallions, green pepper, herb blend, and brown sugar, **stirring** to combine.

Microwave, **uncovered,** on HIGH for 5 to 7 minutes (LW 6 to 8¼ minutes), stirring every 2 minutes, until vegetables are tender-crisp. (**Rotate** dish ¼ turn when stirring if not using a turntable.)

Pour mixture over eggplant cubes, cover again, and cook on 80 percent power or MEDIUM-HIGH for 3 to 4 minutes (LW 3½ to 4¾ minutes). **Uncover** dish, sprinkle with shredded cheese, and cook on HIGH for 2 to 3 minutes (LW 2¼ to 3½ minutes), until cheese melts and dish is bubbly.

Troubleshooting: Cut eggplant into uniformly sized pieces for even cooking.

For less restricted diets: If you're not watching your salt intake, substitute regular canned tomatoes, which add 115 mg sodium per serving.

FOR EACH SERVING:
140 calories
164 mg sodium
18 mg cholesterol
3 g fat

OYSTERS

Oysters are good sources of protein, and although they do contain cholesterol, its form is similar to that in fish; it does not clog the arteries. Oysters are also good sources of phosphorus, calcium, thiamine, riboflavin, vitamin A, and niacin.

Ocean Eggplant

SERVES 6

EQUIPMENT:	2- or 3-quart casserole dish, 6 individual-serving casserole dishes
COOKING TIME:	9 to 13 minutes (Low Wattage ovens 11 to 15¾ minutes)
STANDING TIME:	none required
NUTRITIONAL PROFILE:	moderate calories, low sodium, low cholesterol

2   medium eggplants, cut uniformly into ½-inch cubes
1   medium onion, diced
½   red bell pepper, diced
1   garlic clove, minced
½   cup white wine
½   pound fresh or frozen shucked oysters
½   pound fresh crabmeat
1   teaspoon Parsley Patch All-Purpose herb blend
½   cup plain dry bread crumbs
2   tablespoons freshly grated Parmesan cheese
6   parsley sprigs

Place eggplant cubes in casserole dish. Add onion, red bell pepper, garlic, and wine. **Cover** with lid or plastic wrap, pulling back one corner to vent steam. (If dish is flat-bottomed, **elevate** on an inverted saucer.) Place on turntable if available. Microwave on HIGH for 4 to 5 minutes (LW 4¾ to 6 minutes), **stirring** every 3 minutes. (**Rotate** dish ½ turn when stirring if not using turntable.)

While vegetables are still crisp, add oysters and crabmeat, mixing to combine. **Cover** and cook on HIGH for 4 to 6 minutes (LW 4¾ to 7½ minutes) or until vegetables are tender and oysters are cooked, **stirring** every 2 minutes. (**Rotate** dish ¼ turn when stirring if not using turntable.)

Fold in herb blend and bread crumbs. Divide mixture evenly into 6 individual casserole dishes. Sprinkle each dish with Parmesan cheese and microwave, **uncovered,** on HIGH for 1 to 2 minutes (LW

1½ to 2¼ minutes) or until hot. Garnish each dish with a sprig of parsley.

FOR EACH SERVING:
141 calories
131 mg sodium
34 mg cholesterol
4 g fat

Eggplant and Tomato Bake

SERVES 6

EQUIPMENT:	2-quart round casserole dish, potato masher, small bowl
COOKING TIME:	13 to 19 minutes (Low Wattage ovens 15½ to 23 minutes)
STANDING TIME:	5 minutes
NUTRITIONAL PROFILE:	low calories, low sodium, low cholesterol

1½ **pounds eggplant, peeled and cut into ¾-inch cubes**
3 **tablespoons water**
½ **cup (about 1 medium) chopped onion**
1 **garlic clove, minced**
3 **tablespoons white wine**
3 **egg whites, lightly beaten**
½ **cup plain dry bread crumbs**
½ **teaspoon dried oregano**
1 **teaspoon Parsley Patch Lemon Pepper herb blend**
1 **large tomato, thinly sliced**
½ **cup shredded part–skim milk mozzarella cheese**
2 **tablespoons freshly grated Parmesan cheese**
⅛ **teaspoon paprika**

Place eggplant cubes in casserole dish and sprinkle with water. **Cover** with lid or plastic wrap, pulling back one corner to vent the steam. (If dish is flat-bottomed, **elevate** on an inverted saucer.) Place on turntable if available. Microwave on HIGH for 7 to 10 minutes (LW 8¼ to 12 minutes) or until eggplant is very tender,

stirring every 3 minutes. (**Rotate** dish ½ turn when stirring if not using turntable.) **Mash** with potato masher and set aside.

In small bowl, place onion, garlic, and white wine. **Cover** dish with plastic wrap, venting back one corner, and cook on HIGH for 2 to 3 minutes (LW 2½ to 3½ minutes) or until tender-crisp. Gently stir into mashed eggplant. Fold in beaten egg whites, bread crumbs, oregano, and herb blend; **stir** well. Top with tomato slices and **cover** dish with wax paper.

Microwave on HIGH for 4 to 6 minutes (LW 4¾ to 7½ minutes) or until heated through. (**Rotate** dish ½ turn every 3 minutes if not using turntable.) Top tomatoes with cheeses and sprinkle with paprika. Let **stand, covered,** for 5 minutes, until cheese melts.

FOR EACH SERVING:
82 calories
117 mg sodium
12 mg cholesterol
6 g fat

MUSHROOMS

When choosing mushrooms, be sure to select those with firm, tightly closed caps. Size has nothing to do with maturity; it only helps determine the proper use. Small caps are best used whole, medium-sized mushrooms are best sliced and used in recipes, while large caps make the best stuffed mushrooms. There are only 60 calories in 1 cup of sliced mushrooms.

Don't store mushrooms in a tightly closed plastic bag, or they will soften quickly. To keep them fresh longer, replace tightly covered containers with a loose covering of plastic wrap or place in a plastic bag before refrigerating.

Don't wash mushrooms or soak them in water, or they will absorb the water and become soft. When ready to use, wipe each cap completely with a damp towel and pat dry. Cut a thin slice off the bottom of the stem, and they're ready to use in your favorite recipe.

Mushrooms in Cream Sauce

SERVES 6

EQUIPMENT:	6-cup glass measure or 1-quart round casserole dish
COOKING TIME:	7 to 10 minutes (Low Wattage ovens 8¼ to 12¼ minutes)
STANDING TIME:	none required
NUTRITIONAL PROFILE:	low calories, low sodium, low cholesterol

- **¾ pound (about 3 cups) fresh mushrooms, sliced**
- **3 tablespoons white wine**
- **1 teaspoon all-purpose flour**
- **½ cup plain yogurt**
- **½ teaspoon onion powder**
- **1 teaspoon Parsley Patch It's a Dilly herb blend**
- **1 teaspoon chopped fresh parsley**
- **1 tablespoon minced fresh chives**

In glass measure or casserole dish, combine mushrooms and white wine. Microwave, **uncovered,** on HIGH for 4 to 6 minutes (LW 4¾ to 7½ minutes) or until mushrooms are tender. **Whisk** in flour until blended. **Whisk** in remaining ingredients. **Cover** with wax paper and microwave on 50 percent power or MEDIUM for 3 to 4 minutes (LW 3½ to 4¾ minutes) or until heated through, **whisking** every 2 minutes.

Troubleshooting: Forgetting to whisk sauce may cause it to be lumpy.

Suggestions: May be served as a side dish or poured over 1 cup cooked broccoli, asparagus, or green beans for a total of approximately 50 calories per serving.

FOR EACH SERVING:
25 calories
12 mg sodium
1 mg cholesterol
trace fat

OKRA

When selecting fresh okra, choose bright green pods that are about 2 to 4 inches long and snap or puncture easily, which indicates tenderness. Avoid hard pods that are dull and pale green, shriveled, or have stiff tips.

Okra isn't a vegetable you usually keep on hand, but because it contains natural low-calorie thickeners, it's the perfect addition to soups, stews, and gumbos. Dried okra will perform the same function.

Okra

SERVES 4

EQUIPMENT:	1-quart round casserole dish
COOKING TIME:	7 to 10 minutes (Low Wattage ovens 8¼ to 12 minutes)
STANDING TIME:	5 minutes
NUTRITIONAL PROFILE:	low calories, low sodium, no cholesterol

1   pound fresh okra
¼   cup water

Wash pods and snip off the tip and stem ends. Slice into uniform ½-inch slices and place in casserole dish. Add water and **cover** with lid or plastic wrap, pulling back one corner to vent steam. (If dish is flat-bottomed, **elevate** on an inverted saucer.) Place on turntable if available.

Microwave on HIGH for 7 to 10 minutes (LW 8¼ to 12 minutes) or until tender, **stirring** every 3 minutes, bringing those from the center of the dish to the outside edges and the pieces along the edges to the center. (**Rotate** dish ½ turn when stirring if not using turntable.) Let **stand, covered,** for 5 minutes.

FOR EACH SERVING:
30 calories
2 mg sodium
0 mg cholesterol
trace fat

Okra and Tomatoes

SERVES 4

EQUIPMENT: 2-quart round casserole dish
COOKING TIME: 10 to 14 minutes (Low Wattage ovens 11¾ to 16¾ minutes)
STANDING TIME: 3 to 5 minutes
NUTRITIONAL PROFILE: low calories, low sodium, no cholesterol

1 **tablespoon olive oil**
1 **pound fresh okra, washed, ends removed, cut uniformly into ½-inch slices**
1 **small onion, diced**
1 **small green bell pepper, diced**
1 **15-ounce can low-sodium whole tomatoes, drained, reserving ½ cup liquid, and chopped**
1 **tablespoon cider vinegar**
½ **teaspoon dark brown sugar**
⅛ **teaspoon garlic powder**
¼ **teaspoon Parsley Patch It's a Dilly herb blend**

Place olive oil, okra, onion, and green bell pepper in casserole dish. **Cover** dish with lid or plastic wrap, pulling back one corner to vent the steam. (If dish is flat-bottomed, **elevate** on an inverted saucer.) Place on turntable if available. Microwave on HIGH for 3 to 4 minutes (LW 3½ to 4¾ minutes) or until onion is tender. Add remaining ingredients and **stir** to combine. (**Rotate** dish ½ turn when stirring if not using turntable.)

   Cover and cook on HIGH for 7 to 10 minutes (LW 8¼ to 12 minutes), **stirring** once, until okra is tender. (**Rotate** dish ½ turn when stirring if not using turntable.) Let **stand, covered,** for 3 to 5 minutes before serving.

For less restricted diets: If you're not watching your salt intake, substitute regular tomatoes, which add 173 mg sodium per serving.

FOR EACH SERVING:
85 calories
20 mg sodium
0 mg cholesterol
2 g fat

GREEN PEPPERS

Have you ever stopped to think how popular the colors red and green are in our lives? Besides reminding us of Christmas, they are also very popular colors in the garden.

The word *pepper* seems to spell *hot* to many people, yet bell peppers are anything but hot. Peppers are low in calories and sodium and contain no cholesterol, but they are a good source of potassium and vitamins B and C. An average-size pepper contains only 14 calories.

When choosing green peppers, be sure they are firm to the touch and shiny bright. Check each one carefully to avoid picking those with soft spots, blemishes, bruises, or cuts in the skin. Sweet bell peppers start out green but turn bright red when they are left on the vine to ripen completely. Once they turn red, you will find they have a sweeter taste—and even more vitamins—than when green. Always remove the stems, seeds, and inner membranes before eating.

Easy Ratatouille

SERVES 6

EQUIPMENT:	deep 3-quart casserole dish
COOKING TIME:	16 to 18 minutes (Low Wattage ovens 19 to 21 minutes)
STANDING TIME:	5 minutes
NUTRITIONAL PROFILE:	moderate calories, low sodium, no cholesterol

   ¼ **cup olive oil**
   1 **large onion, sliced**
   3 **garlic cloves, crushed**
   1 **medium red or yellow bell pepper, diced**
   1 **medium green bell pepper, diced**
   1 **small eggplant (1 pound), cut into ½-inch cubes**
   ½ **pound (about 2 cups) fresh mushrooms, sliced**
   3 **medium zucchini, sliced**
   1 **tomato, seeded and diced**
   ¼ **teaspoon freshly ground pepper**
   ¼ **teaspoon dried basil**
   ½ **teaspoon dried oregano**
   2 **tablespoons chopped fresh parsley**
      whole fresh basil leaves for garnish

Place all ingredients except whole basil leaves in casserole dish and **cover** with lid or plastic wrap, pulling back one corner to vent the steam. (If dish is flat-bottomed, **elevate** on an inverted saucer.) Place on a turntable if available.

Microwave on HIGH for 16 to 18 minutes (LW 19 to 21 minutes) or until vegetables are tender, **stirring** every 5 minutes. (**Rotate** dish ¼ turn when stirring if not using a turntable.) Let **stand, covered,** for 5 minutes, and garnish with whole basil leaves.

Troubleshooting: Cut vegetables into uniform sizes so they will cook in the same length of time.

When stirring, bring the less cooked areas from the center of the dish to the outside edges and those from the edges into the center.

FOR EACH SERVING:
122 calories
8 mg sodium
0 mg cholesterol
7 g fat

POTATOES

Potatoes form the backbone of our family meals. They are considered a vegetable source because of their excellent nutritional value, especially their phosphorus, potassium, and vitamin C content.

Scrub potatoes well and pierce each end with the tines of a fork. Why? If you don't allow the steam to escape from foods enclosed in a casing, such as sausage, egg yolks, squash, hot dogs, and potatoes, they will explode when the steam builds up.

Baked Potatoes

SERVES 4

EQUIPMENT: meat rack if available
COOKING TIME: approximately 4 minutes per potato (Low Wattage ovens approximately 4½ minutes per potato)
STANDING TIME: 5 to 10 minutes
NUTRITIONAL PROFILE: low calories, low sodium, no cholesterol

4   medium white potatoes

Scrub and pierce each potato with the tines of a fork. Place on 2 **layers** of paper towels on the floor of your oven or on a paper-towel-covered meat rack. Point smallest end to the center of the oven and largest end to the outside, like the spokes of a wagon wheel.

Microwave on HIGH as follows:
1 potato: 4 to 6 minutes (LW 4½ to 7 minutes)
2 potatoes: 7 to 8 minutes (LW 8 to 9 minutes)
3 potatoes: 11 to 13 minutes (LW 13 to 15 minutes)
4 potatoes: 14 to 16 minutes (LW 16 to 19 minutes)

When microwaving finishes, potatoes should still be a bit firm in the center. Remove potatoes from the oven and **wrap** individually in aluminum foil, shiny side toward potato, or place under an inverted bowl. This will help keep the potatoes hot for 25 to 30 minutes and allow them to finish cooking. Let **stand, covered,** for 5 to 10 minutes before serving.

FOR EACH POTATO:
100 calories
5 mg sodium
0 mg cholesterol
0 g fat

Perfect Scalloped Potatoes

SERVES 6

EQUIPMENT: 6-cup glass measure, deep 3-quart casserole dish

COOKING TIME: 24¾ to 32 minutes (Low Wattage ovens 29¾ to 38 minutes)

STANDING TIME: 5 minutes

NUTRITIONAL PROFILE: moderate calories, low sodium, no cholesterol

2	tablespoons soft-spread margarine
3½	tablespoons all-purpose flour
2½	cups skim milk
1	teaspoon Parsley Patch Lemon Pepper herb blend
2	pounds (6 medium) potatoes, thinly sliced
2	large onions, thinly sliced
1	tablespoon chopped fresh parsley

In glass measure, melt margarine, **uncovered,** on HIGH for 45 to 55 seconds (LW 50 to 60 seconds). **Whisk** in flour, milk, and herb blend. Cook, **uncovered,** on HIGH for 4 to 6 minutes (LW 4¾ to 7 minutes), whisking every minute until sauce is thickened and coats whisk.

In casserole dish, **layer** ⅓ of potatoes and onions and cover with ⅓ of sauce. Continue layering until vegetables and sauce are used up. **Cover** with wax paper. (If dish is flat-bottomed, **elevate** on an inverted saucer.) Place on turntable if available.

Microwave on HIGH for 20 to 25 minutes (LW 24 to 30 minutes) or until potatoes are tender, **stirring** carefully every 10 minutes. (**Rotate** dish ½ turn when stirring if not using turntable.) Let **stand, covered,** for 5 minutes and sprinkle with parsley before serving.

FOR EACH SERVING:
180 calories
97 mg sodium
0 mg cholesterol
2 g fat

ACORN AND BUTTERNUT SQUASH

Most of the squash family are low-calorie and low-sodium vegetables, but the acorn or winter squash is an exception. It contains 50 calories per ½ cup, which is double the calories in the summer squash variety, but still low. You also get more nutrition for your calories—winter squash has much more vitamin A and potassium than the summer variety.

Acorn Squash

SERVES 4

COOKING TIME:	8 to 12 minutes (Low Wattage ovens 9½ to 14¼ minutes)
STANDING TIME:	5 minutes
NUTRITIONAL PROFILE:	low calories, low sodium, no cholesterol

1 whole acorn squash

Method 1. Pierce skin several times with a sharp knife and place on 2 **layers** of paper towels on the floor of microwave. Microwave on HIGH for 8 to 12 minutes (LW 9½ to 14¼ minutes) or until soft. Remove from microwave and let **stand** for 5 minutes.

Method 2. Cut squash in half, scoop out the seeds, **cover** each half with plastic wrap, and place on 2 **layers** of paper towels on microwave floor. Microwave half a squash on HIGH for 5 to 8 minutes (LW 6 to 9½ minutes), 2 halves for 8 to 11 minutes (LW 9½ to 13¼ minutes), and 4 halves for 13 to 16 minutes (LW 15½ to 19½ minutes), allowing them to **stand, covered,** for 5 minutes before serving.

FOR EACH SERVING:
50 calories
14 mg sodium
0 mg cholesterol
trace fat

Butternut Squash

SERVES 4

EQUIPMENT:	9 × 13-inch baking dish
COOKING TIME:	3 to 12 minutes (Low Wattage ovens 3½ to 14¼ minutes)
STANDING TIME:	5 minutes
NUTRITIONAL PROFILE:	low calories, low sodium, no cholesterol

2 pounds butternut squash

Cut squash into 4 ½-pound pieces and scoop out seeds and fiber.

For one ½-pound piece: Place 2 **layers** of paper towels on the floor of the microwave to absorb any moisture. Wrap squash in plastic wrap and microwave on HIGH for 3 to 4 minutes (LW 3½ to 4¾ minutes) or until fork-tender. Let **stand, covered,** for 5 minutes.

For 2 pieces: Wrap each piece in plastic wrap, place on 2 **layers** of paper towels on floor of microwave, and cook on HIGH for 4 to 7 minutes (LW 4¾ to 8¼ minutes) or until fork-tender. Let **stand, covered,** for 5 minutes.

For 4 pieces: Place them in baking dish and **cover** dish with plastic wrap, pulling back one corner to vent the steam. (If dish is flat-bottomed, **elevate** on an inverted saucer.) Microwave 4 pieces for 6 to 12 minutes (LW 7½ to 14¼ minutes) or until fork-tender, **rearranging** pieces and **rotating** dish ½ turn every 4 minutes. Let **stand, covered,** for 5 minutes.

FOR EACH SERVING:
50 calories
14 mg sodium
0 mg cholesterol
trace fat

CUTTING HARD-SKINNED SQUASH

Acorn and butternut squash both tend to have very hard skins that can be a real problem to cut through. To make this task easier, place the whole squash on 2 layers of paper towels on the floor of your microwave. Microwave on HIGH for 1 to 2 minutes (LW 1¼ to 2¼ minutes), and you will find cutting through the skins much easier.

As with any food that has a casing, you must pierce the casing if you want to completely microwave the whole squash. By piercing the skin you allow an escape route for the steam that builds up inside; otherwise the squash will explode inside your microwave. It is not necessary to pierce the skin if you are microwaving only to soften the skin enough to cut.

Plain Yellow Squash

SERVES 4

Yellow or summer squash can be found in supermarkets year-round, but the peak of the season is, of course, the summer. When selecting squash, avoid the larger ones; you may think you're getting more for your money, but don't be fooled. Look for the young, small, tender squash with shiny, smooth skin and a well-shaped form. They are sweeter and contain smaller seeds than their grown-up sisters. Squash may be served in many delicious ways: baked, mashed, or sprinkled with various seasonings.

Summer squash are very low in calories, only 25 per ½-cup serving, but that's without all the extras. Conventionally boiled, squash loses most of its vitamin content into the water, but when microwaved the nutrients stay intact.

EQUIPMENT:	2-quart round casserole dish
COOKING TIME:	4 to 8 minutes (Low Wattage ovens 4¾ to 9½ minutes)
STANDING TIME:	2 to 3 minutes
NUTRITIONAL PROFILE:	low calories, low sodium, no cholesterol

    4 small yellow or summer squash, cut uniformly into ¼-inch slices
    2 tablespoons water

Place squash slices in casserole dish. Sprinkle with water and **cover** with lid or plastic wrap, pulling back one corner to vent the steam. (If dish is flat-bottomed, **elevate** on an inverted saucer.) Place on turntable if available. Microwave on HIGH for 4 to 8 minutes (LW 4¾ to 9½ minutes) or until tender-crisp. **Stir** every 3 minutes, bringing the less cooked slices from center of the dish to outside edges and those along outside edges to the center. Let **stand, covered,** for 2 to 3 minutes.

Troubleshooting: Be sure to cut uniformly sized slices to ensure even cooking.

For less restricted diets: Substitute 2 tablespoons soft-spread margarine for water, which adds 30 calories and 27 mg sodium per serving.

    FOR EACH SERVING:
    45 calories
    3 mg sodium
    0 mg cholesterol
    trace fat

Summer Squash Puff

SERVES 6

EQUIPMENT:	small and large bowls, 2-quart round casserole dish, 1-cup glass measure, potato masher
COOKING TIME:	12½ to 15¾ minutes (Low Wattage ovens 14¾ to 18¼ minutes)
STANDING TIME:	none required
NUTRITIONAL PROFILE:	moderate calories, moderate sodium, low cholesterol

3   **pounds small yellow squash, cut into ¼-inch slices
    and cooked (see recipe on page 93)**
2   **tablespoons white wine**
½   **cup (about 4) chopped scallions**
1   **large garlic clove, minced**
¾   **cup plain dry bread crumbs**
¼   **teaspoon dried basil**
¼   **teaspoon dried oregano**
3   **egg whites, slightly beaten**
¼   **cup skim milk**
¼   **cup soft-spread margarine, melted**
1   **tablespoon Parsley Patch All-Purpose herb blend**
¼   **cup freshly grated Parmesan cheese**

TOPPING
1   **tablespoon soft-spread margarine**
¼   **cup plain dry bread crumbs**
½   **teaspoon paprika**
1   **tablespoon finely chopped fresh parsley**

Drain cooked squash well and **mash** with potato masher. Place wine, scallions, and garlic in a small bowl. **Cover** with plastic wrap, pulling back one corner to vent the steam. (If dish is flat-bottomed, **elevate** on an inverted saucer.) Microwave on HIGH for 3 to 4 minutes (LW 3½ to 4½ minutes) or until tender-crisp. In large bowl, combine scallion mixture with prepared squash, crumbs, basil, oregano, egg whites, milk, melted margarine, herb blend, and Parmesan cheese. Mix together well and spoon mixture into casserole dish.

For topping, place margarine in glass measure and microwave, **uncovered,** on HIGH for 30 to 40 seconds (LW 35 to 45 seconds) or until melted. Stir in crumbs, paprika, and parsley. Sprinkle over casserole. **Cover** dish with lid or plastic wrap, pulling back one corner to vent the steam. (If dish is flat-bottomed, **elevate** on an inverted saucer.) Place on turntable if available.

Microwave on HIGH for 9 to 11 minutes (LW 10¾ to 13 minutes) or until hot and bubbly. (**Rotate** dish ½ turn every 5 minutes if not using turntable.)

Suggestion: This is a lovely side dish to accompany beef, poultry, or fish.

FOR EACH SERVING:
172 calories
230 mg sodium
18 mg cholesterol
11 g fat

Mixed Squash Bake

SERVES 4

EQUIPMENT:	2-quart round casserole dish, 4-cup glass measure, custard cup
COOKING TIME:	12½ to 17¾ minutes (Low Wattage ovens 15 to 22 minutes)
STANDING TIME:	1 minute
NUTRITION PROFILE:	moderate calories, low sodium, no cholesterol

2 small yellow or summer squash, cut into ½-inch cubes
2 small or medium zucchini, cut into ½-inch cubes
1 large onion, chopped
¼ cup hot water
2 tablespoons all-purpose flour
1 teaspoon low-sodium chicken bouillon granules
1 cup skim milk
1 tablespoon soft-spread margarine
¼ cup plain dry bread crumbs
1 tablespoon snipped fresh parsley
1 tablespoon Parsley Patch All-Purpose herb blend

Place yellow squash, zucchini, onion, and water in casserole dish. **Cover** with lid or plastic wrap, pulling back one corner to vent the steam. (If dish is flat-bottomed, **elevate** on an inverted saucer.) Place on turntable if available. Microwave on HIGH for 4 to 6 minutes (LW 4¾ to 7½ minutes) or until vegetables are tender-crisp. (**Rotate** dish ½ turn every 3 minutes if not using turntable.)

In glass measure, **whisk** flour, bouillon granules, and milk together. Microwave, **uncovered,** on HIGH for 4 to 6 minutes (LW 4¾ to 7½ minutes), **whisking** every minute until thickened. **Drain** squash well and pour sauce over squash, tossing lightly.

In custard cup, microwave margarine, **uncovered,** on HIGH for 30 to 40 seconds (LW 40 to 50 seconds) or until melted. Toss bread crumbs, parsley, and herb blend with melted margarine and sprinkle over squash. **Cover** dish with wax paper and place on turntable if available. Cook on HIGH for 4 to 5 minutes (LW 4¾ to 6 minutes) or until heated through. Let **stand, covered,** for 1 minute before serving.

Troubleshooting: Failing to whisk sauce may cause it to be lumpy.

For less restricted diets: If you're not watching your salt intake, substitute regular bouillon granules, which add 225 mg sodium per serving.

FOR EACH SERVING:
120 calories
86 mg sodium
0 mg cholesterol
2 g fat

SWEET POTATOES

Did you know that the sweet potato's cousin is the morning glory and not the yam, as most folks believe? However, yams and sweet potatoes are often treated interchangeably. The yam grows only in the tropics, and the sweet potato was born and bred on American soil. The word *sweet* in sweet potato is a sign of its high sugar content and calories. One sweet potato contains 170 calories versus 90 calories for a white potato. But it's also higher in calcium, phosphorus, and iron than white potatoes. It's an excellent source of vitamin A, which is needed to prevent night blindness and dry skin and may aid in the prevention of some forms of cancer.

Baked Sweet Potatoes

SERVES 4

EQUIPMENT:	2 layers of paper towels, squares of aluminum foil large enough to hold potato or large bowl
COOKING TIME:	3 to 5 minutes per potato (Low Wattage ovens 3½ to 6 minutes)
STANDING TIME:	5 to 10 minutes
NUTRITIONAL PROFILE:	moderate calories, low sodium, no cholesterol

1 pound uniformly shaped sweet potatoes

Scrub the potatoes and pierce the skin several times with a fork. Place them in a circle, pointing toward the center of the oven like the spokes of a wagon wheel, on 2 **layers** of paper towels on the oven floor. Place the larger end of each potato toward the outside of the oven, the smaller end toward the center of the oven.

Microwave on HIGH as follows:

1 sweet potato: 3 to 5 minutes (LW 3½ to 6 minutes)
2 sweet potatoes: 6 to 8 minutes (LW 7½ to 9½ minutes)
3 sweet potatoes: 7 to 10 minutes (LW 8¼ to 12 minutes)
4 sweet potatoes: 10 to 14 minutes (LW 12 to 16¾ minutes)

Once finished microwaving, potatoes should feel slightly firm in the center. **Remove** from the oven and wrap in aluminum foil, shiny side toward the potato, or place under an inverted bowl. Allow them to **stand, covered,** for 5 to 10 minutes before serving.

FOR EACH SERVING:
170 calories
14 mg sodium
0 mg cholesterol
trace fat

Sweet Potatoes Kahlua

SERVES 5

EQUIPMENT: small and medium bowls, 1-quart round casserole dish, electric mixer
COOKING TIME: 3 to 4 minutes (Low Wattage ovens 3¼ to 4¾ minutes)
STANDING TIME: 1 minute
NUTRITIONAL PROFILE: moderate calories, low sodium, no cholesterol

1 pound sweet potatoes, cooked (see recipe on page 98), peeled, and cut up
¼ cup white wine
⅛ cup Kahlua

TOPPING
1 teaspoon packed dark brown sugar
1 teaspoon soft-spread margarine
½ teaspoon water
¼ teaspoon ground cinnamon
⅛ teaspoon freshly grated nutmeg
¾ cup miniature marshmallows

In medium bowl, **whip** potatoes with electric mixer until light and fluffy. Blend in wine and Kahlua. Spoon mixture into casserole dish and set aside.

In small bowl, place brown sugar, margarine, water, cinnamon, and nutmeg. Microwave, **uncovered,** on HIGH for 50 to 60 seconds (LW 1 to 1¼ minutes) or until margarine is melted, stirring once. Add the marshmallows and toss to coat. Spoon marshmallow mixture over top of sweet potatoes and microwave, **uncovered,** on HIGH for 2 to 3 minutes (LW 2¼ to 3½ minutes) or until marshmallows are puffed. Let **stand** on a hard heatproof surface for 1 minute before serving.

FOR EACH SERVING:
186 calories
15 mg sodium
0 mg cholesterol
2 g fat

Sweet Potato Orange Cups

My sister says that once you have prepared this recipe you will never fix sweet potatoes any other way.

SERVES 8

EQUIPMENT:	6-cup glass measure, electric mixer, 13 × 9-inch casserole dish
COOKING TIME:	4½ to 6 minutes (Low Wattage ovens 5¼ to 7 minutes)
STANDING TIME:	3 minutes
NUTRITIONAL PROFILE:	moderate calories, low sodium, no cholesterol

> 4 **large oranges**
> 1 **pound sweet potatoes, cooked (page 98), peeled, and cut into ½-inch slices**
> ¼ **cup soft-spread margarine**
> 2 **tablespoons dark brown sugar**
> ¼ **cup skim milk**
> 4 **teaspoons low-sugar orange marmalade**
> 3 **large marshmallows, cut in half**
>   **freshly grated nutmeg**

Cut oranges in half, fluting the edges with a sharp paring knife, and remove the pulp; set aside.

Place sliced potatoes and margarine in glass measure and **cover** with plastic wrap, pulling back one corner to vent the steam. Cook on HIGH for 2½ to 3 minutes (LW 3 to 3½ minutes) or until potatoes are warm and margarine is melted. With electric mixer, whip potatoes and margarine until light and fluffy. Add brown sugar and milk, blending well.

Spoon mixture evenly into prepared orange cups. Spread ½ teaspoon of marmalade over potato mixture in each cup and top with a marshmallow half. Sprinkle marshmallows with nutmeg. Arrange filled cups in casserole dish and cook, **uncovered,** on HIGH for 2 to 3 minutes (LW 2¼ to 3½ minutes) or until heated through and marshmallows soften. Let **stand** for 3 minutes before serving.

Suggestions: Use these attractive filled oranges to decorate a Thanksgiving turkey or surround a platter of sliced turkey, chicken, or roast beef.

FOR EACH SERVING:
169 calories
26 mg sodium
0 mg cholesterol
4 g fat

TURNIPS AND RUTABAGAS

The turnip and rutabaga are two interchangeable vegetables that very seldom get much mention. Turnips are similar to potatoes in texture but stronger in flavor and smaller than their big cousin, the rutabaga. Small to medium-sized turnips are best, as large ones tend to be woody.

Rutabagas, which are sometimes labeled turnips, are large yellow-fleshed vegetables that usually are coated with a thin layer of wax to prevent loss of moisture and to keep them from shriveling up. As a rule, rutabagas are sweeter than turnips, but you can easily substitute one for the other.

Stem and peel both turnips and rutabagas just before cooking. Both varieties keep well for long periods of time when stored in the refrigerator. Turnips can be cubed or sliced, but rutabagas microwave best when cut uniformly into ½-inch cubes.

To slice the hard rutabaga, cut off the top, making a flat surface. Place the flat surface on a cutting board and cut several slices from one side, forming another flat surface. Place the second flat surface against your cutting board and continue cutting slices. Peel off the waxed skin and cube.

Both turnips and rutabagas are low in calories, providing 18 calories per ½ cup. They are also low in sodium and contain no cholesterol. They do provide calcium, potassium, vitamin C, and the B vitamins.

Steamed Turnips

My reader Frank Clarke wrote me, "Your Goof-Proof Cookbook has been such a help to this 75-year-old guy who is trying to learn something new and having fun at it. My turnips are hard, hard, hard, when I microwave them; please help me solve my problem." Well, Frank, the following recipes are for you and others who enjoy turnips and rutabagas as much as we do. Be careful not to cut these vegetables into very large chunks—or microwave them much longer to avoid the "hard, hard, hard" problem Frank had.

SERVES 4

EQUIPMENT:	1-quart round casserole dish
COOKING TIME:	slices—9 to 11 minutes (Low Wattage ovens 11 to 13 minutes); cubes—12 to 14 minutes (Low Wattage ovens 14 to 16 minutes)
STANDING TIME:	3 minutes
NUTRITIONAL PROFILE:	low calories, low sodium, no cholesterol

4   medium turnips (about 1½ pounds)
¼   cup water

Peel turnips and either **slice** them into ¼-inch slices or **cube** them into ½-inch pieces; place in casserole dish. Drizzle water over the dish and **cover** with the lid or plastic wrap, pulling back one corner to vent the steam. (If dish is flat-bottomed, **elevate** on an inverted saucer.) Place on turntable if available.

Microwave slices on HIGH for 9 to 11 minutes (LW 11 to 13 minutes) or cubes on HIGH for 12 to 14 minutes (LW 14 to 16 minutes) or until soft, **stirring** every 6 minutes. (**Rotate** dish ½ turn when stirring if not using turntable.) Let **stand, covered,** for 3 minutes.

Troubleshooting: Whether cubing or slicing, cut small, uniformly sized pieces to ensure even cooking.

Stir by bringing the less cooked pieces from the center of the dish to the outside edges and the ones along the edges to the center.

Suggestions: Peel and slice raw turnips into thin slices and add to vegetable salads or use raw or leftover cooked cubes in vegetable soups or pot roasts. Season cooked turnips with chopped chives or scallions.

FOR EACH SERVING:
27 calories
2 mg sodium
0 mg cholesterol
trace fat

Rutabagas

SERVES 4

EQUIPMENT:	2-quart round casserole dish
COOKING TIME:	14 to 18 minutes (Low Wattage ovens 17 to 21 minutes)
STANDING TIME:	3 minutes
NUTRITIONAL PROFILE:	low calories, low sodium, no cholesterol

1 medium rutabaga, cut into ½-inch cubes (about 3 to 4 cups)
¼ cup water

Peel rutabaga, cut into ½-inch cubes, place in casserole dish, and drizzle with water. **Cover** with lid or plastic wrap, pulling back one corner to vent the steam. (If dish is flat-bottomed, **elevate** on an inverted saucer.) Place on turntable if available.

Microwave on HIGH for 14 to 18 minutes (LW 17 to 21 minutes) or until tender, **stirring** every 5 minutes. (**Rotate** dish ¼ turn when stirring if not using turntable.) Let **stand, covered,** for 3 minutes.

Troubleshooting: Cube into uniformly sized pieces to ensure even cooking.

Stir by bringing the less cooked cubes from the center to the outside edges and the cubes along the edges to the center.

Suggestion: Season cooked rutabagas with chopped chives or scallions.

FOR EACH SERVING:
27 calories
2 mg sodium
0 mg cholesterol
trace fat

Turnip Medley

SERVES 6

EQUIPMENT:	2-quart round casserole dish, 4-cup glass measure
COOKING TIME:	23 to 28 minutes (Low Wattage ovens 27¼ to 33½ minutes)
STANDING TIME:	3 minutes
NUTRITIONAL PROFILE:	low calories, low sodium, no cholesterol

1   **16-ounce bag frozen peas and carrots**
4   **medium turnips (1½ pounds), cut into ½-inch cubes**
¼   **cup water**
2   **tablespoons white wine**
4   **scallions, diced**
½   **teaspoon Parsley Patch Lemon Pepper herb blend**
1   **teaspoon fresh lemon juice (see tip, page 124)**

Cut an X in the top of the bag of frozen vegetables and place on 2 **layers** of paper towels. Microwave on HIGH for 8 to 10 minutes (LW 9½ to 12 minutes) or until tender, **rotating** bag ½ turn after 4 minutes.

Place peeled and cut turnip in casserole dish and drizzle with water. **Cover** with lid or plastic wrap, pulling back one corner to vent the steam. (If dish is flat-bottomed, **elevate** on an inverted saucer.) Place on turntable if available. Microwave on HIGH for 12 to 14 minutes (LW 14¼ to 16¾ minutes) or until soft, **stirring** every 5 minutes. (**Rotate** dish ½ turn when stirring if not using turntable.) Let **stand, covered,** for 3 minutes, and drain.

In glass measure, combine wine and scallions. Microwave, **uncovered,** on HIGH for 3 to 4 minutes (LW 3½ to 4¾ minutes) or until soft. Mix in herb blend and lemon juice. Gently mix peas and carrots with the cooked turnip and add scallion mixture, tossing lightly.

Troubleshooting: Cut uniformly sized cubes to ensure even cooking.
When stirring, bring the less cooked cubes from the center to the outside edges and the cubes along the edges to the center.

FOR EACH SERVING:
61 calories
76 mg sodium
0 mg cholesterol
trace fat

Mom's Mashed Rutabagas

SERVES 6

EQUIPMENT:	deep 2- or 3-quart round casserole dish, potato masher
COOKING TIME:	16 to 20 minutes (Low Wattage ovens 19½ to 24 minutes)
STANDING TIME:	3 minutes
NUTRITIONAL PROFILE:	low calories, low sodium, no cholesterol

3 cups (about 1 medium) ½-inch-cubed rutabaga
2 cups (about 8) thinly sliced carrots
¼ cup water
1 tablespoon soft-spread margarine
freshly ground pepper to taste

Combine rutabagas with carrots in casserole dish. Drizzle with water and **cover** with lid or plastic wrap, pulling back one corner to vent the steam. (If dish is flat-bottomed, **elevate** on an inverted saucer.) Place on turntable if available. Microwave on HIGH for 16 to 20 minutes (LW 19½ to 24 minutes) or until tender, **stirring** every 5 minutes. (**Rotate** dish ½ turn when stirring if not using turntable.) Once tender, let **stand, covered,** for 3 minutes. Add margarine and **mash** completely with potato masher. Add pepper to taste.

Troubleshooting: Cube into uniformly sized pieces for even cooking.
When stirring, bring the less cooked cubes from the center to the outside edges and the ones along the edges to the center.

FOR EACH SERVING:
44 calories
12 mg sodium
0 mg cholesterol
2 g fat

ZUCCHINI

Zucchini is a good source of vitamin A and provides potassium and calcium. Select small to medium firm squash with tender skins. Large squash have tough skin and contain many large seeds.

Zucchini Deluxe

SERVES 4

EQUIPMENT:	2-quart round casserole dish
COOKING TIME:	11 to 15 minutes (Low Wattage ovens 13 to 18 minutes)
STANDING TIME:	5 minutes
NUTRITIONAL PROFILE:	low calories, low sodium, low cholesterol

1¼ **pounds fresh zucchini, cut into ¼-inch slices**
  1 **large onion, thinly sliced**
  2 **tablespoons white wine**
  ½ **cup plain yogurt**
  2 **tablespoons skim milk**
  1 **teaspoon Parsley Patch Lemon Pepper herb blend**
  1 **teaspoon paprika**

In casserole dish, place zucchini, onion, and wine. **Cover** dish with lid or plastic wrap, pulling back one corner to vent the steam. (If dish is flat-bottomed, **elevate** on an inverted saucer.) Place on a turntable if available. Microwave on HIGH for 9 to 11 minutes (LW 10¾ to 13¼ minutes) or until tender, **stirring** every 3 minutes. (**Rotate** dish ½ turn when stirring if not using turntable.) Mix yogurt, milk, herb blend, and paprika together and **stir** gently into zucchini mixture. **Cover** and cook on HIGH for 2 to 4 minutes (LW 2¼ to 4¾ minutes) or until heated through. Let **stand, covered,** for 5 minutes before serving.

FOR EACH SERVING:
57 calories
31 mg sodium
2 mg cholesterol
trace fat

Vegetable Cheese Italiano

SERVES 6

EQUIPMENT:	6-cup glass measure, food processor or electric mixer, 2-quart flat baking dish, small bowl
COOKING TIME:	13½ to 19¾ minutes (Low Wattage ovens 16 to 24 minutes)
STANDING TIME:	3 minutes
NUTRITIONAL PROFILE:	low calories, low sodium, low cholesterol

  3 **tablespoons white wine**
  1 **medium onion, chopped**
  2 **tablespoons all-purpose flour**
  1 **cup skim milk**
 ½ **cup low-fat cottage cheese**
  1 **pound broccoli, cauliflower, or green beans, cooked and cut into bite-size pieces (see recipe, page 68)**
  1 **tablespoon freshly grated Parmesan cheese**
  1 **tablespoon soft-spread margarine**
 ¼ **cup plain dry bread crumbs**
 ½ **teaspoon Parsley Patch Garlicsaltless herb blend**

In glass measure, combine wine and onion. Microwave, **uncovered,** on HIGH for 4 to 5 minutes (LW 4¾ to 6 minutes) or until soft. **Whisk** in flour until smooth, then **whisk** in milk. Microwave, **uncovered,** on HIGH for 4 to 6 minutes (LW 4¾ to 7½ minutes) or until thickened, **whisking** every minute.

Whip cottage cheese in food processor or with electric mixer until smooth and **whisk** into sauce. Microwave, **uncovered,** on HIGH for 2 to 3 minutes (LW 2¼ to 3½ minutes), **whisking** every minute until hot and smooth. Arrange cooked vegetables in baking dish and cover with sauce. Sprinkle Parmesan cheese over top.

In small bowl, melt margarine, **uncovered,** on HIGH for 35 to 45 seconds (LW 45 to 55 seconds). Stir in bread crumbs and herb blend. Sprinkle crumb mixture over casserole and **cover** with plastic wrap, pulling back one corner to vent steam. (If dish is flat-bottomed, **elevate** on an inverted saucer.) Microwave on 80 percent power or MEDIUM-HIGH for 3 to 5 minutes (LW 3½ to 6 minutes) or until heated through. Let **stand, covered,** for 3 minutes before serving.

Troubleshooting: Forgetting to whisk sauce may cause it to be lumpy.

Whip cottage cheese until as smooth as possible, but be aware that you will not be able to whip all of the curd smooth.

Suggestions: You can combine any vegetables you like in this casserole. To save time, cook a double batch of vegetables one night and turn it into Vegetable Cheese Italiano the next.

FOR EACH SERVING:
87 calories
107 mg sodium
6 mg cholesterol
2 g fat

Poultry

CHICKEN

Chicken is a relatively low-cost, healthy source of high protein. Knowing how to select a chicken can benefit the quality of your finished dinner. Look for plump fryers weighing no less than 2½ pounds, in moisture-free packaging. You can tell a great deal from the packaging of the chicken. If there are any holes or tears in the package, avoid it; if you see a significant amount of pink liquid in the package, it may mean the chicken was frozen and defrosted.

Never freeze chicken you plan to microwave in the store packaging, as it may have a freshness packet underneath it. Microwaves are attracted to liquid before ice, and this flat freshness packet defrosts very quickly, taking the defrosting energy away from the chicken. Be sure to remove the neck and liver packet before freezing, because it too adds time to the defrosting process. Wash and pat the chicken dry, then place in plastic wrap or a heavy plastic bag for freezing. If you aren't careful when defrosting, and fear you might forget to remove the metal twist tie, use a plastic bread closure tab to secure the bag for freezing.

I have found, through much experimenting, that the best way

to defrost anything is to **elevate** it on a meat rack or an inverted small micro-safe bowl and microwave on 30 percent power or LOW for **short** periods of time, then allow the frozen item to **stand** for several minutes. When you defrost for long periods of time, all at once, you wind up actually cooking the defrosting parts while the balance of the food remains frozen. **Elevate** your frozen chicken, defrost for 5 minutes on 30 percent power or LOW, and let it **stand** for 3 or 4 minutes. Rotate the chicken and **repeat** the process. You may have to repeat this process several times, but you should finish with a defrosted bird and not a partially cooked one.

When roasting chicken in your conventional oven, you need the fat-laden skin to keep the meat from drying out and sticking to the cooking container, but this **won't** happen in the microwave. Feel free to **skin** a whole chicken before cooking, but be aware that the finished look will be similar to a boiled chicken. In order to get an appealing oven-brown look to a whole chicken you must apply some type of browning sauce or glaze. The large oven roasters, once glazed, microwave beautifully and, because they cook so long in the microwave, 7 to 9 minutes per pound, finish beautifully browned, just as though they were baked conventionally.

Roast Chicken

SERVES 4

EQUIPMENT:	meat rack (or 2 custard cups), casserole dish large enough to hold chicken, small bowl
COOKING TIME:	21 to 27 minutes (Low Wattage ovens 25 to 32¼ minutes)
STANDING TIME:	10 minutes
NUTRITIONAL PROFILE:	low calories, low sodium, low cholesterol

1 **3-pound whole frying chicken**
2 **tablespoons low-sugar peach preserves**
2 **tablespoons Dijon mustard**
1 **teaspoon low-salt soy sauce**

Wash chicken, removing any excess fat from interior cavity, and pat dry with paper towels. Place chicken on meat rack or balance between 2 inverted custard cups, or place a small inverted bowl under the chicken, and place in casserole dish to catch the drippings. Place preserves, mustard, and soy sauce in small bowl; mix to combine. Spread mixture evenly all over the outside of the chicken.

Microwave, **uncovered,** on HIGH for 21 to 27 minutes (LW 25 to 32¼ minutes), **basting** and **rotating** dish ½ turn every 10 minutes. Chicken is done when the cavity juices run clear and the legs move freely at the joint; when you pierce the skin between the leg and the breast, the pocket of juices you find should be completely clear with no trace of pink. Once done, **remove** chicken from microwave and let **stand, covered** with aluminum foil, shiny side toward the chicken, for 10 minutes to complete cooking and tenderizing process.

Troubleshooting: Should the wing tips begin to overcook, place a small, completely flat piece of aluminum foil over them and secure with a toothpick. Foil that is crimped, folded, or touching itself will arc, so be sure the small piece you use is completely flat and that your manufacturer allows its use in your oven.

Suggestion: When serving a portion, remove the skin.

FOR EACH SERVING:
280 calories
286 mg sodium
105 mg cholesterol
11 g fat

Cheesy Chicken Rolls

SERVES 8

EQUIPMENT: meat mallet or rolling pin, food processor or electric mixer, small wide-mouthed bowl, meat rack

COOKING TIME: 12¾ to 15 minutes (Low Wattage ovens 15¼ to 17¾ minutes)

STANDING TIME: 5 minutes

NUTRITIONAL PROFILE: low calories, low sodium, low cholesterol

4   6-ounce boneless and skinless chicken breasts, excess fat removed
½   cup low-fat cottage cheese
1   teaspoon Parsley Patch Lemon Pepper herb blend
½   teaspoon dried thyme
½   teaspoon dried marjoram
3   tablespoons soft-spread margarine
½   cup crushed cornflake cereal
1   teaspoon Parsley Patch All-Purpose herb blend

With meat mallet or rolling pin, **flatten** chicken breasts between 2 sheets of wax paper and cut in half. **Whip** cottage cheese in food processor or with electric mixer until as smooth as possible. Combine whipped cottage cheese with Lemon Pepper herb blend, thyme, and marjoram. Spread mixture over one side of each chicken piece and roll up jelly-roll style, securing with toothpick if necessary.

In small bowl, heat margarine, **uncovered,** on HIGH for 45 to 55 seconds (LW 50 to 60 seconds) or until melted. Combine cornflake crumbs and All-Purpose herb blend on sheet of wax paper. Dip top of chicken rolls into melted margarine and then into cornflake crumbs.

Place rolls on meat rack, arranged like the spokes of a wagon wheel, with the broader ends to the outside of the dish, and **cover** with wax paper. Microwave on HIGH for 12 to 14 minutes (LW 14¼ to 16¾ minutes) or until chicken loses its pink color and is tender. **Rotate** dish ½ turn every 6 minutes, but do not turn rolls over. Let **stand, covered,** for 5 minutes before serving.

Troubleshooting: Whip cottage cheese until as smooth as possible, but be aware you will not be able to whip all of the curd smooth.

If meat rack isn't available, place rolls in 9-inch round glass baking dish, like the spokes of a wagon wheel, rearranging but not turning rolls over, every 5 minutes.

FOR EACH SERVING:
205 calories
98 mg sodium
64 mg cholesterol
5 g fat

Chicken the Donnkenny Way

My friend Vicki Regensburg at Donnkenny, Inc., recently became a mother, and eating healthy has become a major concern for her and for many others in the office. They asked me to put together an easy recipe they could prepare fresh for lunch in the office microwave. Chicken topped the list of favorites, so I came up with this recipe, which allows everyone to bring in a chicken portion and one other ingredient. Not only is lunch healthy, but the delicious cooking smells tempt many of the buyers in the showroom.

SERVES 6

EQUIPMENT:	11 × 13-inch flat baking dish
COOKING TIME:	29 to 35 minutes (Low Wattage ovens 34½ to 42 minutes)
STANDING TIME:	5 minutes
NUTRITIONAL PROFILE:	low calories, low sodium, low cholesterol

- 1 **10-ounce paper-covered box frozen artichoke hearts**
- 6 **7-ounce chicken legs with thighs attached, skin and excess fat removed**
- ½ **pound (about 2 cups) fresh mushrooms, sliced**
- 1 **cup (about 4) thinly sliced carrots**
- 1 **teaspoon Parsley Patch All-Purpose herb blend**
- 1 **15-ounce can low-sodium whole tomatoes, chopped, with their juice**
- ¼ **cup white wine**

Place **paper-covered** box of artichokes on 2 **layers** of paper towels on the floor of the microwave. (If box has a foil wrapper, **remove** it first.) Microwave on HIGH for 4 to 5 minutes (LW 4½ to 6 minutes) or until thawed.

To ensure that the chicken leg and thigh cook completely, **break** thigh bones at joint of chicken legs. Place chicken pieces in baking dish, meatiest portions to the outside of the dish and leg bones pointing toward the center. Sprinkle sliced mushrooms over and around chicken pieces. Arrange thawed artichoke hearts and carrot slices around chicken legs. Add herb blend to can of chopped tomatoes and mix to combine. Pour tomatoes over and around chicken and sprinkle with wine.

Cover dish with plastic wrap, pulling back one corner to vent the steam. (If dish is flat-bottomed, **elevate** on an inverted saucer). Microwave on HIGH for 15 minutes (LW 18 minutes). Turn over and **rearrange** chicken pieces, bringing the less cooked areas to the outside of the dish and the ones along the edges to the center, and **baste** with sauce.

Cover and cook on HIGH for 10 to 15 minutes (LW 12 to 18 minutes) or until meat is no longer pink and vegetables are tender. Let **stand, covered,** for 5 minutes before serving.

Troubleshooting: If joints are not broken, add 2 to 3 minutes (LW 2¼ to 3½ minutes) to the final cooking time.

Suggestion: Serve each portion over ½ cup cooked long-grain rice which adds 70 calories per serving.

For less restricted diets: If you're not watching your salt intake, substitute regular tomatoes, which add 115 mg sodium per serving.

FOR EACH SERVING:
168 calories
137 mg sodium
50 mg cholesterol
6 g fat

Chicken Dressing Casserole

SERVES 4

EQUIPMENT: 2-quart round casserole dish, 2-cup glass measure

COOKING TIME: 16 to 21 minutes (Low Wattage ovens 18½ to 24¾ minutes)

STANDING TIME: 5 minutes

NUTRITIONAL PROFILE: low calories, low sodium, low cholesterol

¼ cup white wine
½ cup (about 1 medium) chopped onion
½ cup (about 2 large) chopped celery
1 cup (about 4 ounces) sliced fresh mushrooms
¼ cup (about 1) grated carrot
1 tablespoon minced fresh parsley
2 slices whole wheat or white bread, toasted and finely diced
¼ teaspoon dried sage
¼ teaspoon dried thyme
2 cups diced cooked chicken or turkey, fat and skin removed
2 egg whites, well beaten
1 teaspoon Parsley Patch All-Purpose herb blend
¼ teaspoon Parsley Patch Lemon Pepper herb blend
¼ teaspoon paprika
1 cup low-sodium chicken broth or homemade chicken stock (page 44)
2 tablespoons all-purpose flour

Place wine, onion, celery, mushrooms, carrot, and parsley in casserole dish. **Cover** with lid or plastic wrap, pulling back one corner to vent the steam. (If dish is flat-bottomed, **elevate** on an inverted saucer.) Place on turntable if available. Microwave on HIGH for 6 to 8 minutes (LW 7 to 9 minutes) or until vegetables are tender-crisp, stirring every 4 minutes. Add diced bread, sage, thyme, diced chicken, beaten egg whites, both herb blends, and paprika. **Stir** well.

In glass measure, **whisk** together chicken broth and flour until flour is completely dissolved. Microwave, **uncovered,** on HIGH for 3 to 4 minutes (LW 3½ to 4¾ minutes), **whisking** every minute, until thickened. Pour over chicken mixture in dish and stir well.

Cover and cook on HIGH for 7 to 9 minutes (LW 8¼ to 11 minutes) or until hot and bubbly. (**Rotate** dish ½ turn every 5 minutes if not using turntable.) Let **stand, covered,** for 5 minutes before serving.

Troubleshooting: Forgetting to whisk sauce may cause it to be lumpy. Be sure to whisk every minute while thickening to keep it smooth.

Suggestion: This is a great way to use up leftover chicken or turkey.

For less restricted diets: If you're not watching your salt intake, substitute regular chicken broth, which adds 225 mg sodium per serving.

FOR EACH SERVING:
279 calories
153 mg sodium
63 mg cholesterol
1 g fat

Chicken in Mushroom Sauce

Except for duck and goose, poultry is a good low-cholesterol protein source. Cornish hens make a good substitute for duck in recipes, but even using these less fatty birds, it is advisable to skin all poultry, since the skin is the major cholesterol source.

SERVES 4

EQUIPMENT:	4-cup glass measure, 12 × 8- or 13 × 9-inch baking dish
COOKING TIME:	10¾ to 16 minutes (Low Wattage ovens 13½ to 19½ minutes)
STANDING TIME:	5 minutes
NUTRITIONAL PROFILE:	low calories, low sodium, low cholesterol

2 tablespoons soft-spread margarine
2 tablespoons all-purpose flour
¼ teaspoon dried tarragon
dash freshly ground pepper
2 tablespoons white wine
¼ teaspoon dry mustard
1 cup skim milk, minus 2 tablespoons
½ cup shredded sharp Cheddar cheese
1 cup (about 4 ounces) sliced fresh mushrooms
2 tablespoons (about 1) chopped scallion
1 pound boneless and skinless chicken breasts, excess fat removed, pounded thin, and cut into 4 pieces
12 cooked fresh or frozen asparagus spears

Place margarine in glass measure and microwave, **uncovered,** on HIGH for 45 to 55 seconds (LW 55 to 60 seconds) or until melted. Add flour, tarragon, and pepper, **whisking** until smooth. **Whisk** in wine and mustard. Gradually add milk, **whisking** until smooth.

Microwave, **uncovered,** on HIGH for 4 to 6 minutes (LW 4¾ to 7½ minutes), **whisking** every minute. When sauce thickens and coats whisk, add ¾ of the cheese, mushrooms, and scallion. Microwave, **uncovered,** on HIGH for 1 minute (LW 1½ minutes) and **whisk** until smooth.

On top of each chicken breast piece, evenly sprinkle remaining cheese. Place 3 asparagus spears over cheese and fold edges of chicken around asparagus. (If necessary, secure with a round-edged toothpick.) Place rolls in baking dish, arranged like the spokes of a wagon wheel, and cover with cheese and mushroom sauce. **Cover** dish with plastic wrap, pulling back one corner to vent the steam. (If dish is flat-bottomed, **elevate** on an inverted saucer.)

Microwave on HIGH for 5 to 8 minutes (LW 6 to 9½ minutes) or until chicken is no longer pink and is tender, **rotating** dish ½ turn after 3 minutes. Let **stand, covered,** for 5 minutes before serving.

Troubleshooting: If you forget to whisk the sauce, it may be lumpy.

Suggestion: One pound of skinless turkey cutlets may be substituted for chicken.

FOR EACH SERVING:
346 calories
295 mg sodium
65 mg cholesterol
13 g fat

Chicken Noodle Bake

SERVES 4

EQUIPMENT:	deep 2- or 3-quart casserole dish, 4-cup glass measure
COOKING TIME:	19¾ to 25¾ minutes (Low Wattage ovens 23 to 30½ minutes)
STANDING TIME:	5 minutes
NUTRITIONAL PROFILE:	low calories, low sodium, low cholesterol

   2   **tablespoons white wine**
  ½   **cup (about 1 medium) chopped onion**
  ½   **cup (about 2 large stalks) chopped celery**
  ½   **cup (about ½ large) chopped red bell pepper**
  ¼   **pound (about 1 cup) fresh mushrooms, sliced**
   2   **tablespoons soft-spread margarine**
   2   **tablespoons all-purpose flour**
 1¾   **cups skim milk**
  ⅛   **teaspoon dried thyme**
  ⅛   **teaspoon dried sage**
  ¼   **teaspoon Parsley Patch Lemon Pepper herb blend**
  ½   **cup shredded Cheddar cheese**
  ¼   **pound eggless noodles, cooked and drained**
   1   **cup diced cooked chicken, fat and skin removed**

TOPPING
  ½   **cup crushed cornflake cereal**
  ½   **teaspoon Parsley Patch Garlicsaltless herb blend**

Place wine, onion, celery, red bell pepper, and mushrooms in casserole dish. **Cover** with lid or plastic wrap, pulling back one corner to vent the steam. (If dish is flat-bottomed, **elevate** on an inverted saucer.) Place on turntable if available. Microwave on HIGH for 5 to 7 minutes (LW 6 to 8¼ minutes) or until vegetables are tender-crisp.

Place margarine in glass measure and melt, **uncovered,** on HIGH for 40 to 50 seconds (LW 50 to 60 seconds). **Whisk** in flour until smooth. **Whisk** in milk, thyme, sage, and Lemon Pepper herb blend. Cook, **uncovered,** on HIGH for 4 to 6 minutes (LW 4¾ to 7 minutes), whisking every minute until thickened. **Whisk** in cheese until melted.

Add sauce to vegetables and stir in noodles and chicken. **Cover** and cook on 70 percent power or MEDIUM-HIGH for 8 to 10 minutes (LW 9 to 12 minutes) or until heated through, **stirring** every 3 minutes. (**Rotate** dish ¼ turn when stirring if not using turntable.) Mix crushed cornflakes with Garlicsaltless herb blend and sprinkle over dish. **Cover** and cook on HIGH for 2 minutes (LW 2¼ minutes). Let **stand, covered,** for 5 minutes before serving.

Troubleshooting: Forgetting to whisk sauce may cause it to be lumpy.

FOR EACH SERVING:
349 calories
372 mg sodium
60 mg cholesterol
15 g fat

CORNFLAKE TOPPING

Cornflake crumbs are packaged already crushed but contain added sodium and sometimes extra fat. If you're concerned about sodium, make your own crumbs by crushing cornflake cereal in a food processor or by placing in plastic bag and rolling several times with a rolling pin.

Chicken à la King

SERVES 4

EQUIPMENT: deep 3-quart casserole dish, 4-cup glass measure
COOKING TIME: 18¾ to 24¾ minutes (Low Wattage ovens 22¼ to 29½ minutes)
STANDING TIME: 2 to 3 minutes
NUTRITIONAL PROFILE: low calories, low sodium, low cholesterol

2 **tablespoons white wine**
¼ **cup (about ¼ large) chopped green bell pepper**
¼ **cup (about ¼ large) chopped red bell pepper**
½ **cup (about ½ large) chopped red onion**
½ **cup (about 2 large stalks) chopped celery**
1 **large garlic clove, minced**
¼ **pound (about 1 cup) fresh mushrooms, sliced**
2 **tablespoons soft-spread margarine**
2 **tablespoons all-purpose flour**
1 **cup skim milk**
½ **teaspoon low-sodium chicken bouillon granules**
1 **teaspoon Parsley Patch All-Purpose herb blend**
2 **cups diced cooked chicken, fat and skin removed**
1 **cup frozen peas, thawed**
   parsley for garnish

In casserole dish, place wine, green bell pepper, red bell pepper, onion, celery, garlic, and mushrooms. **Cover** with lid or plastic wrap, pulling back one corner to vent the steam. (If dish is flat-bottomed, **elevate** on an inverted saucer.) Place on turntable if available. Cook on HIGH for 6 to 8 minutes (LW 7½ to 9½ minutes) or until vegetables are tender-crisp.

Place margarine in glass measure and melt, **uncovered,** on HIGH for 40 to 50 seconds (LW 50 to 60 seconds). **Whisk** in flour until smooth, then **whisk** in milk, bouillon granules, and herb blend. Cook, **uncovered,** on HIGH for 4 to 6 minutes (LW 4¾ to 7 minutes), whisking every minute until thickened.

Add sauce, chicken, and thawed peas to cooked vegetable mixture. **Cover** and cook on HIGH for 8 to 10 minutes (LW 9½ to

12 minutes) or until heated through and peas are tender, **stirring** every 3 to 4 minutes. (**Rotate** dish ¼ turn when stirring if not using turntable.) Let **stand, covered,** for 2 to 3 minutes and garnish with parsley.

Suggestions: Serve each portion over ½ cup cooked long-grain rice or 1 slice of white or whole wheat bread, toasted and cut into points, which adds 70 calories per serving. Serving over bread will also add 117 mg sodium per serving.

If peas are frozen, microwave paper-covered box on 2 layers of paper towels on HIGH for 2 to 3 minutes (LW 2¼ to 3¼ minutes) until thawed.

For less restricted diets: If you're not watching your salt intake, substitute regular chicken bouillon granules, which add 112 mg sodium per serving.

FOR EACH SERVING:
297 calories
163 mg sodium
63 mg cholesterol
4 g fat

Chicken Oriental

SERVES 6

EQUIPMENT:	9 × 13-inch casserole dish, 2-cup glass measure
COOKING TIME:	22 to 25 minutes (Low Wattage ovens 26¼ to 30 minutes)
STANDING TIME:	15 minutes
NUTRITIONAL PROFILE:	low calories, low sodium, low cholesterol

3 **pounds cut-up chicken fryer parts, skin and excess fat removed**

1 **cup pineapple chunks in natural juice, drained and juice reserved**

¼ **cup (about 2) chopped scallions**

2 **garlic cloves, minced**

½ **teaspoon ground ginger**

1 **tablespoon low-salt soy sauce**

2 **tablespoons honey**

2 **tablespoons white wine**

¼ **teaspoon freshly ground pepper**

1 **teaspoon Parsley Patch Sesame All-Purpose herb blend**

Arrange chicken pieces in casserole dish with the larger and meatier portions to the outside of the dish and thinner sections pointed toward the center of the dish. Place reserved pineapple juice in glass measure and add scallions, garlic, ginger, soy sauce, honey, wine, pepper, and herb blend. **Whisk** these ingredients together well and allow to **stand** for 10 minutes.

Pour mixture over and around chicken pieces. **Cover** dish with wax paper. (If dish is flat-bottomed, **elevate** on an inverted saucer.) Cook on HIGH for 10 minutes (LW 12 minutes), **rotating** dish ½ turn after 5 minutes. **Rearrange** chicken pieces and baste with sauce.

Cover and cook on HIGH for 10 to 12 minutes (LW 12 to 14½ minutes) or until chicken is firm and no longer pink near the bone, **rotating** dish ½ turn every 5 minutes. Top dish with pineapple chunks, **cover,** and cook on HIGH for 2 to 3 minutes (LW 2¼ to 3½ minutes) or until pineapple is hot. Let **stand, covered,** for 5 minutes before serving.

RICE

Check the labels on the boxes of instant rice as some may contain up to 200 mg of sodium for each ½ cup serving as compared to regular long-grain rice. If you're not watching your sodium intake, you can substitute instant rice in any recipe. Regular long-grain rice is really the healthy alternative to instant rice and tastes even better. New products are coming into the market every day. If you prefer to use instant rice, check the labels on boxes, since you may find some without added salt.

Troubleshooting: When rearranging chicken pieces, bring the less cooked pieces from the center of the dish to the outside edges and the pieces along the outer edges to the center.

Suggestion: Serve each portion over ½ cup cooked long-grain rice, which adds 70 calories per serving.

For less restricted diets: If you're not on a low-salt diet, substitute regular soy sauce, which adds 60 mg sodium per serving.

FOR EACH SERVING:
269 calories
158 mg sodium
84 mg cholesterol
trace fat

Lemon and Wine Chicken

SERVES 4

EQUIPMENT:	2-quart round casserole dish, 12 × 8-inch baking dish
COOKING TIME:	19 to 27 minutes (Low Wattage ovens 22¾ to 32¼ minutes)
STANDING TIME:	5 minutes
NUTRITIONAL PROFILE:	low calories, low sodium, low cholesterol

- **1 cup (about ½ medium) cauliflower flowerets**
- **1 cup (about 4) sliced carrots**
- **1 cup (about 4 large stalks) sliced celery**
- **1 cup frozen sliced green beans**
- **¾ cup (about ¾ large) diced green and/or red bell pepper**
- **1 medium onion, sliced**
- **3 tablespoons white wine**
- **2 tablespoons fresh lemon juice (see tip, page 124)**
- **¼ teaspoon low-sodium chicken bouillon granules**
- **¼ teaspoon dried thyme**
- **1 teaspoon parsley flakes**
  pinch freshly ground pepper
- **2 6-ounce boneless and skinless chicken breasts, cut in half, with excess fat removed**
- **6 large iceberg lettuce leaves, washed and drained**

Combine all ingredients except chicken and lettuce leaves in casserole dish. **Cover** with lid or plastic wrap, pulling back one corner to vent the steam. (If dish is flat-bottomed, **elevate** on an inverted saucer.) Place on turntable if available. Cook on HIGH for 5 to 9 minutes (LW 6 to 10¾ minutes) or until vegetables are tender-crisp, **stirring** every 3 minutes. (**Rotate** dish ¼ turn every 3 minutes if not using turntable.)

Place chicken pieces in baking dish, meatiest parts to the outside of the dish. Spread vegetables over and around chicken and completely cover everything with lettuce leaves.

Cover dish with wax paper and cook on HIGH for 14 to 18 minutes (LW 16¾ to 21½ minutes), **rearranging** chicken pieces halfway through cooking. (**Rotate** dish ½ turn every 7 minutes if not using turntable.) When chicken is tender and no longer pink, remove lettuce leaves and let chicken **stand, covered,** for 5 minutes. **Skim** any remaining fat from liquid before serving.

Troubleshooting: When rearranging chicken pieces, bring the less cooked ones from the center of the dish to the outside edges and the ones along the edges to the center.

CITRUS FRUIT JUICE

To extract more juice and flavor from your citrus fruits, microwave lemons, limes, oranges, and grapefruit on HIGH for 15 to 20 seconds per piece of fruit on the floor of your microwave (LW 18 to 20 seconds). Should you do more than one at a time, arrange them in a circle. Allow the fruit to stand for 1 to 2 minutes and then rub them between the palms of your hands. The fruit will not get hot, but this process does produce more juice and aroma; the grated zest will have a great deal more flavor.

If you have a cut lemon or lime that looks dried out, wrap it in a paper towel and microwave on HIGH for 10 seconds (LW 12 seconds); that dried-out fruit will now yield lots of juice.

For less restricted diets: If you're not watching your salt intake, substitute regular chicken bouillon granules, which add 56 mg sodium per serving.

FOR EACH SERVING:
204 calories
76 mg sodium
36 mg cholesterol
trace fat

Smothered Chicken with Mushrooms

SERVES 6

EQUIPMENT:	deep 3-quart casserole dish, 6-cup glass measure
COOKING TIME:	38¾ to 45¾ minutes (Low Wattage ovens 46¾ to 55 minutes)
STANDING TIME:	5 minutes
NUTRITIONAL PROFILE:	low calories, low sodium, low cholesterol

1½ **cups long-grain rice**
1 **cup water**
2 **tablespoons soft-spread margarine**
3 **tablespoons all-purpose flour**
1 **cup low-sodium chicken broth or homemade chicken stock (page 44)**
2 **cups skim milk**
½ **cup red or white wine**
½ **cup (about 1 medium) chopped onion**
½ **cup (about 2 large stalks) chopped celery**
½ **teaspoon onion powder**
1 **teaspoon Parsley Patch All-Purpose herb blend**
2 **pounds cut-up skinless chicken fryer parts, with excess fat removed**
2 **cups small whole fresh mushrooms**

In casserole dish, combine rice and water. **Cover** with lid or plastic wrap, pulling back one corner to vent the steam. (If dish is flat-bottomed, **elevate** on an inverted saucer.) Place on turntable if available.

Microwave on HIGH for 5 minutes (LW 6 minutes). **Reduce** to 50 percent power or MEDIUM and cook for 10 to 13 minutes (LW 12 to 15½ minutes), until almost tender; fluff with a fork.

Place margarine in glass measure and melt, **uncovered,** on HIGH for 40 to 50 seconds (LW 50 to 60 seconds). **Whisk** in flour until smooth. **Whisk** in broth, milk, and wine. Cook on HIGH for 3 to 5 minutes (LW 4 to 6 minutes) or until slightly thickened, **whisking** every minute. Stir in onion, celery, onion powder, and herb blend. Pour ½ this mixture over rice layer. Arrange chicken pieces on top of rice with meatiest portions to the outside of the dish. Arrange mushrooms around chicken pieces and pour remaining sauce mixture over all.

Cover dish with wax paper and microwave on HIGH for 20 to 22 minutes (LW 24 to 26½ minutes) or until chicken is tender and no longer pink near the bone and rice is soft. **Rearrange** chicken pieces every 10 minutes, bringing the less cooked areas from the center of the dish to the outside edges and the ones along the edges to the center of the dish. (**Rotate** dish ½ turn every 10 minutes if not using turntable.) Let **stand, covered,** for 5 minutes before serving.

Troubleshooting: Forgetting to whisk sauce may cause it to lump.

For less restricted diets: If you're not watching your salt intake, substitute regular chicken broth, which adds 150 mg sodium per serving.

FOR EACH SERVING:
360 calories
129 mg sodium
84 mg cholesterol
3 g fat

HOT SPOTS

Hot spots are areas in the oven that have a heavy concentration of microwave energy. You will know if you have one—the food always overcooks in that particular spot of the oven. The only way to beat this problem is to use a turntable or to rotate the food out of that particular area frequently.

Stuffed Chicken Rolls

SERVES 4

EQUIPMENT:	4-cup glass measure, 8- or 9-inch round baking dish, custard cup, small bowl
COOKING TIME:	18½ to 26 minutes (Low Wattage ovens 22¼ to 31¼ minutes)
STANDING TIME:	3 minutes
NUTRITIONAL PROFILE:	low calories, low sodium, low cholesterol

- **2 tablespoons soft-spread margarine**
- **½ cup (about 1 medium) minced onion**
- **¼ cup (about 1 large stalk) minced celery**
- **¼ teaspoon dried sage**
- **¼ teaspoon dried thyme**
- **¼ teaspoon Parsley Patch Lemon Pepper herb blend**
- **2 slices white or whole wheat bread, toasted and finely cubed**
- **¼ cup low-sodium chicken broth or homemade chicken stock (page 44)**
- **2 6-ounce skinless and boneless chicken breasts, cut in half and pounded thin**
- **¼ pound (about ½ bunch) fresh broccoli, cooked and divided into 4 portions**
- **2 tablespoons soft-spread margarine**

SAUCE

- **1 tablespoon soft-spread margarine**
- **2 tablespoons all-purpose flour**
- **1 cup low-sodium chicken broth or homemade chicken stock (page 44)**
- **⅛ teaspoon dried sage**
- **⅛ teaspoon dried thyme**
- **¼ teaspoon Parsley Patch Lemon Pepper herb blend**
- **1 tablespoon white wine**
- **1 tablespoon chopped pimiento**
  parsley to taste

Place 2 tablespoons margarine, onion, celery, ¼ teaspoon sage, ¼ teaspoon thyme, and ¼ teaspoon herb blend in glass measure. Microwave, **uncovered,** on HIGH for 4 to 6 minutes (LW 4¾ to 7½ minutes), until vegetables are tender-crisp. Stir in bread cubes and ¼ cup stock to moisten.

Place ¼ of stuffing mixture on each chicken piece and place broccoli over stuffing. Roll up jelly-roll style. (You may fasten with a wooden pick if necessary.) Arrange rolls, seam side down, in baking dish in a ring like the spokes of a wagon wheel. Melt 2 tablespoons margarine in custard cup, **uncovered,** on HIGH for 40 to 50 seconds (LW 50 to 60 seconds). Brush chicken rolls with melted margarine, **cover** loosely with wax paper, and set aside.

For sauce, place margarine in small bowl, and melt, **uncovered,** on HIGH for 45 to 55 seconds (LW 50 to 60 seconds). **Whisk** in flour until smooth. **Whisk** in 1 cup broth, ⅛ teaspoon sage, ⅛ teaspoon thyme, ¼ teaspoon herb blend, and wine. Microwave, **uncovered,** on HIGH for 4 to 6 minutes (LW 4¾ to 7½ minutes), whisking every minute, until thickened.

Place wax **paper–covered** dish of chicken rolls in microwave. (If dish is flat-bottomed, **elevate** on an inverted saucer.) Place on turntable if available. Cook on HIGH for 5 minutes (LW 6 minutes). **Rearrange** rolls, bringing the less cooked areas to the outside of the dish, and pour sauce over and around rolls. **Cover** and cook on HIGH for 4 to 7 minutes (LW 4¾ to 8¼ minutes) or until chicken is tender and no longer pink. (**Rotate** dish ½ turn every 4 minutes if not using turntable.) Let **stand, covered,** for 3 minutes, remove wooden picks, and garnish with pimiento and parsley.

For less restricted diets: If you're not watching your salt intake, substitute regular chicken broth, which adds 281 mg sodium per serving.

FOR EACH SERVING:
301 calories
198 mg sodium
37 mg cholesterol
8 g fat

Chinese Stew

SERVES 6

EQUIPMENT: deep 3-quart casserole dish, 1-cup glass measure
COOKING TIME: 17 to 20 minutes (Low Wattage ovens 20 to 24¼ minutes)
STANDING TIME: 5 minutes
NUTRITIONAL PROFILE: low calories, low sodium, low cholesterol

2 large onions, sliced
1 large green bell pepper, sliced
1 pound fresh bean sprouts
1 8-ounce box frozen snow peas, thawed and drained
1 pound (about 4 cups) fresh mushrooms, sliced
1 cup (about 4 large stalks) diagonally sliced celery
1 garlic clove, minced
¼ teaspoon dried thyme
¼ teaspoon dried sage
½ teaspoon freshly ground pepper
3 cups cubed cooked chicken or turkey, skin and fat removed
3 tablespoons cornstarch
2 tablespoons low-salt soy sauce
¾ cup low-sodium chicken broth or homemade chicken stock (page 44)

In casserole dish, combine onions, green bell pepper, bean sprouts, snow peas, mushrooms, celery, garlic, thyme, sage, and pepper.

Cover with lid or plastic wrap, pulling back one corner to vent the steam. (If dish is flat-bottomed, **elevate** on an inverted saucer.) Place on turntable if available. Cook on HIGH for 6 minutes (LW 7 to 7½ minutes), **stirring** every 3 minutes. Add cooked poultry and **stir** ingredients together well.

In glass measure, **whisk** together cornstarch, soy sauce, and chicken broth. Microwave, **uncovered,** on HIGH for 3 to 4 minutes (LW 3½ to 4¾ minutes) to thicken, **whisking** every minute. **Stir** cornstarch mixture into casserole, combining well.

Cover and cook on HIGH for 8 to 10 minutes (LW 9½ to 12 minutes) or until vegetables are tender-crisp, **stirring** every 4 minutes. (**Rotate** dish when stirring if not using turntable.) Let **stand, covered,** for 5 minutes before serving.

Suggestions: Serve each portion over ½ cup cooked long-grain rice or eggless noodles, which add 70 calories per serving.

For less restricted diets: If you're not watching your salt intake, substitute regular soy sauce, which adds 180 mg sodium per serving, and regular chicken broth, which adds 113 mg of sodium per serving.

FOR EACH SERVING:
300 calories
202 mg sodium
79 mg cholesterol
1 g fat

TURKEY BREAST

Although turkey and Thanksgiving seem to be made for each other, turkey isn't just for the holidays.

A whole turkey is often too much for many families, especially those interested only in using the leftover white meat for sandwiches. Give some thought to trying just a turkey breast and leaving the rest of the turkey for bigger families or those who are creative with leftovers. Turkey breasts microwave beautifully, and if you add a bit of glaze to the skin, it also browns just as nicely as it would in a conventional oven.

Start with a completely defrosted turkey breast—if yours is frozen, we can fix that. As in microwaving any meat or poultry, the food must be **elevated** off the flat cooking surface. If you don't have a meat rack made for the microwave, a simple inverted micro-safe bowl or coffee cup set into a casserole dish will work. Remove all the wrappings from your frozen turkey breast and place it skin side down on a meat rack or balanced on top of a small micro-safe bowl or between custard cups. Multiply the weight by 4, and that will be the number of minutes necessary to defrost on 50 percent or MEDIUM power.

Let's use a 5-pound turkey breast as an example. Microwave the **elevated** breast, skin side down, for 10 minutes (LW 12 minutes). Carefully remove any gravy or giblet package that may be tucked inside, turn the breast skin side up, and microwave for another 10 minutes on 50 percent or MEDIUM power. Rinse the entire piece in cold water and let it **stand** for 10 minutes. If it is still icy, microwave, breast side up, for 4 to 5 minutes (LW 5 to 7 minutes) on 30 percent power or LOW and let **stand** for another 5 to 10 minutes. Allow 45 minutes for proper defrosting; if you attempt to rush the process on a higher setting, some areas will begin to cook before others are defrosted.

If you're dieting and watching your cholesterol, leaving the skin on and glazing isn't necessary, but if the appearance of the finished product is important to your presentation, try this tasty glaze. Remember, you can always remove the skin once the turkey slice is on your plate.

Glazed Roast Turkey Breast

SERVES 8

EQUIPMENT:	2-cup glass measure, meat rack or 2 custard cups and casserole dish to catch the drippings
COOKING TIME:	1¼ to 1¾ hours (Low Wattage ovens 1¾ to 2 hours)
STANDING TIME:	10 to 20 minutes
NUTRITIONAL PROFILE:	moderate calories, low sodium, moderate cholesterol

1   **teaspoon low-salt soy sauce**
2   **tablespoons honey**
4   **tablespoons low-sugar apricot preserves**
1   **tablespoon soft-spread margarine**
2   **tablespoons orange-flavored liqueur**
1   **5-pound bone-in turkey breast, thawed**

Place all ingredients except turkey in glass measure and **cover** with wax paper. Microwave on HIGH for 2 to 3 minutes (LW 2½ to 3½ minutes), **whisking** every minute, until all ingredients are well blended. Place turkey breast, skin side down (if skinned, backbone down), on a meat rack or balanced on 2 custard cups set into a casserole dish to catch the drippings. Microwave, **uncovered,** for 13 to 16 minutes (LW 15½ to 19¼ minutes) per pound on 50 percent power or MEDIUM, as follows.

Calculate cooking time and divide into fourths. Start the turkey on HIGH for the first 5 minutes of the first quarter's cooking time, then lower power to 50 percent or MEDIUM for the balance of the first quarter of time.

Turn breast on its side and brush on the glaze. Microwave on 50 percent power or MEDIUM for the second quarter of cooking time.

Turn breast on the opposite side, brush with glaze, and continue on 50 percent power or MEDIUM for the third quarter of cooking time.

For the final quarter of cooking time, **turn** turkey skin side up, cover breast with glaze, and finish the cooking time at 50 percent power or MEDIUM. When microwaving has finished, the internal temperature should be 170 degrees if using a micro-safe thermometer.

Remove turkey from the microwave and tent with aluminum foil, shiny side toward the meat. Let **stand, covered,** for 10 to 20 minutes to finish tenderizing and cooking before slicing.

Troubleshooting: Forgetting to elevate will cause uneven cooking. Be sure to balance turkey between 2 custard cups if a meat rack is not available.

Failing to lower the power setting to 50 percent or MEDIUM will cause the breast to dry out and toughen.

Suggestions: Should you want to use only legs or thighs, just elevate them on a meat rack in a circle like the spokes of a wagon wheel. Microwave them, brushed with glaze, on 70 percent power or MEDIUM-HIGH for 13 to 17 minutes (LW 15 to 20 minutes) a pound, turning them over and rearranging halfway through cooking time. If turntable is available, use it.

To reduce calories by ⅓, eliminate the orange-flavored liqueur. In its place grate the peel of an orange, using the orange zest for the recipe flavoring. Be sure to microwave the orange on HIGH power for 15 seconds, let stand for 1 minute, and roll between the palms of your hands before grating to concentrate the flavor.

FOR EACH SERVING:
485 calories
142 mg sodium
165 mg cholesterol
11 g fat

SOY SAUCE

Soy sauce is very high in sodium. While greatly increasing your salt intake, it does give a distinctive flavor you can't duplicate. There are low-salt forms of soy sauce, and if you're watching your salt intake, read the label, as this version will give you ½ the salt found in regular soy sauce.

Turkey Divan Casserole

SERVES 6

EQUIPMENT:	6-cup glass measure, 2-quart round casserole dish, 2-cup glass measure
COOKING TIME:	17¼ to 23½ minutes (Low Wattage ovens 20½ to 29 minutes)
STANDING TIME:	2 minutes
NUTRITIONAL PROFILE:	low calories, low sodium, low cholesterol

1   16-ounce bag frozen broccoli cuts
2   tablespoons soft-spread margarine
2   tablespoons all-purpose flour
½   teaspoon Parsley Patch All-Purpose herb blend
2   cups skim milk
½   cup shredded Swiss cheese
2   cups diced cooked turkey, skin and fat removed
1   tablespoon soft-spread margarine
¼   cup plain dry bread crumbs
2   tablespoons freshly grated Parmesan cheese

Make a slit in the top of frozen broccoli bag and place on 2 layers of paper towels. Microwave on HIGH for 8 to 10 minutes (LW 9½ to 12 minutes) or until tender-crisp, **turning** bag over and **rotating** ½ turn after 5 minutes.

In 6-cup glass measure, melt 2 tablespoons margarine, **uncovered,** on HIGH for 45 to 55 seconds (LW 50 to 60 seconds). **Whisk** in flour and herb blend. **Whisk** in milk until blended and microwave, **uncovered,** on HIGH for 4 to 6 minutes (LW 4¾ to 7½ minutes), **whisking** every minute, until slightly thickened. Add Swiss cheese, whisking until melted, then add turkey cubes.

Arrange broccoli in casserole dish and cover with turkey mixture. In 2-cup glass measure, microwave, **uncovered,** 1 tablespoon margarine on HIGH for 30 to 40 seconds (LW 40 to 50 seconds) or until melted. Add bread crumbs and Parmesan cheese, mixing to combine. Sprinkle bread crumb mixture over casserole. (If dish is flat-bottomed, **elevate** on an inverted saucer.) Place on turntable if available. **Cover** dish with wax paper and microwave on HIGH for 4 to 6 minutes (LW 4½ to 7½ minutes) or until heated through. Let **stand, covered,** for 2 minutes before serving.

Troubleshooting: Failing to whisk sauce may cause it to be lumpy.

Suggestions: Substitute green beans or asparagus for broccoli if you prefer.

FOR EACH SERVING:
290 calories
233 mg sodium
92 mg cholesterol
15 g fat

Turkey-Pineapple Curry

SERVES 6

EQUIPMENT:	6-cup glass measure, deep 2-quart casserole dish
COOKING TIME:	11 to 16 minutes (Low Wattage ovens 13 to 18¾ minutes)
STANDING TIME:	none required
NUTRITIONAL PROFILE:	low calories, low sodium, low cholesterol

⅓ **cup white wine**
½ **cup (about 1 medium) chopped onion**
⅓ **cup all-purpose flour**
1 **teaspoon curry powder**
1 **teaspoon Parsley Patch All-Purpose herb blend**
1 **quart (4 cups) low-sodium chicken broth or home-made chicken stock (page 44)**
3 **cups cubed cooked turkey, skin and fat removed**
1 **cup drained pineapple tidbits packed in natural juices**

Place wine and onion in glass measure and microwave, **uncovered,** on HIGH for 3 to 4 minutes (LW 3¼ to 4½ minutes) or until soft. **Whisk** in flour, curry powder, and herb blend, whisking until smooth. Add broth, whisking well. Microwave, **uncovered,** on HIGH for 6 to 8 minutes (LW 7½ to 9½ minutes) or until mixture thickens, **whisking** every minute.

Place turkey and pineapple in casserole dish, cover with sauce, and stir carefully. (If dish is flat-bottomed, **elevate** on an inverted saucer.) Microwave, **uncovered,** on HIGH for 2 to 4 minutes (LW 2¼ to 4¾ minutes) or until heated through.

Suggestions: If you feel you are missing flavor, add another good sprinkle of Parsley Patch herb blend.

Serve each portion over ½ cup cooked long-grain rice, which adds 70 calories to each serving.

For less restricted diets: If you're not watching your salt intake, substitute regular chicken broth, which adds 608 mg of sodium per serving.

FOR EACH SERVING:
231 calories
52 mg sodium
88 mg cholesterol
7 g fat

GROUND TURKEY

I don't think there is anyone who can't think of at least one way to prepare hamburger. But have you noticed ground turkey in the meat case and drawn a complete blank? Here are four good recipes to get you started—but be sure the ground turkey doesn't have fat added; some commercial brands grind the skin in, too.

If you plan to freeze fresh ground turkey, do it as you would ground beef or ground pork. Place the meat in a plastic bag and make a **depression** in the center of the bag with your fist or form the meat into a ring shape before freezing so that the microwaves can get in and around the meat from all sides, defrosting it faster.

To defrost, **remove** the twist tie from the frozen bag, set it onto an inverted saucer, and microwave on 30 percent power or LOW for 3 to 4 minutes (LW 3½ to 4½ minutes). Allow the defrosting meat to **stand** in the microwave for 3 or 4 minutes and **repeat** the process.

Depending on the quantity of meat you are defrosting, you may have to repeat the process once or twice. By defrosting for short periods of time and allowing the meat to stand you will defrost the entire package evenly, without cooking the outside edges before the center area defrosts.

Turkey Stroganoff

SERVES 4

EQUIPMENT:	small and medium bowls, dinner plate or round baking dish, 3-quart casserole dish
COOKING TIME:	16 to 22 minutes (Low Wattage ovens 19 to 26 minutes)
STANDING TIME:	none required
NUTRITIONAL PROFILE:	low calories, low sodium, low cholesterol

  4 slices white or whole wheat bread, cut into cubes
  ¼ teaspoon dried thyme
  ¼ teaspoon dried sage
  ¼ teaspoon freshly ground pepper
  **½ cup low-sodium chicken broth or homemade chicken
     stock (page 44)**
  2 egg whites, slightly beaten
  1 pound fresh lean ground turkey
  1 cup (about 4 ounces) sliced fresh mushrooms
  ½ cup plain yogurt
1½ cups skim milk
  ¼ cup white wine
  4 tablespoons all-purpose flour

Combine bread cubes, thyme, sage, pepper, broth, and egg whites in medium bowl. Add ground turkey and mix well. Shape into about 38 1-inch balls. Arrange balls in circles on plate or in baking dish. (If dish is flat-bottomed, **elevate** on an inverted saucer.) Microwave, **uncovered,** on HIGH for 3 minutes (LW 3½ minutes).

  Drain any liquid and **rearrange,** moving the balls from around the outside edges to the center and bringing the ones in the center to the outside edges. Microwave, **uncovered,** on HIGH for 3 to 5 minutes (LW 3½ to 6 minutes) or until the balls are no longer pink in the center. **Drain** any liquid and set aside.

  Place mushrooms in casserole dish. In a small bowl, combine yogurt, milk, wine, and flour, **whisking** well to blend ingredients. Pour liquid over mushrooms. **Cover** dish with lid or plastic wrap, pulling back one corner to vent the steam. (If dish is flat-bottomed,

elevate on an inverted saucer.) Place on turntable if available. Microwave on HIGH for 5 to 7 minutes (LW 6 to 8¼ minutes) or until boiling, **whisking** several times.

Add turkey meatballs, cover, and cook on HIGH for 5 to 7 minutes (LW 6 to 8¼ minutes) or until balls are heated through, carefully **stirring** once. (**Rotate** dish ½ turn when stirring if not using turntable.)

Troubleshooting: Forgetting to whisk sauce may cause it to be lumpy.

Suggestions: Serve each portion over ½ cup cooked long-grain rice or eggless noodles, which add 70 calories per serving.

For less restricted diets: If you're not watching your salt intake, substitute regular chicken broth, which adds 112 mg sodium per serving.

FOR EACH SERVING:
329 calories
291 mg sodium
89 mg cholesterol
7 g fat

Turkey Burgers

SERVES 4

EQUIPMENT:	medium bowl, 9-inch glass pie plate
COOKING TIME:	7 to 9 minutes (Low Wattage ovens 8¼ to 10¾ minutes)
STANDING TIME:	5 minutes
NUTRITIONAL PROFILE:	low calories, low sodium, low cholesterol

  1 **pound fresh lean ground turkey**
  ¼ **cup (about 1 small) chopped onion**
  ¼ **cup (about 1 large stalk) chopped celery**

⅓ **cup skim milk**
2 **egg whites, slightly beaten**
1 **small garlic clove, minced**
¼ **cup plain dry bread crumbs**
1 **teaspoon paprika**
2 **tablespoons minced fresh parsley**
¼ **teaspoon dried thyme**
¼ **teaspoon freshly ground pepper**
4 **slices spiced apple rings for garnish**

Combine all ingredients except apple rings in medium bowl. Shape mixture into 4 uniformly sized patties and place flat in pie plate. **Cover** dish with wax paper. (If dish is flat-bottomed, **elevate** on an inverted saucer.) Place on a turntable if available. Microwave on HIGH for 7 to 9 minutes (LW 8¼ to 10¾ minutes). (**Rotate** dish ½ turn every 4 minutes if not using turntable.) Let **stand, covered,** for 5 minutes and garnish with spiced apple rings.

Troubleshooting: Be sure to divide meat evenly and shape meat into uniformly sized patties to ensure even cooking.

FOR EACH SERVING:
187 calories
146 mg sodium
87 mg cholesterol
3 g fat

Turkey Porcupines

SERVES 4

EQUIPMENT:	small and medium bowls, deep 10-inch round casserole dish, 6-cup glass measure
COOKING TIME:	22½ to 30¾ minutes (Low Wattage ovens 27¼ to 37 minutes)
STANDING TIME:	none required
NUTRITIONAL PROFILE:	low calories, low sodium, moderate cholesterol

2 tablespoons white wine
½ cup (about 1 medium) chopped onion
½ cup (about 2 large stalks) chopped celery
2 tablespoons minced fresh parsley
1 garlic clove, minced
1¼ pounds fresh lean ground turkey
1 cup cooked long-grain rice
2 egg whites, slightly beaten
¼ teaspoon dried thyme
¼ teaspoon freshly ground pepper
½ cup (about 2 ounces) sliced fresh mushrooms
1 tablespoon burgundy
2 tablespoons soft-spread margarine
2 tablespoons all-purpose flour
1 cup skim milk
½ teaspoon low-salt soy sauce
¼ cup shredded sharp Cheddar cheese
   fresh parsley sprigs for garnish

Place white wine, onion, celery, parsley, and garlic in a small bowl and microwave, **uncovered,** on HIGH for 3 to 5 minutes (LW 3½ to 6 minutes) or until vegetables are tender-crisp.

In medium bowl, combine turkey, rice, egg whites, thyme, pepper, and vegetable mixture. Mix well and shape uniformly into 2-inch balls. Place balls in casserole dish and **cover** with wax paper. (If dish is flat-bottomed, **elevate** on an inverted saucer.) Place on turntable if available.

Cook on HIGH for 6 minutes (LW 7½ minutes). (**Rotate** dish ½ turn after 3 minutes if not using turntable.) **Drain** liquid and **rearrange** turkey balls, moving the less cooked ones in the center to the outside edges and the ones along the edges into the center of the dish.

Cover and cook on HIGH for 3 to 5 minutes (LW 3½ to 6 minutes) or until centers are no longer pink. (**Rotate** dish ½ turn after 3 minutes if not using turntable.) Set aside.

Place mushrooms and wine in small bowl. **Cover** with wax paper and microwave on HIGH for 3 to 4 minutes (LW 3½ to 4½ minutes) or until mushrooms are soft.

Place margarine in glass measure and melt, **uncovered,** on HIGH for 35 to 45 seconds (LW 50 to 60 seconds). **Whisk** in flour until smooth. **Whisk** in skim milk, soy sauce, and mushrooms. Microwave, **uncovered,** on HIGH for 4 to 5 minutes (LW 4½ to 6 minutes), **whisking** every minute, until thick enough to coat whisk.

Add shredded Cheddar and **whisk** until melted. Pour gravy mixture over turkey balls and **cover** with lid or plastic wrap, pulling back one corner to vent the steam. Microwave on HIGH for 3 to 5 minutes (LW 3¾ to 6 minutes) or until hot and bubbly. Garnish with sprigs of parsley.

Troubleshooting: Forgetting to whisk sauce may cause it to be lumpy.

If cheese doesn't melt completely while whisking, microwave for 1 minute on HIGH and whisk well.

Suggestion: White wine may be substituted for burgundy.

For less restricted diets: If you're not watching your sodium intake, substitute regular soy sauce, which adds 15 mg sodium per serving.

> FOR EACH SERVING:
> 342 calories
> 295 mg sodium
> 117 mg cholesterol
> 14 g fat

Turkey Loaf Supreme

SERVES 6 (WITH 2½ CUPS SAUCE)

EQUIPMENT:	large bowl; gelatin mold with open center, bundt pan, tube pan, or drinking glass to form a round shape with an open center; meat or bacon rack; 6-cup glass measure
COOKING TIME:	turkey loaf—8 to 10 minutes (Low Wattage ovens 9½ to 12 minutes); sauce—4 to 6 minutes (Low Wattage ovens 5 to 7 minutes)
STANDING TIME:	5 minutes
NUTRITIONAL PROFILE:	moderate calories, low sodium, low cholesterol

> 1¼ **pounds fresh lean ground turkey**
> ½ **cup (about 1 medium) diced onion**
> ½ **cup (about 2 large stalks) diced celery**
> ½ **cup (about 2) grated carrots**
> 2 **egg whites, well beaten**
> ⅓ **cup skim milk**
> ⅓ **cup water**
> ½ **cup plain dry bread crumbs**
> ¼ **cup freshly grated Parmesan cheese**
> ½ **teaspoon dried oregano**
> ½ **teaspoon dried basil**
> ¼ **teaspoon freshly ground pepper**
> 1 **teaspoon paprika**
> 1 **garlic clove, minced**
> 1 **tablespoon minced fresh parsley**

> SAUCE
> 1 **cup skim milk**
> 2 **tablespoons cornstarch**
> 1 **cup low-sodium chicken broth or homemade chicken stock (page 44)**
> ½ **cup white wine**

Combine all turkey loaf ingredients in large mixing bowl and mix well. Mold mixture into a ring shape, using a mold, bundt pan, or tube pan, or shaping a ring around a drinking glass. Pack tightly and **invert** molded loaf onto meat rack. Microwave, **uncovered,** on HIGH for 8 to 10 minutes (LW 9½ to 12 minutes) or until the top begins to brown, **rotating** dish ½ turn after 4 minutes. Remove from microwave and tent with aluminum foil, shiny side toward the meat. Let **stand, covered,** for 5 minutes.

While the turkey is standing, prepare the sauce. Place milk in glass measure and **whisk** in cornstarch until completely dissolved. **Whisk** in chicken broth and wine, whisking together well. Cook, **uncovered,** on HIGH for 4 to 6 minutes (LW 5 to 7 minutes), **whisking** every minute, until sauce thickens and coats whisk. Transfer meat to serving platter and serve with sauce.

Troubleshooting: It is very important that you mold the loaf into a round shape with the center open.

If you don't have a meat rack, unmold the loaf on a flat cooking container and drain any excess juices frequently. If you allow the loaf to cook in the molding container, the excess juices will build up and the loaf will not form a crust.

Forgetting to whisk sauce may cause it to be lumpy.

The loaf continues to cook while standing; to prevent it from drying out, cook it until top of meat is brown and no longer pink but not crisp and hard.

Suggestions: Prepare vegetable of your choice and use it to fill center of loaf, making a very attractive presentation. To save 50 calories per serving, eliminate the sauce and substitute low-sodium chicken broth to moisten the turkey loaf slightly.

For less restricted diets: If you're not watching your salt intake, substitute regular chicken broth, which adds 150 mg sodium per serving.

FOR EACH SERVING:
372 calories
262 mg sodium
88 mg cholesterol
8 g fat

Turkey-Stuffed Cabbage

SERVES 6

EQUIPMENT:	deep 3- or 4-quart casserole, colander, large mixing bowl, drinking glass, 9 × 13- or 12 × 8-inch casserole dish
COOKING TIME:	52 to 66 minutes (Low Wattage ovens 62 to 78 minutes)
STANDING TIME:	5 to 10 minutes
NUTRITIONAL PROFILE:	low calories, low sodium, low cholesterol

1   3-pound large-leafed cabbage
¼   cup water

FILLING
1½   pounds fresh lean ground turkey
2   egg whites
1   cup cooked long-grain rice
1   teaspoon Parsley Patch All-Purpose herb blend
¼   cup plain dry bread crumbs
¼   teaspoon dried basil
1   tablespoon low-salt ketchup
2   tablespoons skim milk
1   tablespoon chopped fresh parsley or parsley flakes
1   medium onion, minced

SAUCE
1   8-ounce can low-salt tomato sauce
1   28-ounce can low-sodium whole tomatoes, chopped, with their juice
1   medium onion, chopped
2   tablespoons dark brown sugar
1   tablespoon vinegar or fresh lemon juice (see box, page 124)

Remove any damaged outer leaves from the cabbage. Make 4 deep cuts all around the core, into the cabbage. Place cabbage, core down, in deep casserole dish. Add water and cover with lid or plastic wrap, pulling back one corner to vent the steam. (If dish is flat-bottomed, **elevate** on an inverted saucer.) Microwave on HIGH for 12 to 16 minutes (LW 14 to 18 minutes). **Drain** in colander and flush with cold water. Once cool enough to touch, **separate** leaves.

In large bowl, blend together all filling ingredients. Place a mound of filling (1 to 2 heaped tablespoons, depending on size of leaf) in center of cabbage leaf. Bring top of leaf over meat, fold in sides, and bring bottom up and tuck it into sides, forming a little package. Distribute filling among leaves and shred any leftover cabbage.

Place a glass in the center of casserole dish and line bottom with shredded cabbage. Place cabbage rolls on top, largest rolls to the outside of the dish and smallest rolls to the center. Remove glass but leave that space open.

Combine sauce ingredients and pour over cabbage rolls. **Cover** dish with lid or plastic wrap, pulling back one corner to vent the steam. (If dish is flat-bottomed, **elevate** on an inverted saucer.) Microwave on HIGH for 5 minutes (LW 6 minutes). **Reduce** power to 80 percent or MEDIUM-HIGH, and cook for 35 to 45 minutes (LW 42 to 54 minutes) or until rolls are tender, **basting** and **rotating** dish ½ turn every 20 minutes. Once cabbage is tender and filling is completely cooked, let **stand, covered,** for 5 to 10 minutes before serving to allow filling to tenderize.

Troubleshooting: Keep rolls basted with sauce to prevent them from drying out.

For less restricted diets: If you're not watching your salt intake, substitute regular ketchup, which adds 30 mg sodium per serving; a can of regular tomato sauce, which adds 215 mg sodium per serving; and a can of regular tomatoes, another 209 mg sodium per serving.

FOR EACH SERVING:
219 calories
112 mg sodium
65 mg cholesterol
3 g fat

ONIONS

If healthy eating is high on your list of priorities, onions should play a large role in your diet. An average onion provides 20 percent of the U.S. RDA of vitamin C and has 2.8 grams of dietary fiber. Onions are a great source of potassium, have no fat or cholesterol, and retain their healthful properties whether eaten cooked or raw. Some studies show that onions help lower blood pressure and reduce cholesterol levels.

Store onions in a dark, dry, cool location that has good ventilation—not with potatoes, or they will spoil each other. Refrigerate only onions that have been cut; to keep them over a long period of time, chop, package securely, and freeze. Peeling onions is easier if you cut off the bottom first, then the top. Make a slash in the onion's side and remove the skin and first outer peel.

Mr. Goober's Turkey-Stuffed Onions

Mr. Goober, a dear friend and a fantastic cook, enjoyed lacing his food with wine and believed that it produced a certain delicate taste and flavor. Using wine in your recipes is also a great way to reduce your need for salt, because the chemicals in wine are quite similar to those in table salt.

SERVES 6

EQUIPMENT:	deep 8-inch round casserole dish, medium mixing bowl, 1-cup glass measure
COOKING TIME:	20 to 24 minutes (Low Wattage ovens 23¾ to 28½ minutes)
STANDING TIME:	3 minutes
NUTRITIONAL PROFILE:	low calories, low sodium, low cholesterol

6 **large white onions (2½ to 3 pounds)**
1 **pound fresh lean ground turkey**
¼ **cup plain dry bread crumbs**
¼ **teaspoon dried basil**

⅓ cup skim milk
3 tablespoons freshly grated Parmesan cheese
2 tablespoons minced fresh parsley
¼ teaspoon freshly ground pepper
½ teaspoon paprika
¼ teaspoon garlic powder

TOPPING
1 tablespoon soft-spread margarine
¼ cup (about ¼ large) finely chopped red bell pepper
¼ cup plain dry bread crumbs
½ cup low-sodium chicken broth or homemade chicken stock (page 44)
2 tablespoons Marsala

Place peeled onions in casserole dish. **Cover** dish with lid or plastic wrap, pulling back one corner to vent the steam. (If dish is flat-bottomed, **elevate** on an inverted saucer.) Place on a turntable if available. Cook on HIGH for 10 to 12 minutes (LW 12 to 14¼ minutes) or until onions are just about tender. (**Rotate** dish ½ turn after 5 minutes if not using a turntable.) When onions are cool enough to handle, scoop out centers, leaving a ¼-inch-thick shell. **Drain** liquid, return onion shells to dish, and set aside.

Chop enough of the removed onion pulp to make ½ cup, discarding remaining pulp. Combine ½ cup onion pulp with turkey, ¼ cup bread crumbs, basil, milk, cheese, parsley, pepper, paprika, and garlic powder in medium mixing bowl, mixing together well. Gently fill each onion shell with turkey mixture, mounding high on top, and return to casserole dish. Any remaining mixture may be shaped into balls and placed around the onions.

Place margarine and red bell pepper in glass measure. Cook, **uncovered,** on HIGH for 45 to 55 seconds (LW 60 seconds) or until margarine melts. Stir in ¼ cup bread crumbs and sprinkle over filled onion tops.

Combine broth and wine, then pour around onions. **Cover** again and place on a turntable if available. Microwave on HIGH for 9 to 11 minutes (LW 10¾ to 13¼ minutes) or until turkey is no longer pink. After 5 minutes of cooking time, **rotate** each onion from the outside of the dish to the center. (**Rotate** dish ½ turn after 5 minutes if not on turntable.) Let **stand, covered,** for 3 minutes.

Suggestion: Check the ground turkey package to be sure it's *lean* turkey; otherwise you will increase the cholesterol and calorie intake. Sometimes the fatty skin is included in packaged ground turkey.

For less restricted diets: If you're not watching your salt intake, substitute regular canned chicken broth, which adds 75 mg sodium per serving.

FOR EACH SERVING:
183 calories
167 mg sodium
63 mg cholesterol
7 g fat

Meats

BEEF BRISKET

Brisket is a perfect cut of beef to microwave because of its flatness and relatively even shape. It's also relatively lean, so it fits into a healthy eating style. Stay away from prime cuts of beef, as they are heavily marbled with fat, unlike brisket.

You can make the pot roast in a microwave-safe roasting bag, but secure the bag loosely with string or dental floss, not a metal twist tie. Leave a small avenue for the steam to escape. Since pot roast needs to steam, you can also use a tightly covered casserole dish. If the cover on your casserole dish doesn't make a tight seal, place a piece of wax paper between the dish and the cover, but be careful when removing the cover; otherwise you could get burned from the sudden release of steam.

To ensure tenderness, you must reduce the power setting on your microwave to 50 percent or MEDIUM and allow the finished roast to **stand tightly covered** for 15 to 20 minutes. While standing, the meat finishes cooking, tenderizes, and the flavors blend.

Sweet and Sour Brisket Pot Roast

SERVES 8

EQUIPMENT: large roasting bag with casserole dish to hold it or 3-quart casserole dish with cover, 4-cup glass measure

COOKING TIME: 80 to 95 minutes (Low Wattage ovens 96 to 114 minutes)

STANDING TIME: 15 to 20 minutes

NUTRITIONAL PROFILE: low calories, low sodium, moderate cholesterol

3 pounds flat-cut beef brisket
1½ cups unsweetened grapefruit juice
1 6-ounce can low-salt tomato paste
1 large onion, thinly sliced
1 garlic clove, minced
1 teaspoon Parsley Patch All-Purpose herb blend
3 carrots, thinly sliced
2 celery stalks, thinly sliced
3 tablespoons dark brown sugar

Deeply pierce both sides of the meat with the tines of a large fork and place in casserole dish or lightly floured roasting bag set into a flat casserole dish. In glass measure, mix together juice, tomato paste, onion, garlic, herb blend, carrots, and celery. Pour mixture over meat and loosely close bag or tightly **cover** casserole dish. (If dish is flat-bottomed, **elevate** on an inverted saucer.) Place on turntable if available. Microwave on HIGH for 5 minutes (LW 6 minutes). **Reduce** power to 50 percent or MEDIUM, **cover,** and microwave for 30 to 40 minutes (LW 36 to 48 minutes). Turn meat over and stir gravy. (**Rotate** dish ½ turn every 10 minutes if not using turntable.)

Cover and microwave on 50 percent power or MEDIUM for 45 to 50 minutes (LW 54 to 60 minutes) or until meat is fork-tender. (**Rotate** dish ½ turn every 20 minutes if not using turntable.)

Let **stand, covered,** for 15 to 20 minutes. After standing, remove roast to carving board and **whisk** brown sugar into drippings. Slice meat and serve with sauce.

Troubleshooting: Meat tenderizes while standing; do not omit this step.

Suggestion: Cut meat into thin slices and fan out on each plate, covered with a tablespoon or 2 of gravy. By filling the plate with thin slices rather than 1 or 2 thick ones, your servings will appear much larger.

For less restricted diets: If you're not watching your salt intake, substitute regular tomato paste, which adds 12 mg sodium per serving.

FOR EACH SERVING:
367 calories
92 mg sodium
154 mg cholesterol
6 g fat

Tangy Sauced Buffet Brisket

SERVES 6

EQUIPMENT:	6-cup measure, 3-quart round casserole dish
COOKING TIME:	20 to 25 minutes (Low Wattage ovens 23¾ to 30 minutes)
STANDING TIME:	5 minutes
NUTRITIONAL PROFILE:	low calories, low sodium, moderate cholesterol

1　**15-ounce can low-salt tomato sauce**
½　**cup low-salt ketchup**
½　**cup water**
2　**large garlic cloves, crushed**
½　**cup (about 1 medium) chopped onion**
¼　**cup red wine vinegar**
1　**tablespoon honey**
1　**tablespoon fresh lemon juice (see box, page 124)**
¼　**cup dark brown sugar**
1　**teaspoon Parsley Patch Sesame All-Purpose herb blend**
2　**pounds flat-cut beef brisket, cooked (see recipe on page 149) and cut into thin strips**

Combine all ingredients except beef in glass measure and **cover** with wax paper. Microwave on HIGH for 8 to 10 minutes (LW 9½ to 12 minutes) or until hot and bubbly. Place a layer of beef strips in casserole dish and spread with a layer of sauce. Continue layering meat and sauce until all of both is used. **Cover** with wax paper. (If dish is flat-bottomed, **elevate** on an inverted saucer.) Cook on HIGH for 12 to 15 minutes (LW 14¼ to 18 minutes) or until heated through. Let **stand, covered,** for 5 minutes before serving.

For less restricted diets: If you're not watching your salt intake, substitute regular tomato sauce, which adds 403 mg sodium per serving, and regular ketchup, which adds 237 mg sodium per serving.

FOR EACH SERVING:
366 calories
89 mg sodium
136 mg cholesterol
5 g fat

Roast Beef Strata with Scallion Curls

The scallion curls can garnish any recipe, but they add particular color and flair to squares of beef strata.

SERVES 6

EQUIPMENT: 2-quart baking dish, medium bowl
COOKING TIME: 50 to 55 minutes (Low Wattage ovens 55 to 61 minutes)
STANDING TIME: 3 to 3½ hours before cooking, 10 minutes after cooking
NUTRITIONAL PROFILE: low calories, low sodium, low cholesterol

5 slices white or whole wheat bread, crusts removed and bread cut into 1-inch cubes
½ cup shredded Swiss cheese
1 cup diced lean cooked roast beef
1 scallion, chopped
1 tablespoon chopped fresh parsley
1 tablespoon chopped pimiento
6 egg whites, slightly beaten
2 cups skim milk
½ teaspoon Parsley Patch All-Purpose herb blend
¼ teaspoon freshly ground pepper
scallion curls for garnish (recipe follows)

Arrange ½ the bread cubes in the bottom of baking dish. Layer cheese and beef over cubes and sprinkle with scallions, parsley, and pimiento. **Cover** with remaining bread cubes.

In bowl, **whisk** together beaten egg whites and milk. Add seasonings and **whisk** well. Pour over bread cubes and **cover** tightly with plastic wrap. Allow dish to **stand** in refrigerator for 3 to 3½ hours or all day if making in advance.

When ready to microwave, **remove** plastic wrap and **cover** dish with wax paper. (If dish is flat-bottomed, **elevate** on an inverted saucer.) Place on turntable if available. Microwave on 40 percent power or MEDIUM for 50 to 55 minutes (LW 55 to 61 minutes) or until a knife inserted in the center comes out clean. (**Rotate** dish ¼ turn every 15 minutes if not using turntable.) Let **stand, covered,** for 10 minutes before cutting.

Suggestion: Excellent dish for brunch, or a buffet table.

FOR EACH SERVING:
277 calories
298 mg sodium
73 mg cholesterol
7 g fat

SCALLION CURLS

**6 scallions
ice water**

Cut stems from scallion bulbs at the point where stems begin to turn green. Trim stems to about 4 inches in length. Reserve bulbs and any remaining stem pieces for use in another recipe. Using a sharp knife or kitchen scissors, cut each individual green stem lengthwise into about 6 very thin strips, almost to the base of the stem. Place prepared stems in a bowl of ice water and place in refrigerator for about 1 hour. **Drain** scallion curls and blot them on paper toweling when ready to use.

Zippy Beef Stew

SERVES 6

EQUIPMENT:	deep 3-quart casserole dish
COOKING TIME:	70 to 80 minutes (Low Wattage ovens 84 to 96 minutes)
STANDING TIME:	15 minutes
NUTRITIONAL PROFILE:	low calories, low sodium, low cholesterol

**1½ pounds lean sirloin, cut into ½-inch cubes
¼ cup all-purpose flour
1 15-ounce can low-sodium tomatoes, chopped, with their juice
½ cup burgundy
1 cup water**

1 tablespoon low-sodium beef bouillon granules
1 garlic clove, minced
1 cup (about 1 large) chopped onion
1 cup (about 4 large stalks) chopped celery
1 cup (about 4 ounces) sliced fresh mushrooms
2 medium potatoes, peeled and cut into eighths
2 carrots, thinly sliced
1 10-ounce box frozen mixed vegetables
1 teaspoon Parsley Patch All-Purpose herb blend
¼ teaspoon freshly ground pepper

Toss beef with flour and place in casserole dish. Stir in tomatoes, wine, water, bouillon granules, and garlic. **Cover** dish with aluminum foil (see tip, page 156), casserole lid, or plastic wrap, pulling back one corner to vent the steam. (If dish is flat-bottomed, **elevate** on an inverted saucer.) Place on turntable if available. Microwave on HIGH for 5 minutes (LW 6 minutes). **Stir, reduce** power to 50 percent or MEDIUM, **cover,** and cook for 30 to 35 minutes (LW 36 to 42 minutes), stirring every 15 minutes. (**Rotate** dish ½ turn when stirring if not using turntable.)

Add all remaining vegetables and seasonings, **cover,** and cook on 50 percent power or MEDIUM for 35 to 40 minutes (LW 42 to 48 minutes) or until meat is fork-tender, carefully **stirring** every 20 minutes. (**Rotate** dish ½ turn when stirring if not using turntable.) Let **stand, covered,** for 15 minutes before serving.

Suggestion: Try buying sirloin steaks on sale and cutting your own stew beef, discarding all the fat around the edges of the steak.

For less restricted diets: If you're not watching your salt intake, substitute regular canned tomatoes, which add 115 mg sodium per serving, and regular beef bouillon granules, which add 450 mg sodium per serving.

FOR EACH SERVING:
345 calories
112 mg sodium
56 mg cholesterol
4 g fat

┌───┐

SLOW COOKING

By placing a *completely flat* (not crimped, bent, molded, or folded)
piece of aluminum foil over the top of the casserole dish, you
force the microwaves to come in from the sides and bottom of
the dish and not the top, making your microwave a slow cooker.
If you're not comfortable using foil, or if your manufacturer does
not recommend its use in your oven, cover dish with casserole
lid or plastic wrap that you have vented, being sure the meat and
vegetables remain *under* the liquid.

└───┘

Burgundy Beef

SERVES 4

EQUIPMENT:	10-inch covered browning dish
COOKING TIME:	21 to 24 minutes (Low Wattage ovens 25¼ to 28½ minutes)
STANDING TIME:	5 minutes
NUTRITIONAL PROFILE:	low calories, low sodium, moderate cholesterol

       1   **tablespoon corn or soybean oil**
       1   **garlic clove, minced**
    1½   **pounds lean sirloin steak, cut uniformly into thin
           1-inch strips**
      ¼   **cup water**
       1   **bay leaf**
       8   **small pearl onions, peeled**
       1   **cup (about 4 ounces) sliced fresh mushrooms**
      ½   **cup burgundy**
       2   **teaspoons cornstarch**
       1   **teaspoon Parsley Patch All-Purpose herb blend**
      ¼   **teaspoon freshly ground pepper**
      ¼   **teaspoon paprika**
       1   **tablespoon drained capers**

Preheat browning dish according to manufacturer's instructions, usually 5 to 7 minutes (LW 6 to 8 minutes). Add oil and garlic, moving them around dish with wooden spoon to prevent sticking. As garlic sizzles, add meat strips, mixing with oil and garlic. Microwave, **uncovered,** on HIGH for 2 minutes (LW 2¼ minutes). **Stir** and add water, gently scraping any brown bits from the bottom of the dish.

Add bay leaf, onions, and mushrooms, mixing to combine. **Cover** dish with lid and microwave on HIGH for 3 to 4 minutes (LW 3½ to 4¾ minutes). **Whisk** burgundy, cornstarch, herb blend, pepper, and paprika together well. Pour wine mixture over meat and vegetables.

Cover and microwave on 80 percent power or MEDIUM-HIGH for 16 to 18 minutes (LW 19½ to 21½ minutes) or until meat and vegetables are tender, **stirring** every 5 minutes and rotating dish ½ turn. Sprinkle with capers and let **stand, covered,** for 5 minutes before serving.

Troubleshooting: If you don't have a covered browning dish, substitute a 2-quart covered casserole dish and omit preheating. Remember, the oil and garlic will not sizzle, the meat won't brown, and you won't be able to scrape the brown bits from the bottom of the dish.

Suggestions: Serve each portion over ½ cup cooked long-grain rice or eggless noodles, which add 70 calories for each serving.

FOR EACH SERVING:
321 calories
91 mg sodium
120 mg cholesterol
8 g fat

Blissfully Swiss

SERVES 4

EQUIPMENT: 2-quart flat casserole dish, 2-cup glass measure

COOKING TIME: 50 to 55 minutes (Low Wattage ovens 60 to 66 minutes)

STANDING TIME: 10 minutes

NUTRITIONAL PROFILE: low calories, low sodium, moderate cholesterol

1½ **pounds lean top round steak, ½ to 1 inch thick**
1 **teaspoon onion powder**
½ **pound (about 2 cups) fresh mushrooms, sliced**
1 **15-ounce can low-sodium whole tomatoes, drained and chopped, with juice reserved**
1 **medium green bell pepper, sliced**
1 **large onion, sliced**
2 **carrots, sliced in julienne**
¼ **teaspoon freshly ground pepper**
1 **tablespoon low-salt ketchup**
1 **tablespoon dark brown sugar**
1 **tablespoon cornstarch**
1 **tablespoon chopped fresh parsley**

Cut steak into 4 uniformly sized serving pieces and arrange in flat casserole dish. Sprinkle onion powder, mushrooms, tomatoes, green bell pepper, onion, carrots, and ground pepper over meat. Place tomato liquid plus enough water to make 1 cup in glass measure. **Whisk** in ketchup, brown sugar, and cornstarch. Pour over meat and vegetables and **cover** with lid or plastic wrap, pulling back one corner to vent the steam. (If dish is flat-bottomed, **elevate** on an inverted saucer.)

Microwave on HIGH for 5 minutes (LW 6 minutes), **reduce** power to 50 percent or MEDIUM, and cook for 45 to 50 minutes (LW 54 to 60 minutes) or until meat is tender, **turning** meat over, **rearranging** pieces, and **rotating** dish ½ turn after 20 minutes. Let **stand, covered,** for 10 minutes to finish cooking and tenderize. Garnish with parsley.

Troubleshooting: Forgetting to whisk sauce may cause it to be lumpy.

When rearranging meat pieces, bring the portions near the center of the dish to the outside edges and the pieces along the outside edges to the center.

For less restricted diets: If you're not watching your salt intake, substitute regular tomatoes, which add 173 mg sodium per serving, and regular ketchup, which adds 78 mg sodium per serving.

FOR EACH SERVING:
314 calories
128 mg sodium
120 mg cholesterol
11 g fat

Sirloin Bake

SERVES 4

EQUIPMENT:	3-quart round casserole dish
COOKING TIME:	62 to 70 minutes (Low Wattage ovens 69 to 83¾ minutes)
STANDING TIME:	5 minutes
NUTRITIONAL PROFILE:	moderate calories, low sodium, moderate cholesterol

1   large onion, chopped
½   pound (about 2 cups) fresh mushrooms, sliced
1   large green bell pepper, cut into strips
2   tablespoons white wine
1½   pounds lean sirloin steak, fat removed and meat cut into thin strips
⅓   cup all-purpose flour
1   teaspoon Parsley Patch Lemon Pepper herb blend
1   15-ounce can low-sodium whole tomatoes, chopped, with their juice
½   cup water
1   tablespoon low-salt soy sauce
3   tablespoons molasses
1   9-ounce package frozen french-cut green beans, thawed

Combine onion, mushrooms, green bell pepper, and wine in casserole dish. **Cover** with lid or plastic wrap, pulling back one corner to vent the steam. (If dish is flat-bottomed, **elevate** on an inverted saucer.) Place on turntable if available.

Microwave on HIGH for 6 to 7 minutes (LW 7½ to 8¼ minutes) or until vegetables are tender-crisp, **stirring** every 3 minutes. (**Rotate** dish ½ turn when stirring if not using turntable.)

In a small plastic or paper bag, mix flour and herb blend together. Add meat strips to bag and toss with flour. **Stir** flour-coated meat strips into the vegetables and add tomatoes with juice, water, soy sauce, and molasses. **Cover** again and microwave on HIGH for 5 minutes (LW 6 minutes). **Stir, reduce** power to 50 percent or MEDIUM, **cover,** and cook for 45 to 50 minutes (LW 48 to 60 minutes), stirring every 15 minutes. (**Rotate** dish ¼ turn when stirring if not using turntable.) **Stir** in green beans, **cover,** and microwave on HIGH for 6 to 8 minutes (LW 7½ to 9½ minutes) or until beans are tender. Let **stand, covered,** for 5 minutes before serving.

Troubleshooting: Slightly frozen steak is easier to cut into strips than soft, thawed meat.

Suggestion: Serve each portion over ½ cup cooked long-grain rice, which adds 70 calories per serving.

For less restricted diets: If you're not watching your salt intake, substitute regular soy sauce, which increases the sodium per serving by 570 mg.

FOR EACH SERVING:
395 calories
313 mg sodium
120 mg cholesterol
11 g fat

SPINACH

Spinach, like all dark green vegetables, is an excellent source of iron, vitamins A and C, potassium, and calcium. Many women have an iron deficiency during their childbearing years. Other good iron sources such as egg yolks and organ meats are not healthy choices because of their high cholesterol content. Spinach and raisins are probably your best bets for boosting your iron level in a healthy way.

Confetti Beef and Spinach Bake

SERVES 6

EQUIPMENT:	plastic dishwasher-safe colander and casserole dish, deep 2- or 3-quart casserole dish
COOKING TIME:	36 to 45 minutes (Low Wattage ovens 42¼ to 54 minutes)
STANDING TIME:	2 minutes
NUTRITIONAL PROFILE:	moderate calories, low sodium, low cholesterol

> 1   **pound lean ground sirloin**
> 1   **garlic clove, minced**
> ¼   **cup (about 1 small) minced onion**
> ¼   **cup (about 1 large stalk) minced celery**
> ¼   **cup (about 1) diced carrots**
> ¼   **cup burgundy**
> 1   **6-ounce can low-salt tomato paste**
> 1   **28-ounce can low-sodium tomatoes, chopped, with their juice**
> 1   **teaspoon Parsley Patch Garlicsaltless herb blend**
> 1   **10-ounce paper-covered box chopped spinach or broccoli**
> ½   **pound eggless noodles, cooked and drained**
> ¼   **cup grated Cheddar cheese**
> 2   **tablespoons freshly grated Parmesan cheese**

Crumble ground sirloin into colander and set in casserole dish. Microwave, **uncovered,** on HIGH for 3 minutes (LW 3½ minutes).

Break up meat chunks with fork and add garlic, onion, celery, and carrots. Microwave, **uncovered,** on HIGH for 4 to 6 minutes (LW 4¾ to 7½ minutes) or until meat is no longer pink.

In deep casserole dish, combine wine, tomato paste, and chopped tomatoes. **Stir** in meat and vegetable mixture and sprinkle with herb blend. **Stir** all ingredients together and **cover** with lid or plastic wrap, pulling back one corner to vent the steam. (If dish is flat-bottomed, **elevate** on an inverted saucer.) Place on turntable if available. Microwave on 80 percent power or MEDIUM-HIGH for 15 to 18 minutes (LW 17 to 21½ minutes), until hot and flavors blend.

Place **paper-covered** box of spinach on 2 layers of paper towels and microwave on HIGH for 6 to 8 minutes (LW 7½ to 9½ minutes). **Drain** well and fold into tomato mixture. Fold in cooked noodles and Cheddar cheese. **Cover** with wax paper and micro-wave on HIGH for 8 to 10 minutes (LW 9½ to 12 minutes), until hot and bubbly. Sprinkle with Parmesan cheese and let **stand, covered,** for 2 minutes before serving.

Troubleshooting: Be sure frozen vegetable box is covered with a **paper** wrapper. If the box has an aluminum foil wrapper, remove it before microwaving, or it will arc and ignite the paper box.

Suggestion: For those who don't like spinach, substitute frozen chopped broccoli.

For less restricted diets: If you're not watching your salt intake, sub-stitute regular tomatoes, which adds 209 mg sodium per serving, and regular tomato paste, which adds 29 mg sodium per serving.

FOR EACH SERVING:
383 calories
266 mg sodium
56 mg cholesterol
11 g fat

Beef and Pizza-Topped Potatoes

SERVES 4

EQUIPMENT: plastic dishwasher-safe colander, 2-quart cas-serole dish

COOKING TIME: 10½ to 13½ minutes (Low Wattage ovens 12½ to 16 minutes)

STANDING TIME: none required

NUTRITIONAL PROFILE: low calories, low sodium, low cholesterol

½ **pound lean ground sirloin**
¼ **cup (about ½ small) chopped green bell pepper**
¼ **cup (about 1 large stalk) chopped celery**
¼ **cup (about 1 ounce) sliced mushrooms**
1 **garlic clove, minced**
1 **medium onion, thinly sliced**
1 **tablespoon burgundy wine**
1 **8-ounce can low-sodium tomato sauce**
⅛ **teaspoon dried oregano**
⅛ **teaspoon dried basil**
⅛ **teaspoon freshly ground pepper**
4 **medium baked potatoes (see recipe on page 89)**
½ **cup (¼ pound) shredded part-skim mozzarella cheese**

Place colander in casserole dish to catch drippings. **Crumble** ground sirloin into colander and microwave, **uncovered,** on HIGH for 3 minutes (LW 4 minutes). Break up meat chunks with a fork and add green pepper, celery, mushrooms, garlic, and onion. Microwave, **uncovered,** on HIGH for 4 to 5 minutes (LW 4¾ to 6 minutes) or until meat is no longer pink.

Place meat in clean casserole dish and add wine, tomato sauce, oregano, basil, and pepper. Microwave, **uncovered,** on HIGH for 3 to 5 minutes (LW 3½ to 6 minutes) or until mixture is hot and flavors blend. Halve potatoes and flake centers. Mound hamburger mixture over flaked potatoes and sprinkle with mozzarella cheese. Microwave, **uncovered,** on HIGH for 25 to 35 seconds (LW 30 to 40 seconds), just until cheese begins to melt.

Troubleshooting: Mozzarella cheese will toughen in the microwave if cooking continues after the cheese begins to melt.

Suggestion: If beef is a dietary problem, try substituting lean ground turkey.

For less restricted diets: If you're not watching your salt intake, substitute regular tomato sauce, which adds 323 mg sodium per serving.

FOR EACH SERVING:
308 calories
168 mg sodium
42 mg cholesterol
10 g fat

OVEN CLEANING

Abrasives and ordinary oven cleaners cannot be used in the microwave. To help remove crusted food particles, stains, and odors, combine 2 cups of water with the juice of a lemon, or 1 teaspoon vanilla extract, or 1 teaspoon of apple pie spice in a 4-cup glass measure. Microwave on HIGH for 12 minutes (LW 15 minutes). This mixture will leave a heavy mist on the walls and ceiling of your oven, and you can just wipe out the interior with a soft cloth or sponge. By adding the lemon juice, vanilla, or spice you will also remove any leftover odors, leaving a clean, sweet-smelling interior. Be sure to keep the door closures clean and free of any grease or food buildup and clean the exterior of the oven with a spray window cleaner.

Sloppy Joes

Notice the healthy approach to cooking hamburger that is possible in the microwave. Meat drippings and grease (better known as artery cloggers) pass through the holes in the plastic colander and are all collected underneath the meat.

SERVES 6

EQUIPMENT: plastic dishwasher-safe colander with casserole dish, deep 3-quart casserole dish
COOKING TIME: 14¾ to 17¾ minutes (Low Wattage ovens 17½ to 21¼ minutes)

STANDING TIME: 5 minutes
NUTRITIONAL PROFILE: low calories, low sodium, low cholesterol

1 pound lean ground sirloin
1 medium onion, minced
1 garlic clove, minced
1 medium green bell pepper, diced
1 28-ounce can low-sodium whole tomatoes, chopped, with their juice
1 8-ounce can low-sodium tomato sauce
½ cup (about 2 ounces) sliced fresh mushrooms
¼ teaspoon dried basil
½ teaspoon dried oregano
3 hamburger buns, split
½ cup grated Cheddar cheese

MICROWAVING GROUND MEATS

Because the microwave extracts ⅓ more fat from meat than conventional cooking does, the best way to microwave ground meat is in a plastic dishwasher-safe colander set in a casserole dish to catch the drippings. All the fat falls through the holes, leaving the meat nearly fat-free. If a plastic colander isn't available, try placing ground meat in a casserole dish lined with 3 thicknesses of paper towels. Place one thickness over the meat and cook for the times given in the recipe. After cooking, drain meat on additional clean paper towels to be sure you have removed as much of the fat as possible.

Crumble ground sirloin into colander and place colander in casserole dish to catch the drippings. Microwave, **uncovered,** on HIGH for 3 minutes (LW 3½ minutes) and break up meat chunks with a fork. Add onion, garlic, and green bell pepper to meat in colander and microwave, **uncovered,** on HIGH for 3 to 4 minutes (LW 3½ to 4¾ minutes), until meat is no longer pink.

Transfer meat and vegetables to deep casserole dish and add tomatoes, tomato sauce, and mushrooms. Sprinkle with basil and oregano, **stirring** together well. **Cover** dish with lid or plastic wrap, pulling back one corner to vent the steam. (If dish is flat-bottomed, **elevate** on an inverted saucer.) Place on turntable if available. Cook on HIGH for 8 to 10 minutes (LW 9½ to 12 minutes) or until the flavors blend, **stirring** well after 5 minutes. (**Rotate** dish ½ turn when stirring if not using turntable.)

Let **stand, covered,** for 5 minutes, then spoon each portion over ½ a hamburger bun and cover with grated Cheddar cheese. Microwave, uncovered, on HIGH for 45 to 50 seconds (LW 60 seconds) or until cheese begins to melt.

Troubleshooting: If a plastic dishwasher-safe colander isn't available, see tip on page 165 for microwaving ground meats.

For less restricted diets: If you're not watching your salt intake, substitute regular tomatoes, which add 209 mg sodium per serving, and regular tomato sauce, another 215 mg per serving.

FOR EACH SERVING:
317 calories
306 mg sodium
70 mg cholesterol
11 g fat

Beef-Crowned Zucchini

SERVES 4

EQUIPMENT:	grapefruit spoon, 12 × 8-inch glass baking dish, medium bowl
COOKING TIME:	9 to 13 minutes (Low Wattage ovens 10¾ to 14¾ minutes)
STANDING TIME:	3 minutes
NUTRITIONAL PROFILE:	low calories, low sodium, low cholesterol

2 medium zucchini (about 1½ pounds)
¾ pound lean ground sirloin
¼ cup plain yogurt
¼ cup (about ¼ large) chopped red onion
1 garlic clove, minced
1 tablespoon freshly grated Parmesan cheese
½ teaspoon dried basil

¼   **teaspoon freshly ground pepper**
1   **teaspoon dried oregano**
1   **tablespoon chopped fresh parsley**
⅔   **cup low-salt meatless spaghetti sauce**

Wash zucchini and trim off ends. Cut zucchini in half lengthwise. Using grapefruit spoon, scoop out the pulp and reserve, leaving a ¼-inch shell. Place halves, cut side down, in baking dish. (If dish is flat-bottomed, **elevate** on an inverted saucer.) Place on turntable if available. **Cover** with wax paper and microwave on HIGH for 3 to 4 minutes (LW 3½ to 6 minutes) or until warm and softened. Remove from dish and **invert** on paper towels to drain.

Chop reserved pulp and place in bowl. Add remaining ingredients except spaghetti sauce. Mix together well. Return zucchini shells to original dish and mound ¼ of meat mixture into each shell. **Cover** dish with wax paper and cook on HIGH for 5 to 7 minutes (LW 6 to 7½ minutes) or until meat is no longer pink and shells are tender. (**Rotate** dish ½ turn after 3 minutes if not using a turntable.)

Top each boat with spaghetti sauce, **cover,** and heat on HIGH for 1 minute (LW 1¼ minutes) or until sauce is hot. Let stand, **covered,** for 3 minutes before serving.

Troubleshooting: If you don't have a grapefruit spoon, carefully scoop out the pulp with an ordinary spoon, taking care to leave the ends closed so that the filling remains in the shells.

Zucchini tends to be a very watery vegetable, and placing boats on a meat or bacon rack to cook may eliminate some of the water buildup you'll find if you use a baking dish.

For less restricted diets: If you're not watching your salt intake, substitute regular spaghetti sauce, which adds 225 mg sodium per serving.

FOR EACH SERVING:
210 calories
141 mg sodium
59 mg cholesterol
9 g fat

Mini Meat Loaves

SERVES 4

EQUIPMENT:	small and medium mixing bowls, 9- or 10-inch glass pie plate
COOKING TIME:	8 to 9 minutes (Low Wattage ovens 9½ to 10¾ minutes)
STANDING TIME:	5 minutes
NUTRITIONAL PROFILE:	low calories, low sodium, low cholesterol

1 pound lean ground sirloin
½ cup plain dry bread crumbs
½ teaspoon dried basil
½ teaspoon dried oregano
½ cup (about 1 medium) minced onion
½ cup skim milk
1 tablespoon freshly grated Parmesan cheese
1 egg white
¼ teaspoon freshly ground pepper
¼ cup low-salt tomato sauce

BARBECUE SAUCE
2 tablespoons packed dark brown sugar
½ teaspoon dry mustard
2 tablespoons low-salt tomato sauce
dash cayenne pepper

Combine ground sirloin, crumbs, basil, oregano, onion, milk, Parmesan cheese, egg white, pepper, and ¼ cup tomato sauce in medium bowl, mixing together well. Divide mixture into 4 equal portions and shape into small, evenly shaped loaves. Arrange loaves in pie plate like the spokes of a wagon wheel and **cover** with wax paper. (If dish is flat-bottomed, **elevate** on an inverted saucer.) Place on a turntable if available. Microwave on HIGH for 7 to 8 minutes (LW 8¼ to 9½ minutes). (**Rotate** dish ½ turn after 3 minutes if not using turntable.)

In small bowl, combine all barbecue sauce ingredients. Brush each loaf with barbecue sauce and cook, **uncovered,** on HIGH for 1 minute (LW 1¼ minutes). Let **stand** for 5 minutes before serving.

Troubleshooting: Divide meat mixture evenly into 4 portions and shape meat uniformly to ensure even cooking.

Suggestions: To prepare individual portions, mix the entire batch of meat, form into loaves, wrap individually, and freeze for quick defrost and preparation. Once defrosted, microwave on HIGH for 2 to 3 minutes (LW 2¼ to 3½ minutes) for each loaf. Add 1 tablespoon of barbecue sauce and cook, **uncovered,** on HIGH for 30 to 45 seconds (LW 40 to 50 seconds) for each serving.

For less restricted diets: If you're not watching your salt intake, substitute regular tomato sauce, which adds 403 mg sodium per serving.

FOR EACH SERVING:
288 calories
162 mg sodium
78 mg cholesterol
10 g fat

Surprise Onion Pie

SERVES 6

EQUIPMENT:	2-quart round casserole dish, medium mixing bowl, 9-inch glass pie plate
COOKING TIME:	21 to 25 minutes (Low Wattage ovens 25¼ to 29¼ minutes)
STANDING TIME:	5 minutes
NUTRITIONAL PROFILE:	low calories, low sodium, low cholesterol

2 **large sweet Spanish onions, peeled and cut into ¼-inch slices (about 5 cups)**
1 **cup (about 4 ounces) sliced fresh mushrooms**
2 **tablespoons soft-spread margarine**
1 **pound lean ground sirloin**
¾ **cup plain dry bread crumbs**
2 **egg whites**
¼ **cup low-salt ketchup**
1 **tablespoon chopped fresh parsley**
1 **garlic clove, minced**
1 **teaspoon Parsley Patch All-Purpose herb blend**
2 **tablespoons freshly grated Parmesan cheese**

Place onions, mushrooms, and margarine in casserole dish. **Cover** with lid or plastic wrap, pulling back one corner to vent steam. (If dish is flat-bottomed, **elevate** on an inverted saucer.) Place on turntable if available. Microwave on HIGH for 6 to 8 minutes (LW 7 to 9 minutes) or until onions are limp; drain any liquid. (**Rotate** dish ½ turn every 3 minutes if not using turntable.)

In medium mixing bowl, combine ground sirloin, bread crumbs, egg whites, ketchup, parsley, garlic, and herb blend. Mix ingredients together well and pat into pie plate as for a pie crust. **Cover** with wax paper. (If dish is flat-bottomed, **elevate** on an inverted saucer.) Place on turntable, if available. Microwave on HIGH for 9 to 10 minutes (LW 10¾ to 12 minutes). (**Rotate** dish ½ turn every 3 minutes if not using turntable.) **Drain** liquid, cover meat shell with onion and mushroom mixture, and sprinkle with Parmesan cheese.

Cover with wax paper and microwave on HIGH for 6 to 7 minutes (LW 7½ to 8¼ minutes) or until meat is firm and no longer pink. (**Rotate** dish ½ turn every 3 minutes if not using turntable.) Let **stand, covered,** for 5 minutes before slicing into wedges.

Troubleshooting: If your oven has a hot spot, an area with a high concentration of microwave energy, you may find the meat overcooking in that area of the oven. If so, rotate the dish out of that area more frequently.

For less restricted diets: If you're not watching your salt intake, substitute regular ketchup, which adds 119 mg sodium per serving.

FOR EACH SERVING:
271 calories
137 mg sodium
47 mg cholesterol
10 g fat

Beef Wedges .

SERVES 4

EQUIPMENT:	medium mixing bowl, 9-inch round baking dish
COOKING TIME:	15 to 17 minutes (Low Wattage ovens 18 to 20 minutes)
STANDING TIME:	5 minutes
NUTRITIONAL PROFILE:	low calories, low sodium, low cholesterol

WEDGES
- 1 pound fresh lean ground sirloin
- 2 egg whites, slightly beaten
- ½ cup plain dry bread crumbs
- ¼ teaspoon dried basil
- ¼ teaspoon dried oregano
- ¼ cup cold water
- ½ cup (about 1 medium) finely chopped onion
- 2 tablespoons low-salt ketchup
- 2 tablespoons freshly grated Parmesan cheese
- ½ teaspoon freshly ground pepper

SAUCE
- 1 10-ounce box frozen whole kernel corn, thawed
- 1 cup low-salt crushed canned tomatoes
- ½ cup (about ½ large) chopped green bell pepper
- ½ cup (about 2 ounces) sliced fresh mushrooms
- 1 garlic clove, minced
- ½ teaspoon dried oregano
- ¼ teaspoon dried basil
- 1 tablespoon snipped fresh parsley
- 1 tablespoon Parsley Patch Popcorn herb blend

Combine all wedge ingredients in medium bowl. **Form** mixture into a flat mound in baking dish. **Score** meat into 4 wedges by using the handle of a wooden spoon or mallet.

Combine all sauce ingredients and pour over and around meat wedges. **Cover** dish with wax paper. (If dish is flat-bottomed, **elevate** on an inverted saucer.) Place on turntable if available. Microwave on HIGH for 15 to 17 minutes (LW 18 to 20 minutes) or until meat loses its pink color and becomes firm. (**Rotate** dish ½ turn every 7 minutes if not using turntable.) Let **stand, covered,** for 5 minutes. Cut into wedges and serve each wedge covered with vegetables and sauce.

Troubleshooting: If corn is frozen, place paper-covered box (if box has an aluminum foil wrapper, remove it) on 2 layers of paper towels on microwave floor and microwave on 30 percent power or LOW for 3 to 4 minutes (LW 3¼ to 4½ minutes), until thawed.

For less restricted diets: If you're not watching your salt intake, substitute regular ketchup, which adds 89 mg sodium per serving, and regular tomatoes, which add 89 mg sodium per serving.

> FOR EACH SERVING:
> 342 calories
> 252 mg sodium
> 91 mg cholesterol
> 12 g fat

VEAL

Veal in the microwave—would I lie to you? Because veal has nearly no fat, it becomes tough and dries out very easily if not coated with a sauce or glaze. Remember, the lower the fat content of meats, the lower the cholesterol level, except for veal, which has *more* cholesterol.

Starting out with nice fresh veal is one key to the quality of the finished dish. Young veal is very pale pink in color—the redder the meat, the older the veal. Should there be any visible fat, it also should be pale in color.

Like all red meat roasts, when microwaved veal must be elevated on a meat rack or balanced on several custard cups and cooked on a low temperature setting to allow it to tenderize and stay moist. For the best results, microwave veal roasts to 160 degrees on a temperature probe or micro-safe thermometer.

Don't forget, if your microwave comes with a probe you must **program** the microwave to cook to 160 degrees on *50 percent* power. Should you just program in temperature, the microwave will automatically cook on HIGH power, guaranteeing you a tough dry roast that cooked much too fast.

Glazed Veal Roast

SERVES 6

EQUIPMENT:	meat rack or 2 custard cups and flat casserole dish, small bowl, micro-safe meat thermometer or oven probe
COOKING TIME:	about 39 to 48 minutes (Low Wattage ovens 46½ to 58½ minutes)
STANDING TIME:	5 to 10 minutes
NUTRITIONAL PROFILE:	moderate calories, low sodium, moderate cholesterol

- **1 3-pound boneless veal roast**
- **1 teaspoon dried rosemary**
- **¼ cup low-sugar orange marmalade**
- **1 teaspoon dark brown sugar**
- **¼ cup white wine**
- **1 tablespoon grated orange zest**

Rub roast with rosemary and place on meat rack (or balance on 2 inverted custard cups) set into a casserole dish to catch the drippings. **Insert** probe or micro-safe thermometer into the center of meat if available. Veal should be microwaved for 13 to 16 minutes per pound (LW 15½ to 19½ minutes per pound).

In a small bowl, combine marmalade, brown sugar, wine, and zest, mixing well. Spread ½ of glaze over meat and microwave, **uncovered,** on HIGH for 5 minutes (LW 6 minutes). **Reduce** power to 50 percent or MEDIUM and continue microwaving, **uncov-ered,** for 34 to 43 minutes (LW 41½ to 53½ minutes) or until meat reaches 160 degrees, turning meat over and coating with remaining glaze mixture after 15 minutes. **Remove** meat from microwave, **tent** with aluminum foil, shiny side toward the meat, and allow to **stand, covered,** for 5 to 10 minutes or until the internal temperature reaches 170 degrees.

Troubleshooting: Remember, the meat continues to cook after the oven shuts off and during standing time. If you microwave until the meat reaches 170 degrees, it will **overcook** and toughen while it stands. If you're using a probe, after standing time you can plug it back into the oven to check the temperature.

If you are using a regular oven meat thermometer, insert and check meat temperature only when meat is removed from microwave.

FOR EACH SERVING:
400 calories
136 mg sodium
172 mg cholesterol
6 g fat

LAMB

The hardest part of preparing a leg of lamb is the carving, but try these tips. Place the shank bone to your right and cut 2 or 3 slices from the thin side, parallel to the leg bone. Turn the leg over so it rests on the cut side. Steady the leg with a carving fork and make vertical slices down to the leg bone. Cut horizontally along the leg bone to release the slices.

ARRANGING SLICED MEATS

How we visualize the size of our servings when cutting down portions has a major influence on our psychological sense of deprivation. To fool your eye, thinly slice meat and fan the slices out on the plate. This attractive arrangement can equal one thick slice of meat, yet the portion appears very generous.

Bone-In Leg of Lamb

SERVES 6

EQUIPMENT: meat rack or 2 custard cups and flat casserole dish
COOKING TIME: 45 to 55 minutes (Low Wattage ovens 64 to
75 minutes)
STANDING TIME: 10 minutes
NUTRITIONAL PROFILE: moderate calories, low sodium, moderate
cholesterol

1   3-pound bone-in leg of lamb
2   to 3 garlic cloves, peeled and thinly sliced
1   teaspoon dried rosemary
1   teaspoon dried basil
½   teaspoon dried oregano
1   tablespoon olive oil

Cut several small slits in the surface of lamb, about ½ inch deep.
Insert a slice of garlic in each slit. Mix the remaining ingredients
and rub ½ the mixture over entire leg of lamb. Place lamb, fat
side down, on a meat rack or balanced on 2 inverted custard cups
set in a casserole dish to catch the drippings. Microwave, **uncovered,** on HIGH for 10 minutes (LW 12 minutes). **Reduce** power to
50 percent or MEDIUM and cook, **uncovered,** for 20 minutes (LW 24
minutes).

Turn lamb over, rub the remaining herb mixture over the
lamb, and cook, **uncovered,** on 50 percent power or MEDIUM for 25
to 35 minutes (LW 30 to 41 minutes). Once done, **remove** from
the microwave, **tent** meat in aluminum foil (shiny side toward the
meat), and let **stand** for 10 minutes to finish cooking and tenderize.

Troubleshooting: The times given will produce a medium-cooked
lamb; should you want medium-rare, reduce cooking time by 1
to 2 minutes. For well done, increase cooking time by 2 to 3
minutes.

Suggestions: Slice thinly and fan out on plate rather than concen-
trating the meat in thick slabs.

Grind any leftovers and use them to stuff green peppers, onions, tomatoes, or zucchini or cube for Lamb and Spinach Casserole (recipe follows).

FOR EACH SERVING:
391 calories
102 mg sodium
140 mg cholesterol
10 g fat

Lamb and Spinach Casserole

SERVES 4

EQUIPMENT:	deep 2- and 3-quart casserole dishes, small bowl
COOKING TIME:	11¾ to 17 minutes (Low Wattage ovens 14½ to 20 minutes)
STANDING TIME:	3 minutes
NUTRITIONAL PROFILE:	low calories, low sodium, moderate cholesterol

1 pound fresh spinach, washed and trimmed
2 tablespoons soft-spread margarine
1 pound (about 2 cups) lean cooked lamb, cut into bite-size pieces
¼ cup plain yogurt
2 tablespoons freshly grated Parmesan cheese
1 tablespoon white wine
¼ teaspoon dry mustard
    dash cayenne pepper

Trim and wash spinach and place in large deep casserole dish. **Cover** with lid or plastic wrap, pulling back one corner to vent the steam. (If dish is flat-bottomed, **elevate** on an inverted saucer.) Place on turntable if available. Microwave on HIGH for 5 to 8 minutes (LW 6 to 9½ minutes), **stirring** every 3 minutes. (**Rotate** dish ½ turn when stirring if not using turntable.) Let **stand, covered,** for 3 minutes. After standing, **drain** completely and set aside.

In small bowl, melt margarine, **uncovered,** on HIGH for 45 to 50 seconds (LW 60 seconds). In medium casserole dish, combine lamb, yogurt, cheese, wine, and mustard. Drizzle melted margarine over mixture, tossing to coat. Fold in the spinach and add cayenne pepper to taste. **Cover** dish with lid or vented plastic wrap. (If dish is flat-bottomed, **elevate** on an inverted saucer.) Place on turntable if available. Microwave on 80 percent power or MEDIUM-HIGH for 6 to 8 minutes (LW 7½ to 9½ minutes) or until completely heated through.

Troubleshooting: To keep margarine from spattering oven when melting, place a napkin or paper towel over dish.

FOR EACH SERVING:
276 calories
153 mg sodium
120 mg cholesterol
14 g fat

ELEVATING
FLAT-BOTTOMED CONTAINERS

Cooking containers made specifically for microwave use all have slightly concave bottoms and sit on little legs or rims to allow the microwaves to get underneath the dish. When using ordinary equipment, such as glassware, be sure to elevate the dish on an inverted saucer or small bowl from your cupboard. Check carefully to make sure there is no metal decoration on the saucer or bowl that will cause arcing and ruin the dish. If you have a meat or bacon rack, you can simply leave it in the oven and use it to elevate whatever you're cooking.

PORK

You may be surprised to learn that—compared to most meats, including chicken and fish—fresh pork isn't high in cholesterol but is high in protein, thiamine, and B vitamins with only 300 calories in a 4-ounce serving. Be sure to select fresh pink cuts of pork with some marbling of fat and always refrigerate or freeze immediately.

Fresh pork can be refrigerated for up to 2 days, while smoked pork (high in sodium) will stay fresh for 1 to 2 weeks when well refrigerated. You can freeze ground pork for 1 to 3 months, and other fresh pork cuts can be frozen for 3 to 6 months.

As a rule of thumb, when purchasing pork allow ¼ to ⅓ pound per person for boneless pork roasts and ⅓ to ½ pound per person for pork chops. Remember, when microwaving pork (except for ground pork) always reduce the temperature setting to 50 percent power or MEDIUM to avoid shrinkage and allow time for tenderizing.

PORK TENDERLOIN

Lean and tender best describes the succulent pork tenderloin. You may have had this cut, smoked and cured in the form of Canadian bacon. The fresh version microwaves beautifully because of its rather uniform shape. Tenderloins usually range from 1 to 1½ pounds in weight and contain no waste or bone. Tenderloin is a particularly lean form of pork that lends itself well to healthy eating.

As with all other red meat, tenderloin must be microwaved at a reduced power setting of 50 percent or MEDIUM to allow enough cooking time for the meat to tenderize.

Roast Pork Tenderloin

SERVES 4

EQUIPMENT:	meat or bacon rack or 2 custard cups and casserole dish
COOKING TIME:	18 to 25 minutes (Low Wattage ovens 21½ to 29½ minutes)
STANDING TIME:	10 minutes
NUTRITIONAL PROFILE:	low calories, low sodium, low cholesterol

1 1½-pound pork tenderloin
¼ teaspoon freshly ground pepper
½ teaspoon garlic powder

Sprinkle outside of tenderloin with pepper and garlic powder. Place tenderloin on meat rack or balance on 2 inverted custard cups, a small bowl, or saucer set into a casserole dish to catch the drippings. Microwave, **uncovered,** on HIGH for 3 minutes (LW 3½ minutes). This is one meat selection best microwaved with a meat probe or micro-safe thermometer, as pork dries out very quickly if overcooked. If probe or thermometer is available, **insert** at this time (see tip, page 181).

Microwave, **uncovered,** on 50 percent power or MEDIUM until the thermometer or probe registers 165 degrees. **Remove** probe, turn meat over, and **reinsert** probe after 8 minutes. **Remove** meat from oven, **tent** in aluminum foil, shiny side toward the meat, and let **stand** for 10 minutes to finish cooking and tenderize. After standing, meat should register 180 degrees.

Should you not have a micro-safe thermometer or probe for your oven, after first 3 minutes (LW 3½ minutes) on HIGH, **reduce** power to 50 percent or MEDIUM for 15 to 22 minutes (LW 18 to 26 minutes), turning over after half of cooking time. Once done, remove meat from oven, **tent** with aluminum foil, shiny side toward the meat, and let **stand** for 10 minutes before slicing.

Suggestion: When serving, carve thin slices and fan out on plate. This will give the impression of a larger serving.

FOR EACH SERVING:
338 calories
100 mg sodium
113 mg cholesterol
17 g fat

Lee-Lee's Pork Tenderloin

This recipe is an adaptation of my aunt Lee-Lee's Vietnamese-style dish.

SERVES 4

EQUIPMENT:	small and large bowls, meat rack or 2 custard cups and casserole dish, 2-quart casserole dish
COOKING TIME:	32 to 38 minutes (Low Wattage ovens 37½ to 47 minutes)
STANDING TIME:	1 hour to overnight for meat; 10 minutes for finished recipe
NUTRITIONAL PROFILE:	moderate calories, low sodium, low cholesterol

1   1½-pound pork tenderloin

MARINADE
- **2   teaspoons low-salt soy sauce**
- **¼   cup Marsala wine**
- **1   tablespoon dark brown sugar**
- **¼   teaspoon ground ginger**
- **2   teaspoons red food coloring**
- **½   teaspoon ground cinnamon**
- **1   garlic clove, crushed**
- **1   scallion, cut into 2-inch pieces**

- **1   pound mixed fresh Oriental vegetables *or* 1 16-ounce bag frozen Japanese vegetables or vegetable combination of your choice**
- **¼   cup water**

Place tenderloin in a plastic bag set into a large bowl. Combine marinade ingredients in a small bowl and pour over pork. Tie bag tightly and let **stand** at room temperature for 1 hour or refrigerate overnight, **turning** bag occasionally to coat the tenderloin well with marinade.

Remove tenderloin, reserving the marinade, and place on a meat rack or balance on 2 inverted custard cups, small bowl, or saucer set in a casserole dish to catch the drippings. **Cover** meat loosely with wax paper and cook on 50 percent power or MEDIUM for 3 minutes (LW 3½ minutes). **Rotate** dish ¼ turn.

Brush meat with marinade, **cover,** and cook for 3 minutes (LW 3½ minutes) longer. **Turn** pork over and brush with reserved marinade. **Cover, insert** meat thermometer or probe if available, and cook on 50 percent power or MEDIUM for 15 to 19 minutes (LW 18 to 24 minutes), **rotating** dish ¼ turn every 3 minutes until meat thermometer registers 165 degrees.

Remove tenderloin to a serving platter, **cover** with aluminum foil, shiny side toward meat, and let **stand** for 10 minutes to finish cooking. Thermometer should register 180 degrees when meat is finished standing. Reserve 2 or 3 tablespoons of pork drippings.

Place fresh or frozen vegetables and water in casserole dish. **Cover** with lid or plastic wrap, pulling back one corner to vent the steam. (If dish is flat-bottomed, **elevate** on an inverted saucer.) Cook on HIGH for 7 to 8 minutes (LW 8 to 10 minutes). **Stir, cover,** and cook for 4 to 5 minutes (LW 4½ to 6 minutes) more or until tender-crisp. Stir undrained cooked vegetables with the reserved pork drippings to coat vegetables. Slice tenderloin diagonally into ¼-inch slices. Spoon vegetables onto serving platter and arrange pork slices on top.

Suggestion: Try varying the combination of vegetables to suit your family's tastes.

FOR EACH SERVING:
380 calories
200 mg sodium
112 mg cholesterol
17 g fat

PROBE OR
MEAT THERMOMETER

When using a meat thermometer or oven probe (if your microwave has one) in meat roasts, always insert it into the center of the meat, away from any bones. If the roast is thin, a tenderloin for instance, insert thermometer or probe at an angle to help prevent it from falling out.

Sweet and Sour Pork

SERVES 6

EQUIPMENT:	2-quart round casserole dish
COOKING TIME:	21 to 25 minutes (Low Wattage ovens 25¼ to 30¼ minutes)
STANDING TIME:	5 minutes
NUTRITIONAL PROFILE:	low calories, low sodium, low cholesterol

- ¼ **cup dark brown sugar**
- 2 **tablespoons cornstarch**
- ¼ **cup cider vinegar**
- 1 **tablespoon low-salt soy sauce**
- 2 **tablespoons low-salt ketchup**
- 1 **20-ounce can pineapple chunks packed in natural juices, drained and juice reserved**
- 1 **pound lean boneless pork, cut into ½-inch cubes**
- 1 **large green bell pepper, cut into 1-inch cubes**
- 1 **medium onion, cut into thin wedges with layers separated**

In casserole dish, **whisk** together brown sugar, cornstarch, vinegar, soy sauce, ketchup, and reserved pineapple juice until smooth. Add pork cubes, stirring to combine with sauce. **Cover** dish with lid or plastic wrap, pulling back one corner to vent the steam. (If dish is flat-bottomed, **elevate** on an inverted saucer.) Place on turntable, if available. Microwave on HIGH for 3 minutes (LW 3½ minutes) and **stir.** (**Rotate** dish ½ turn if not using turntable.)

Reduce power to 50 percent or MEDIUM, **cover,** and cook for 12 to 14 minutes (LW 14½ to 17 minutes) or until pork is no longer pink, stirring every 5 minutes. (**Rotate** dish ½ turn when stirring if not using turntable.)

Add green bell pepper and onion, **cover,** and cook on 80 percent power or MEDIUM-HIGH for 5 to 7 minutes (LW 6 to 8½ minutes) or until vegetables are tender-crisp, **stirring** every 3 minutes. (**Rotate** dish ½ turn when stirring if not using turntable.) Add pineapple chunks and heat, **uncovered,** on HIGH for 1 minute (LW 1¼ minutes). Let **stand** for 5 minutes before serving.

Suggestion: Serve each portion over ½ cup cooked long-grain rice, which adds 70 calories per serving.

For less restricted diets: If you're not watching your salt intake, substitute regular soy sauce, which adds 60 mg sodium per serving, and regular ketchup, which adds 59 mg sodium per serving.

FOR EACH SERVING:
268 calories
158 mg sodium
50 mg cholesterol
2 g fat

Sausage Mélange

SERVES 6

EQUIPMENT:	plastic dishwasher-safe colander with casserole dish, deep 3-quart casserole dish
COOKING TIME:	31 to 37 minutes (Low Wattage ovens 37 to 44¼ minutes)
STANDING TIME:	5 to 10 minutes
NUTRITIONAL PROFILE:	low calories, low sodium, low cholesterol

1 teaspoon paprika
1 tablespoon fennel seed
½ teaspoon freshly ground pepper
1 pound lean ground pork
2 pounds (about 6) small potatoes, cut into quarters
3 medium onions, cut into quarters
2 medium green and/or red bell peppers, cut into 1-inch chunks
½ pound (about 2 cups) sliced fresh mushrooms
1 teaspoon dried oregano
¼ teaspoon freshly ground pepper
1 teaspoon snipped fresh parsley
½ teaspoon low-sodium beef bouillon granules
¼ cup white wine

Blend paprika, fennel, and ½ teaspoon pepper into pork. **Crumble** meat into colander and set in casserole dish to catch the drippings (see tip, page 165). Microwave, **uncovered,** on HIGH for 3 minutes (LW 3½ minutes). Break meat up into small chunks with fork. Cook, **uncovered,** on HIGH for 3 to 4 minutes (LW 3½ to 4¾ minutes), until meat is no longer pink.

In deep casserole dish, **alternate** layers of potatoes, drained pork mixture, onions, peppers, and mushrooms, seasoning each layer with a sprinkle of oregano, pepper, and parsley. **Whisk** bouillon into wine and pour over the sausage and potatoes. **Cover** dish with lid or plastic wrap, pulling back one corner to vent the steam. (If dish is flat-bottomed, **elevate** on an inverted saucer.) Place on turntable if available.

Microwave on HIGH for 15 minutes (LW 18 minutes). Turn over all ingredients carefully, **cover,** and cook on HIGH for 10 to 15 minutes (LW 12 to 18 minutes) or until potatoes are tender. Let **stand, covered,** for 5 to 10 minutes before serving.

For less restricted diets: If you're not watching your salt intake, use regular beef bouillon, which adds 75 mg sodium per serving.

FOR EACH SERVING:
339 calories
46 mg sodium
50 mg cholesterol
5 g fat

UNIFORMLY CUT FOOD

When cutting meat and vegetables, be sure to cut them into uniform size pieces to ensure that the entire dish cooks evenly.

Pasta and Rice

PASTA

It's been said that pasta originated with the Arabs, who devised it as a method of preserving flour in the desert. Today pasta and noodles come in many shapes and sizes. Even the Chinese serve their own type of pasta in lo mein, wonton skins, and egg roll wrappers. Pasta is low in fat and sodium and easily digested. Eggless pasta is the healthiest choice; virtually all spaghetti on the market is eggless, and most imported pasta is eggless, too.

Cooking pasta in the microwave doesn't save you time, and unless you are cooking a very small amount, you also need a very large container. Cook macaroni products on your conventional stove in double batches and freeze half, in tightly sealed plastic bags, for easy defrosting and use in other recipes.

Chicken Pasta Italiano

SERVES 6

EQUIPMENT:	9 × 13-inch flat casserole dish, 6-cup glass measure
COOKING TIME:	22 to 25 minutes (Low Wattage ovens 26¼ to 30 minutes)
STANDING TIME:	3 to 5 minutes
NUTRITIONAL PROFILE:	moderate calories, low sodium, low cholesterol

3 **pounds cut-up skinless chicken fryer parts, with excess fat removed**
1 **15-ounce can low-sodium stewed tomatoes, sliced, with their juice**
½ **teaspoon onion powder**
½ **teaspoon Parsley Patch Lemon Pepper herb blend**
1 **8-ounce can low-sodium tomato sauce**
2 **garlic cloves, crushed**
1 **medium carrot, cut into 2 × ¼-inch strips**
1 **large green bell pepper, chopped**
½ **pound (about 2 cups) fresh mushrooms, sliced**
1 **teaspoon dried oregano**
6 **cups hot cooked eggless spaghetti**
2 **tablespoons freshly grated Parmesan cheese**

Wash and pat chicken pieces dry with paper towels. Place chicken pieces in casserole dish with thickest portions toward the outside of the dish. Place tomatoes, onion powder, herb blend, tomato sauce, garlic, carrot, green bell pepper, mushrooms, and oregano in glass measure. Mix together well. Pour mixture over and around chicken pieces. **Cover** dish with plastic wrap, pulling back one corner to vent the steam. (If dish is flat-bottomed, **elevate** on an inverted saucer.)

Cook on HIGH for 22 to 25 minutes (LW 26¼ to 30 minutes) or until chicken is tender and no longer pink, **rotating** dish ½ turn, basting pieces with sauce, and **rearranging** chicken every 10 minutes. Let **stand, covered,** for 3 to 5 minutes and serve chicken and sauce over hot cooked spaghetti, sprinkling grated cheese over the top.

Troubleshooting: When rearranging chicken pieces, bring the less cooked ones from the center of the dish to the outside edges and the ones along the edges to the center.

For less restricted diets: If you're not watching your salt intake, substitute regular stewed tomatoes, which add 115 mg per serving, and regular tomato sauce, another 215 mg sodium per serving.

FOR EACH SERVING:
482 calories
110 mg sodium
84 mg cholesterol
4 g fat

Spaghetti with Italian Meat Sauce

SERVES 6

EQUIPMENT:	colander with dish to catch drippings, deep 3-quart casserole dish
COOKING TIME:	51 to 63 minutes (Low Wattage ovens 61½ to 75½ minutes)
STANDING TIME:	5 minutes
NUTRITIONAL PROFILE:	moderate calories, low sodium, low cholesterol

1   pound lean ground sirloin
2   garlic cloves, minced
1   medium onion, diced
1   medium green bell pepper, diced
2   28-ounce cans low-sodium crushed tomatoes
1   8-ounce can low-sodium tomato sauce
¼   cup burgundy wine
1   tablespoon dried oregano
1   teaspoon dried basil
1   teaspoon Parsley Patch All-Purpose herb blend
¼   teaspoon fennel seed
6   cups cooked spaghetti, drained

Crumble ground sirloin into colander and set in casserole dish to catch the drippings. Microwave, **uncovered,** on HIGH for 3 minutes (LW 3½ minutes). Break up meat chunks with fork and add garlic, onion, and green bell pepper. Microwave, **uncovered,** on HIGH for 3 to 5 minutes (LW 4 to 6 minutes) or until meat is no longer pink.

Discard fat and transfer meat to deep casserole dish. Stir in remaining ingredients. **Cover** with lid or plastic wrap, pulling back one corner to vent the steam. (If dish is flat-bottomed, **elevate** on an inverted saucer.) Place on turntable, if available. Microwave on HIGH for 5 minutes (LW 6 minutes), **reduce** power to 50 percent or MEDIUM (if you have only HIGH on your oven, see tip, page 188) and cook, **uncovered,** for 40 to 50 minutes (LW 48 to 60 minutes) or until flavors blend, **stirring** every 10 minutes. (**Rotate** dish ¼ turn when stirring if not using turntable.) Let **stand, covered,** for 5 minutes before serving.

Troubleshooting: Sauce should be cooked uncovered to allow it to thicken; however, if it's spattering your oven, cover with a paper towel.

If you have a hot spot in your oven, you may find the sauce overcooking in that area. To avoid this, rotate dish more frequently.

For less restricted diets: If you're not watching your salt intake, substitute regular crushed tomatoes, which add 625 mg sodium per serving, and regular tomato sauce, which adds 323 mg sodium per serving.

FOR EACH SERVING:
406 calories
79 mg sodium
37 mg cholesterol
6 g fat

OVENS WITH ONLY HIGH POWER

Some of these recipes call for a reduced power setting. If your oven has only HIGH power, try placing a glass of water next to the food you're cooking. Some of the microwaves will be drawn to the water and away from the cooking food, thereby reducing the amount of power going to the food. Unfortunately, there's no accurate way to measure how much power the water draws from the food.

LOW-FAT CHEESES

When a cheese label reads "part-skimmed milk," you are assured of a lower-calorie and lower-cholesterol cheese that looks and tastes pretty much like whole-milk cheese.

Ricotta and cottage cheese are similar, but ricotta has more calcium. The added calcium is an advantage, for it aids in the prevention of osteoporosis (the thinning bone disease), a health concern for women.

Triple-Cheese Lasagne Swirls

You may be surprised to see a low-calorie lasagne, but you can reduce the calories even further, almost in half by substituting uncreamed low-fat cottage cheese in place of the ricotta. Keep in mind that the finished product will not be as rich and creamy when made with the cottage cheese.

SERVES 6

EQUIPMENT:	12 × 8- or 13 × 9-inch baking dish, medium mixing bowl
COOKING TIME:	6 to 7 minutes (Low Wattage ovens 8 to 9 minutes)
STANDING TIME:	5 minutes
NUTRITIONAL PROFILE:	low calories, low sodium, low cholesterol

- **2 cups low-salt meatless spaghetti sauce**
- **1 16-ounce container part-skim ricotta cheese**
- **1 cup shredded part-skim mozzarella cheese**
- **2 egg whites, slightly beaten**
- **¼ teaspoon freshly ground pepper**
- **¾ teaspoon dried oregano**
- **¼ teaspoon freshly grated nutmeg**
- **1 tablespoon minced fresh parsley**
- **6 lasagne noodles, cooked and drained**
- **¼ cup freshly grated Parmesan cheese, with 2 tablespoons reserved for topping**

Spread 1 cup of spaghetti sauce over the bottom of baking dish and set aside. In mixing bowl, combine all ingredients except noodles, reserved Parmesan, and remaining spaghetti sauce. Blend well.

Lay lasagne strips flat on counter top and spread 2 to 3 tablespoons of cheese mixture along length of each strip. Roll up each strip, jelly-roll style. Arrange rolls seam side down in prepared dish. Top rolls with remaining sauce.

Cover dish with plastic wrap, pulling back one corner to vent the steam. (If dish is flat-bottomed, **elevate** on an inverted saucer.) Microwave on HIGH for 6 to 7 minutes (LW 8 to 9 minutes) or until the dish is hot and bubbly, **rotating** dish ½ turn after 3 minutes. Let **stand, covered,** for 5 minutes. Remove plastic wrap and sprinkle top of each roll with reserved Parmesan cheese.

Suggestions: Conventionally cook the entire package of lasagne strips, drain, and cool. Freeze unused strips by placing a sheet of wax paper between each strip to keep them from sticking. Wrap the entire bundle in plastic wrap or place in a tightly sealed plastic bag. Having cooked lasagne strips on hand makes this main dish ready to prepare at a moment's notice.

For less restricted diets: If you're not watching your salt intake, substitute regular jarred spaghetti sauce, which adds 450 mg of sodium per serving.

FOR EACH SERVING:
350 calories
246 mg sodium
47 mg cholesterol
23 g fat

Vegetarian Lasagne .

Whenever I demonstrate this recipe, everyone is amazed that lasagne cooks so beautifully using raw noodles right out of the box.

SERVES 6

EQUIPMENT:	12 × 8- or 13 × 9-inch casserole dish or 2-quart flat casserole dish, medium mixing bowl
COOKING TIME:	40 to 48 minutes (Low Wattage ovens 48 to 56¾ minutes)
STANDING TIME:	10 minutes
NUTRITIONAL PROFILE:	moderate calories, low sodium, low cholesterol

1   **16-ounce bag frozen broccoli cuts**
1   **pound part-skim ricotta cheese**
2   **egg whites**
1   **tablespoon chopped fresh parsley**
½   **teaspoon garlic powder**
2   **tablespoons freshly grated Parmesan cheese**
1   **quart low-salt meatless spaghetti sauce**
8   **uncooked lasagne noodles**
1   **cup shredded part-skim mozzarella cheese**
¼   **cup freshly grated Parmesan cheese**

Cut a slit or an X in the top of the plastic bag of frozen broccoli cuts. Place bag on 2 **layers** of paper towels on microwave floor. Microwave on HIGH for 4 to 6 minutes (LW 4¾ to 7½ minutes) or until defrosted but still crisp.

Combine ricotta cheese, egg whites, parsley, garlic powder, and 2 tablespoons of Parmesan cheese in bowl. Mix well and set aside. Pour 1⅓ cups of sauce into casserole dish and place 4 uncooked noodles evenly over sauce, overlapping noodles if necessary. Spread 1⅓ cups of sauce over noodles and sprinkle with ½ the broccoli cuts, ½ the cheese mixture, and ½ cup of the mozzarella cheese. Layer remaining noodles over mozzarella and cover with remaining sauce. Sprinkle sauce with remaining mozzarella and broccoli cuts. Spread remaining cheese mixture over broccoli and **cover** dish with plastic wrap, pulling back one corner to vent the steam. (If dish is flat-bottomed, **elevate** on an inverted saucer.) Microwave on HIGH power for 15 minutes (LW 18 minutes), rotating dish ½ turn every 7 minutes.

Reduce power to 60 percent or MEDIUM, cover, and cook for 20 to 25 minutes (LW 24 to 28 minutes) or until noodles are tender, **rotating** the dish ½ turn every 10 minutes. Sprinkle top with ¼ cup Parmesan cheese and microwave, **uncovered,** on HIGH for 1 to 2 minutes (LW 1¼ to 2¼ minutes) or until cheese melts. **Cover** dish with plastic wrap and let **stand** for 10 minutes before serving.

Troubleshooting: If you have only HIGH power on your oven, when the recipe calls for MEDIUM, microwave for 4 minutes and let rest for 2 minutes. Repeat this twice more and let stand on a hard heatproof surface for 10 minutes. Check doneness of noodles and, if necessary, microwave for 2 to 4 minutes more. Once noodles are done, go on with the last step of melting the Parmesan cheese.

If the sauce is overcooking in spots, you could have a hot spot in your oven, which means you need to rotate the dish more often.

If you are using a square-cornered dish, try not to fill up the corners, as the microwaves overcook things in square corners.

If the noodles in the center of the dish aren't done, you used a flat-bottomed dish and forgot to elevate it.

Mozzarella cheese toughens if it is exposed to the microwaves, so be sure to place the top layer of mozzarella cheese *under* the ricotta mixture.

Suggestions: Substitute thawed chopped spinach or french-cut green beans for the broccoli cuts.

For less restricted diets: If you're not watching your salt intake, substitute regular meatless spaghetti sauce, which adds 449 mg sodium per serving.

FOR EACH SERVING:
478 calories
298 mg sodium
54 mg cholesterol
24 g fat

Orzo with Vegetables

There seem to be hundreds of different brands, varieties, and shapes of macaroni products on the market today. One you may not have used often is orzo, a small pasta grain that looks like rice and tastes like a cross between the two.

SERVES 6

EQUIPMENT: deep 3-quart casserole dish, small bowl
COOKING TIME: 12 to 17 minutes (Low Wattage ovens 14¼ to 20¼ minutes)
STANDING TIME: 2 to 3 minutes
NUTRITIONAL PROFILE: low calories, low sodium, no cholesterol

1   16-ounce box orzo macaroni
1   large onion, chopped
1   large green bell pepper, chopped
½   pound (about 2 cups) fresh mushrooms, sliced
½   cup (about 2) grated carrots
1   garlic clove, minced
½   cup white wine
1   teaspoon low-sodium chicken bouillon granules
1½   teaspoons Parsley Patch All-Purpose herb blend
2   cups crushed cornflake cereal
¼   teaspoon onion powder

Cook orzo al dente on your stove top according to box instructions. (It doesn't save time to cook it in the microwave.) **Drain** and place in a covered container to keep warm while you prepare the vegetables. In casserole dish, place onion, green pepper, mushrooms, carrots, garlic, and wine.

Cover dish with lid or plastic wrap, pulling back one corner to vent the steam. (If dish is flat-bottomed, **elevate** on an inverted saucer.) Place on turntable if available. Microwave on HIGH for 7 to 10 minutes (LW 8¼ to 12 minutes) or until vegetables are tender-crisp.

Stir bouillon into vegetables until dissolved. Add herb blend, stirring to combine. Fold in cooked orzo. Combine cornflake crumbs and onion powder in small bowl. Add ¾ of the mixture to the orzo and vegetables, **stirring** to combine. **Cover** and cook on HIGH for 5 to 7 minutes (LW 6 to 8¼ minutes) or until heated through. (**Rotate** dish ½ turn every 3 minutes if not using turntable.) Let **stand, covered,** for 2 to 3 minutes. Sprinkle remaining cornflake mixture over casserole before serving.

For less restricted diets: If you're not watching your salt intake, substitute regular bouillon granules, which add 300 mg sodium per serving.

FOR EACH SERVING:
219 calories
95 mg sodium
0 mg cholesterol
trace fat

Mushroom Linguine

SERVES 4

EQUIPMENT:	4-cup glass measure, 2-quart round casserole dish
COOKING TIME:	13 to 19 minutes (Low Wattage ovens 15¼ to 23¼ minutes)
STANDING TIME:	none required
NUTRITIONAL PROFILE:	low calories, low sodium, no cholesterol

- ¼ **cup water**
- 1 **low-sodium beef bouillon cube**
- ¼ **cup white wine**
- ¾ **pound (about 3 cups) fresh mushrooms, sliced**
- ½ **cup (about 4) diced scallions**
- 3 **tablespoons all-purpose flour**
- 1 **cup skim milk**
- 1 **teaspoon Parsley Patch Garlicsaltless herb blend**
- ¼ **teaspoon dried basil**
- 1 **teaspoon chopped fresh parsley**
- 4 **cups cooked linguine, drained**

Place water in glass measure and microwave, **uncovered,** on HIGH for 2 to 3 minutes (LW 2¼ to 3½ minutes) or until boiling. Dissolve bouillon cube in boiling water and set aside.

Place wine, mushrooms, and scallions in casserole dish. Microwave, **uncovered,** on HIGH for 4 to 6 minutes (LW 4¾ to 7½ minutes) or until vegetables are tender-crisp. **Whisk** flour into dissolved bouillon. Add milk, herb blend, basil, and parsley, whisking until completely blended. Microwave, **uncovered,** on HIGH for 4 to 6 minutes (LW 4¾ to 7½ minutes), **whisking** every minute until sauce is thickened and coats whisk.

Pour sauce over vegetables, stir, and **cover** with wax paper. (If dish is flat-bottomed, **elevate** on an inverted saucer.) Microwave on 80 percent power or MEDIUM-HIGH for 3 to 4 minutes (LW 3½ to 4¾ minutes), until hot and flavors blend, **stirring** once. Serve over hot linguine.

Troubleshooting: Forgetting to whisk sauce may cause it to be lumpy.

For less restricted diets: If you're not watching your salt intake, substitute a regular beef bouillon cube, which adds 225 mg sodium per serving.

> FOR EACH SERVING:
> 288 calories
> 50 mg sodium
> 0 mg cholesterol
> trace fat

Mussels and Spaghetti

SERVES 6

EQUIPMENT:	4-cup glass measure, deep 3-quart casserole dish
COOKING TIME:	21 to 29 minutes (Low Wattage ovens 24¾ to 35 minutes)
STANDING TIME:	2 minutes
NUTRITIONAL PROFILE:	low calories, low sodium, low cholesterol

48   **small fresh mussels in their shells**
2   **tablespoons olive oil**
1   **teaspoon finely chopped garlic**
¼   **cup (about 1 small) chopped onion**
¼   **cup (about 1 large stalk) chopped celery**
1   **teaspoon dried basil**
1   **tablespoon chopped fresh parsley**
½   **cup white wine**
1   **28-ounce can low-sodium crushed tomatoes**
6   **cups cooked eggless spaghetti or linguine, drained**

Scrub mussels well with a stiff brush, discard any broken or open ones, and remove the beards on the outside of the shell. Place oil, garlic, onion, celery, basil, and parsley in glass measure. Microwave, **uncovered,** on HIGH for 4 to 6 minutes (LW 4½ to 7½ minutes) or until vegetables are tender-crisp, **stirring** every 2 minutes. Add wine and cook, **uncovered,** on HIGH for 2 to 3 minutes (LW 2¼ to 3½ minutes) or until rapidly boiling.

Empty tomatoes into casserole dish and stir in wine and vegetable mixture. **Cover** with wax paper. (If dish is flat-bottomed, **elevate** on an inverted saucer.) Place on turntable if available. Microwave on 70 percent power or MEDIUM-HIGH for 10 to 12 minutes (LW 12 to 14½ minutes), stirring every 5 minutes. (**Rotate** dish ½ turn when stirring if not using turntable.)

Add scrubbed mussels, **cover** with lid or plastic wrap, pulling back one corner to vent steam, and cook on HIGH for 5 to 8 minutes (LW 6 to 9½ minutes) or until mussels are open, stirring once. If all mussels aren't open, microwave 1 minute more on HIGH. (**Rotate** dish ½ turn when stirring if not using turntable.) Let **stand, covered,** for 2 minutes and discard any mussels that aren't open before serving. Serve over 1 cup spaghetti or linguine.

For less restricted diets: If you're not watching your salt intake, substitute regular crushed tomatoes, which add 209 mg sodium per serving.

FOR EACH SERVING:
350 calories
113 mg sodium
40 mg cholesterol
6 g fat

Veal and Peppers on Spaghetti

SERVES 4

EQUIPMENT: deep 3-quart round casserole dish
COOKING TIME: 23 to 30 minutes (Low Wattage ovens 27¾ to 34½ minutes)
STANDING TIME: 10 minutes
NUTRITIONAL PROFILE: moderate calories, low sodium, low cholesterol

1 **pound veal cutlets, cut into thin strips**
1 **medium onion, chopped**
1 **large green bell pepper, cut into strips**
1 **medium red bell pepper, cut into strips**
1 **teaspoon minced garlic**
1 **cup (about 4 ounces) sliced fresh mushrooms**
¼ **cup burgundy**
1 **28-ounce can low-sodium crushed tomatoes**
   dash cayenne pepper
½ **teaspoon dried oregano**
½ **teaspoon dried basil**
1 **tablespoon snipped fresh parsley**
¼ **teaspoon Parsley Patch All-Purpose herb blend**
4 **cups cooked eggless spaghetti, drained**

Combine veal, onion, green and red peppers, garlic, mushrooms, and wine in casserole dish. Microwave, **uncovered,** on HIGH for 5 to 7 minutes (LW 6 to 8¼ minutes) or until vegetables are tender-crisp. Add crushed tomatoes, cayenne pepper, oregano, basil, parsley, and herb blend, stirring to combine. **Cover** dish with lid or plastic wrap, pulling back one corner to vent the steam. (If dish is flat-bottomed, **elevate** on an inverted saucer.) Place on turntable if available.

Microwave on HIGH for 6 to 8 minutes (LW 7½ to 9½ minutes) or until bubbling. **Reduce** power to 50 percent or MEDIUM, **cover,** and cook for 12 to 14 minutes (LW 14¼ to 16¾ minutes) or until meat is tender and flavors blend. Let **stand, covered,** for 10 minutes before serving over hot spaghetti.

Troubleshooting: If you don't cut the meat and vegetables uniformly, they won't cook in the same length of time.

For less restricted diets: If you're not watching your salt intake, substitute regular crushed tomatoes, which add 313 mg sodium per serving.

FOR EACH SERVING:
473 calories
119 mg sodium
86 mg cholesterol
9 g fat

Rice

SERVES 4

EQUIPMENT:	deep 2-quart casserole dish
COOKING TIME:	16 to 20 minutes (Low Wattage ovens 19¼ to 23 minutes)
STANDING TIME:	3 minutes
NUTRITIONAL PROFILE:	low calories, low sodium, no cholesterol

1   cup long-grain white rice
2   cups water

Place rice and water in casserole dish and **stir. Cover** with lid or plastic wrap, pulling back one corner to vent the steam. (If dish is flat-bottomed, **elevate** on an inverted saucer.) Place on turntable if available.
Microwave on HIGH for 5 minutes (LW 6 minutes). (**Rotate** dish ½ turn if not using turntable.) Stir and **reduce** power to 50 percent or MEDIUM, cover, and cook for 11 to 15 minutes (LW 13¼ to 17 minutes) or until liquid is absorbed and rice is tender. (**Rotate** dish ¼ turn every 5 minutes if not using turntable.) Let **stand, covered,** for 3 minutes and fluff with a fork before serving.

FOR EACH SERVING:
70 calories
2 mg sodium
0 mg cholesterol
trace fat

Polka Dot Rice

SERVES 6

EQUIPMENT: deep 2½- or 3-quart casserole dish
COOKING TIME: 23 to 29 minutes (Low Wattage ovens 27½ to 34½ minutes)
STANDING TIME: 5 minutes
NUTRITIONAL PROFILE: moderate calories, low sodium, no cholesterol

2 cups water
4 teaspoons low-sodium chicken bouillon granules
2 tablespoons soft-spread margarine
1 cup raw long-grain rice
1 scallion, chopped
1 tablespoon snipped fresh parsley
½ pound (about 2 cups) fresh mushrooms, sliced
½ cup frozen green peas, thawed
1 tablespoon diced pimiento

Place water in casserole dish. Microwave, **uncovered,** on HIGH for 3 to 4 minutes (LW 3½ to 4½ minutes) or until hot. Add bouillon and margarine, stirring until both are dissolved. **Stir** in rice, scallion, parsley, and mushrooms. **Cover** with lid or plastic wrap, pulling back one corner to vent the steam. (If dish is flat-bottomed, **elevate** on an inverted saucer.) Place on turntable if available. Microwave on HIGH for 5 minutes (LW 6 minutes). (**Rotate** dish ½ turn after 3 minutes if not using turntable.) **Stir.**

Reduce power to 50 percent or MEDIUM, cover, and cook for 15 to 20 minutes (LW 18 to 24 minutes) or until liquid is absorbed and rice is tender. (**Rotate** dish ¼ turn every 5 minutes if not using turntable.) Add thawed peas and pimiento, folding in with fork. Let **stand, covered,** for 5 minutes. Fluff with fork before serving.

For less restricted diets: If you're not watching your salt intake, substitute regular chicken bouillon granules, which add 600 mg sodium per serving.

FOR EACH SERVING:
174 calories
45 mg sodium
0 mg cholesterol
3 g fat

Stir-Frys

Scallops and Broccoli in Pepper Sauce

I just can't give you this recipe without telling you what happened when I microwaved a scallop stir-fry as a guest on a morning television show. I was on tour with my first book, on television in many cities across the country. In each city an escort brought all the food and dishes to the television station for me, as I couldn't carry everything on the plane.

On this particular day the escort picked me up in the morning and told me she had had trouble making the recipe the night before, because the garlic and oil didn't sizzle as I described in my recipe. I told her she must not have preheated the browning dish long enough, but she assured me she had. I was very puzzled, as that had never happened to me, but thought I would try it myself. Before going on the air all the supplies she brought were put on a table for me to prepare. I hoped what I saw wasn't true, but yes, she had brought me a regular brown *glass* dish, not a microwave browning dish. The show must go on, so I microwaved the scallop stir-fry in the brown dish, explaining what a browning dish is and telling the viewers that if you don't have one, a regular round casserole will work—it did.

SERVES 4

EQUIPMENT:	10-inch covered browning dish, small bowl
COOKING TIME:	11 to 15 minutes (Low Wattage ovens 12¾ to 17¾ minutes)
STANDING TIME:	3 minutes
NUTRITIONAL PROFILE:	low calories, low sodium, low cholesterol

2 **tablespoons peanut oil**
1 **teaspoon finely minced garlic**
1 **teaspoon finely minced fresh ginger**
4 **whole scallions, cut into ¼-inch pieces**
2 **cups (about 1 bunch) fresh broccoli flowerets**
2 **tablespoons white wine**
2 **tablespoons low-salt soy sauce**
1 **teaspoon sugar**
⅛ **teaspoon crushed red pepper flakes**
2 **tablespoons low-salt ketchup**
1 **tablespoon cornstarch**
2 **tablespoons low-sodium chicken broth or home-made chicken stock (page 44)**
1 **pound fresh bay scallops**

Preheat browning dish for 5 to 7 minutes (LW 6 to 8 minutes) or according to manufacturer's instructions. Remove hot dish from microwave, using pot holders, and add oil, swirling to coat dish. Immediately add garlic, ginger, and scallions, stirring with wooden spoon.

Microwave, **uncovered,** on HIGH for 2 minutes (LW 2¼ minutes). Add broccoli, stirring to coat with garlic mixture, cover, and microwave on HIGH for 3 to 4 minutes (LW 3½ to 4¾ minutes) or until broccoli is tender-crisp.

In small bowl, whisk together wine, soy sauce, sugar, red pepper flakes, ketchup, cornstarch, and chicken stock. Add sauce to broccoli, stirring to combine. **Cover** and microwave on HIGH for 4 to 5 minutes (LW 4¾ to 6 minutes) or until mixture boils. Add scallops, **stirring** to combine with sauce and vegetables, **cover,** and cook on HIGH for 2 to 4 minutes (LW 2¼ to 4¾ minutes) or until scallops are tender. Let **stand, covered,** for 3 minutes before serving.

Troubleshooting: This recipe works best in a microwave browning dish, but you can substitute a round casserole dish, remembering that the oil and garlic will not sizzle, which blends the flavors better.

Suggestion: Serve over ½ cup cooked long-grain rice, which adds 70 calories per serving.

For less restricted diets: If you're not watching your salt intake, substitute regular soy sauce, which adds 60 mg sodium per serving; regular ketchup, which adds 27 mg sodium per serving; and regular chicken broth, which adds 28 mg sodium per serving.

FOR EACH SERVING:
207 calories
163 mg sodium
22 mg cholesterol
8 g fat

THE BROWNING DISH

Microwave browning dishes are specially coated with a material that absorbs the microwaves, so that the surface of the dish gets hot like a frying pan. Use pot holders to remove the very hot dish from the oven and place on a heatproof pad, or you might burn your counter top. When stir-frying, you need a deep browning dish with a cover. If you have one that is flat, use a regular casserole dish, because covering a hot browning dish with plastic wrap or wax paper may start a fire.

Fruity Scallop Stir-Fry

SERVES 4

EQUIPMENT: 10-inch covered browning dish, small bowl
COOKING TIME: 10 to 11 minutes (Low Wattage ovens 11½ to 12¾ minutes)
STANDING TIME: 3 minutes
NUTRITIONAL PROFILE: moderate calories, low sodium, low cholesterol

1 **10-ounce box frozen snow peas**
1 **tablespoon peanut oil**
1 **garlic clove, minced**
1 **cup (about 4 large stalks) diagonally sliced celery**
1 **medium onion, sliced, with rings separated**
1 **pound fresh bay scallops**
2 **large pears, peeled, cored, and cut into wedges**
½ **cup cider vinegar**
2 **tablespoons dark brown sugar**
1 **tablespoon low-salt soy sauce**
2 **tablespoons low-salt ketchup**
1 **tablespoon cornstarch**
½ **cup natural unsalted cashews**

Remove plastic pouch from box of snow peas, cut an X in plastic to vent the steam, and place on 2 layers of paper towels. Microwave on 30 percent power or LOW for 2 to 3 minutes (LW 2¼ to 3½ minutes) to defrost. **Drain** on several paper towels.

Preheat 10-inch browning dish on HIGH for 5 to 7 minutes (LW 6 to 8 minutes) or according to manufacturer's instructions. Using pot holders, **remove** dish from microwave and add oil, swirling to coat dish. Add garlic, celery, onion, and scallops. **Cover** and microwave on HIGH for 3 minutes (LW 3½ minutes). Add pears and snow peas, **cover,** and cook on HIGH for 2 minutes (LW 2¼ minutes) or until vegetables are tender-crisp.

In a small bowl, whisk together vinegar, brown sugar, soy sauce, ketchup, and cornstarch. Add sauce to scallops and vegetables, stirring well. Microwave, **uncovered,** on HIGH for 3 minutes

(LW 3½ minutes) or until sauce thickens. Sprinkle dish with cashews. Let **stand** for 3 minutes before serving.

Troubleshooting: If browning dish isn't available, use 2-quart casserole dish, eliminating the preheating step.

Suggestion: Serve over ½ cup cooked long-grain rice, which adds 70 calories per serving.

For less restricted diets: If you're not watching your salt intake, substitute regular soy sauce, which adds 90 mg sodium per serving, and regular ketchup, which adds 89 mg sodium per serving.

FOR EACH SERVING:
450 calories
267 mg sodium
22 mg cholesterol
13 g fat

NUTS

Cashews, like all nuts, are excellent sources of protein, potassium, phosphorus, and niacin. They do, however, contain substantial calories and a lot of fat (600 calories per ½ cup), so don't overdo it when watching your weight. Natural unsalted nuts are just as nutritious as the salted variety and will save you 173 mg of sodium per ounce, with the same high calories.

Stir-Fried Beef and Mushrooms

SERVES 4

EQUIPMENT:	medium bowl, 10-inch covered browning dish
COOKING TIME:	5 to 7 minutes (Low Wattage ovens 5¾ to 8¼ minutes)
STANDING TIME:	3 minutes
NUTRITIONAL PROFILE:	low calories, low sodium, low cholesterol

½ **pound sirloin steak, sliced into thin ½-inch strips**
2 **teaspoons low-salt soy sauce**
1 **tablespoon white wine**
2 **teaspoons cornstarch**
⅛ **teaspoon ground ginger**
1 **teaspoon sugar**
1 **garlic clove, minced**
3 **to 4 drops dark sesame oil**
2 **tablespoons peanut oil**
½ **pound fresh mushrooms, sliced**
4 **scallions, including tops, cut into 1-inch pieces**

Combine sirloin in medium bowl with soy sauce, white wine, cornstarch, ginger, sugar, garlic, and sesame oil. Allow to marinate at room temperature 1 hour or all day in the refrigerator.

Preheat browning dish on HIGH for 5 to 7 minutes (LW 6 to 8 minutes) or according to manufacturer's instructions. Remove dish from oven, using pot holders, and add peanut oil, meat, and marinade. To prevent sticking, move meat around dish with wooden spoon. Microwave, **uncovered,** on HIGH for 2 minutes (LW 2¼ minutes). **Stir,** add mushrooms and scallions, **cover,** and microwave on HIGH for 3 to 5 minutes (LW 3½ to 6 minutes) or until meat and mushrooms are tender. Let **stand, covered,** for 3 minutes before serving.

Troubleshooting: If covered browning dish isn't available, use 2-quart flat casserole dish and eliminate preheating time and peanut oil, but be aware that meat will not have a fried effect. Without peanut oil, each serving will have 50 fewer calories.

Suggestion: Serve over ½ cup cooked long-grain rice and add 70 calories per serving.

For less restricted diets: If you're not watching your salt intake, substitute regular soy sauce, which adds 60 mg sodium per serving.

FOR EACH SERVING:
170 calories
139 mg sodium
40 mg cholesterol
8 g fat

Chicken with Pineapple and Almonds

SERVES 4

EQUIPMENT:	10-inch covered browning dish, small bowl
COOKING TIME:	12 to 16 minutes (Low Wattage ovens 14 to 19¼ minutes)
STANDING TIME:	3 minutes
NUTRITIONAL PROFILE:	low calories, low sodium, low cholesterol

- 2 **tablespoons peanut oil**
- 1 **teaspoon minced fresh garlic**
- ½ **teaspoon finely minced fresh ginger**
- 1 **pound boneless and skinless chicken breasts, with excess fat removed, sliced into thin 1-inch strips**
- 3 **cups chopped bok choy**
- 1 **cup (about 4 ounces) sliced fresh mushrooms**
- ½ **cup low-sodium chicken broth or homemade chicken stock (page 44)**
- 1½ **tablespoons white wine**
- ½ **teaspoon Parsley Patch Garlicsaltless herb blend**
- 1 **tablespoon cornstarch**
- 2 **teaspoons low-salt soy sauce**
- 1½ **teaspoons sugar**
- 4 **unsweetened canned or fresh pineapple slices**
- ¼ **cup unsalted almonds**

Preheat browning dish on HIGH for 5 to 7 minutes (LW 6 to 8 minutes) or according to manufacturer's instructions. Using pot holders, remove hot dish from oven and add oil, swirling to coat dish. Immediately add garlic and ginger, **stirring** with wooden spoon. Add chicken strips, stirring to prevent sticking. **Cover** and microwave on HIGH for 3 minutes (LW 3½ minutes). **Stir** and add bok choy and mushrooms. **Cover** and cook on HIGH for 3 to 4 minutes (LW 3½ to 4¾ minutes) or until vegetables are tender-crisp.

In small bowl, whisk together broth, wine, herb blend, cornstarch, soy sauce, and sugar until well blended. Pour sauce over chicken and vegetables, **stir, cover,** and cook on HIGH for 4 to 6 minutes (LW 4¾ to 7½ minutes) or until sauce is hot. Add pineapple and almonds, **stirring** to combine, and microwave, **uncovered,** for 2 to 3 minutes (LW 2¼ to 3½ minutes) or until hot and bubbly. Let **stand** for 3 minutes before serving.

Troubleshooting: If you don't have a covered browning dish, substitute a 2- or 3-quart casserole dish and omit preheating and oil. Be aware that garlic and ginger flavors will not blend as well and that each serving will have 50 fewer calories when omitting oil.

Suggestion: Serve each portion over ½ cup cooked long-grain rice, which adds 70 calories per serving.

For less restricted diets: If you're not watching your salt intake, substitute regular chicken broth, which adds 113 mg sodium per serving, and regular soy sauce, which adds 60 mg sodium per serving.

FOR EACH SERVING:
316 calories
155 mg sodium
63 mg cholesterol
12 g fat

Sweet and Sour Fish Combination

SERVES 4

EQUIPMENT:	deep 3-quart casserole dish, 4-cup glass measure
COOKING TIME:	12 to 17 minutes (Low Wattage ovens 14¼ to 20½ minutes)
STANDING TIME:	3 minutes
NUTRITIONAL PROFILE:	low calories, low sodium, low cholesterol

1   tablespoon peanut oil
1   teaspoon finely minced garlic

1   teaspoon finely minced fresh ginger
1   green bell pepper, cut into ½-inch squares
1   carrot, thinly sliced on diagonal
1   medium onion, cut into ¾-inch pieces
½   pound fresh bay scallops
¼   pound scrod fillets, cut into 1-inch squares
¼   pound fresh crabmeat
1   cup low-sodium chicken broth or homemade chicken
    stock (page 44)
4   tablespoons rice wine vinegar
4   tablespoons sugar
1   teaspoon low-salt soy sauce
¼   teaspoon freshly ground pepper
1   tablespoon white wine
2   tablespoons cornstarch
3   unsweetened canned or fresh pineapple slices, cut
    into ¾-inch pieces
6   maraschino cherries

Place oil, garlic, ginger, green bell pepper, carrot, and onion in casserole dish. **Cover** with lid or plastic wrap, pulling back one corner to vent steam. (If dish is flat-bottomed, elevate on an inverted saucer.) Place on turntable if available. **Microwave** on HIGH for 4 to 6 minutes (LW 4¾ to 7½ minutes) or until vegetables are tender-crisp. Carefully fold in scallops, scrod, and crabmeat. **Cover** and cook on HIGH for 3 to 4 minutes (LW 3½ to 4¾ minutes) or until scallops are opaque.

In glass measure, whisk together broth, vinegar, sugar, soy sauce, pepper, wine, and cornstarch until well blended. Add pineapple and cherries to fish and cover with sauce, carefully stirring together. Microwave, **uncovered,** on HIGH for 5 to 7 minutes (LW 6 to 8¼ minutes) or until sauce thickens and fish is completely cooked, carefully **stirring** every 2 minutes. (**Rotate** dish ½ turn when stirring if not using turntable.) Let **stand** for 3 minutes before serving.

Troubleshooting: Forgetting to whisk sauce ingredients may cause sauce to be lumpy.

Suggestion: Serve over ½ cup cooked long-grain rice, which adds 70 calories per serving.

For less restricted diets: If you're not watching your salt intake, substitute regular chicken broth, which adds 225 mg sodium per serving, and regular soy sauce, which adds 30 mg sodium per serving.

FOR EACH SERVING:
260 calories
130 mg sodium
26 mg cholesterol
5 g fat

Fish

Crabmeat Bake

SERVES 4

EQUIPMENT:	2-quart round casserole dish, small bowl, custard cup
COOKING TIME:	16¼ to 20½ minutes (Low Wattage ovens 20 to 25¼ minutes)
STANDING TIME:	3 to 5 minutes
NUTRITIONAL PROFILE:	low calories, low sodium, low cholesterol

---

IMITATION CRABMEAT

Imitation crabmeat, also called *surimi* or *seafood chunks* or *sealegs*, is less expensive than real crabmeat, and as long as it contains only pollack or any other type of white fish it is almost as good a source of protein as regular crabmeat. Read labels carefully to be sure the product contains only fish products. Also watch for sugar and salt levels; depending on the brand, these can be substantial.

½ cup (about 2 large stalks) chopped celery
½ cup (about 1 medium) chopped onion
¼ cup (about ¼ large) chopped green bell pepper
1 garlic clove, minced
  dash dried dill
  dash cayenne pepper
2 tablespoons white wine
2 tablespoons all-purpose flour
1 cup skim milk
1 pound fresh crabmeat
½ cup (about 2 ounces) sliced fresh mushrooms
2 teaspoons fresh lemon juice (see box, page 124)
1 tablespoon chopped fresh parsley
1 tablespoon soft-spread margarine
¼ teaspoon Parsley Patch Popcorn herb blend
¼ cup plain dry bread crumbs
  paprika

In casserole dish, combine celery, onions, green bell pepper, garlic, dill, cayenne pepper, and wine. **Cover** dish with lid or plastic wrap, pulling back one corner to vent the steam. (If dish is flat-bottomed, **elevate** on an inverted saucer.) Place on turntable if available. Cook on HIGH for 5 minutes (LW 6 minutes) or until vegetables are tender-crisp, stirring after 3 minutes.

In small bowl, **whisk** flour into milk until completely combined. Stir milk mixture into vegetables. **Cover** and cook on HIGH for 2 to 4 minutes (LW 3 to 5 minutes) or until mixture is heated through and slightly thickened. Add crabmeat, mushrooms, lemon juice, and parsley. **Stir** and **cover**. Cook on HIGH for 7 to 9 minutes (LW 8 to 11 minutes) or until hot and bubbly, stirring every 3 minutes. (**Rotate** dish ½ turn when stirring if not using turntable.)

Place margarine and herb blend in custard cup and melt, **uncovered,** on HIGH for 25 to 35 seconds (LW 35 to 45 seconds). **Stir** in crumbs, top casserole with crumb mixture, and sprinkle paprika over all. Cook, **uncovered,** on HIGH for 2 minutes (LW 2½ minutes), until just hot. Let dish **stand** for 3 to 5 minutes.

Troubleshooting: Forgetting to whisk sauce may cause it to be lumpy. Always whisk sauces in the microwave.

To keep margarine from spattering oven, cover top of custard cup with a paper napkin or paper towel.

FOR EACH SERVING:
211 calories
141 mg sodium
50 mg cholesterol
4 g fat

Crabmeat-Stuffed Peppers

SERVES 4

EQUIPMENT:	2-quart casserole dish, 6-cup glass measure, 12 × 8-inch flat casserole dish
COOKING TIME:	18 to 22 minutes (Low Wattage ovens 21¼ to 25¾ minutes)
STANDING TIME:	3 minutes
NUTRITIONAL PROFILE:	low calories, low sodium, low cholesterol

4   large green bell peppers
¼   cup water
½   cup (about 1 medium) finely chopped onion
2   scallions, chopped
¼   cup (about 1 large stalk) chopped celery
2   garlic cloves, minced
1   cup (about 4 ounces) chopped fresh mushrooms
¼   cup white wine
⅛   teaspoon dried dill
1   pound chopped fresh crabmeat
1   cup cooked long-grain rice
1   teaspoon Parsley Patch It's A Dilly herb blend
1   large fresh tomato, chopped
4   lemon wedges for garnish

Wash peppers; remove tops, seeds, and pith. Place pepper shells open side up in casserole dish. Pour water into bottom of dish and **cover** with lid or plastic wrap, pulling back one corner to vent the steam. (If dish is flat-bottomed, **elevate** on an inverted saucer.) Microwave on HIGH for 2 minutes (LW 2¼ minutes). Remove peppers from dish and place upside down on paper towels to drain.

Place onion, scallions, celery, garlic, mushrooms, wine, dill, and crabmeat in glass measure. Microwave, **uncovered,** on HIGH for 6 to 8 minutes (LW 7 to 9¼ minutes) or until vegetables are tender.

Add rice and herb blend to seafood and vegetable mixture. Mix well and stuff mixture into drained pepper shells, mounding tops if necessary. Place filled shells in flat casserole dish, pour chopped fresh tomato around peppers, and **cover** again. Microwave on HIGH for 10 to 12 minutes (LW 12 to 14¼ minutes) or until peppers are tender, **rotating** dish ½ turn every 5 minutes. Let **stand, covered,** for 3 minutes and garnish each pepper top with a lemon wedge.

Suggestion: If your garden holds an abundance of peppers, remove the stems and seeds, wash, pat dry, and cut into small chunks or strips. Place cut-up peppers in an airtight container and freeze for use in cooking all winter.

FOR EACH SERVING:
225 calories
74 mg sodium
25 mg cholesterol
2 g fat

Fillet of Flounder Bake

SERVES 4

EQUIPMENT:	6-cup glass measure, 2-quart flat casserole dish, small bowl
COOKING TIME:	30¾ to 37 minutes (Low Wattage ovens 36½ to 43 minutes)
STANDING TIME:	rice—5 minutes; finished dish—1 to 2 minutes
NUTRITIONAL PROFILE:	low calories, low sodium, low cholesterol

2 tablespoons soft-spread margarine
2 tablespoons all-purpose flour
1 cup skim milk

   2 **cups hot water**
   1 **cup long-grain rice**
   1 **teaspoon soft-spread margarine**
   ¼ **pound (about 1 cup) fresh mushrooms, sliced**
   1 **tablespoon white wine**
   1 **tablespoon chopped pimiento**
   1 **tablespoon snipped fresh parsley**
   ½ **teaspoon Parsley Patch Popcorn herb blend**
   ⅛ **teaspoon freshly ground pepper**
   ¾ **cup plain yogurt**
   1¼ **pounds flounder fillets**
   paprika

Place 2 tablespoons margarine in glass measure and melt, **uncovered,** on HIGH for 45 to 55 seconds (LW 50 to 60 seconds). **Whisk** in flour, then milk, until well blended. Microwave, **uncovered,** on HIGH for 3 to 5 minutes (LW 3½ to 6 minutes), **whisking** every minute until thickened. Set aside to cool.

Place hot water, rice, and 1 teaspoon margarine in casserole dish and stir. (If dish is flat-bottomed, **elevate** on an inverted saucer.) Microwave, **uncovered,** on HIGH for 5 minutes (LW 6 minutes). **Stir, cover** dish with wax paper, and cook on 40 percent power or MEDIUM for 10 minutes (LW 12 minutes). Let **stand, covered,** for 5 minutes.

Place mushrooms and wine in small bowl and microwave, **uncovered,** on 60 percent power or MEDIUM-HIGH for 3 to 4 minutes (LW 3½ to 4¾ minutes) or until tender. **Drain.** Add mushrooms, pimiento, parsley, herb blend, and pepper to rice, stirring well. **Whisk** yogurt into cooled white sauce. Reserve ¾ cup and add the remainder to the rice mixture.

Arrange fish fillets over the rice, spread the reserved sauce over the fish, and sprinkle with paprika. **Cover** dish with plastic wrap, pulling back one corner to vent the steam, and microwave on HIGH for 9 to 11 minutes (LW 10¾ to 13¼ minutes) or until fish flakes easily, **rotating** dish ½ turn every 5 minutes. Let **stand, covered,** for 1 to 2 minutes before serving.

Troubleshooting: Forgetting to whisk sauce may cause it to be lumpy.

To keep pointed tips of fish from overcooking, tuck them underneath the fillets.

FOR EACH SERVING:
350 calories
99 mg sodium
31 mg cholesterol
13 g fat

Fish with Summer Vegetables

SERVES 4

EQUIPMENT: 9-inch glass baking dish, 6-cup glass measure, custard cup
COOKING TIME: 13½ to 17½ minutes (Low Wattage ovens 16½ to 21¼ minutes)
STANDING TIME: 1 to 2 minutes
NUTRITIONAL PROFILE: low calories, low sodium, low cholesterol

1¼ **pounds flounder, sole, or cod fillets**
¼ **cup white wine**
1 **medium onion, thinly sliced and separated into rings**
½ **medium green bell pepper, thinly sliced**
½ **cup (about 2 large stalks) thinly sliced celery**
1 **small tomato, seeded and diced**
1 **tablespoon snipped fresh parsley**
1 **tablespoon fresh lemon juice (see tip, page 124)**
¼ **teaspoon freshly ground pepper**

TOPPING
1 **tablespoon soft-spread margarine**
¼ **cup plain dry bread crumbs**
½ **teaspoon paprika**
½ **teaspoon Parsley Patch Popcorn herb blend**

Arrange fish pieces in baking dish, with the **thickest** portions to the outside of the dish and tips tucked under fillets. Combine wine, onion, green bell pepper, celery, tomato, and parsley in glass measure and cook, **uncovered,** on HIGH for 6 to 8 minutes (LW 7½ to 9½ minutes) or until tender-crisp. Blend in lemon juice and pepper. Pour sauce over fillets.

Place margarine in custard cup and melt, **uncovered,** on HIGH for 30 to 35 seconds (LW 40 to 60 seconds). **Stir** in crumbs, paprika, and herb blend. Sprinkle topping over fish and cover dish with wax paper. (If dish is flat-bottomed, **elevate** on an inverted saucer.) Place on turntable if available. Cook on HIGH for 7 to 9 minutes (LW 8¼ to 10¾ minutes) or until fish flakes easily with a fork. (**Rotate** dish ½ turn every 3 minutes if not using turntable.) Let **stand, covered,** for 1 to 2 minutes, before serving.

Troubleshooting: Be sure to tuck thin or pointed tips of fillets under center of the fillet to prevent the ends from overcooking.

To prevent margarine from spattering oven, cover custard cup with paper towel or napkin.

FOR EACH SERVING:
234 calories
110 mg sodium
75 mg cholesterol
6 g fat

HALIBUT

Usually found cut into steaks, halibut is white, firm, and mild-flavored. The nearly black outer skin and center bone are both easily removed once the fish is cooked. As with all fish in the microwave, cook halibut just until it begins to flake and let it finish cooking while it stands.

Garlic Baked Halibut

SERVES 4

EQUIPMENT:	1-cup glass measure, 12 × 8- or 13 × 9-inch flat baking dish
COOKING TIME:	12½ to 16½ minutes (Low Wattage ovens 14¾ to 19¾ minutes)
STANDING TIME:	5 minutes
NUTRITIONAL PROFILE:	low calories, low sodium, low cholesterol

2 tablespoons white wine
1 scallion, finely chopped
1 tablespoon minced garlic
2 tablespoons chopped fresh parsley
1 teaspoon paprika
4 ¾-inch-thick halibut steaks (about 1½ pounds)
½ teaspoon Parsley Patch Garlicsaltless herb blend
freshly ground pepper to taste
4 lemon slices

Place wine, scallions, garlic, parsley, and paprika in glass measure and microwave, **uncovered,** on HIGH for 2 to 3 minutes (LW 2½ to 3¾ minutes) or until scallions are tender.

Arrange halibut steaks in baking dish, with broader ends to the outside of the dish and smaller ends pointing toward the center. Spread ¼ of the vegetable mixture over each steak and sprinkle with herb blend and pepper. **Cover** dish with plastic wrap, pulling back one corner to vent the steam. (If dish is flat-bottomed, **elevate** on an inverted saucer.)

Microwave on 70 percent power or MEDIUM-HIGH for 7 to 9 minutes (LW 8¼ to 10¾ minutes) per pound, **rearranging** fish and **rotating** dish ½ turn every 5 minutes, until fish flakes. Let **stand, covered,** for 5 minutes and garnish each steak with a slice of lemon before serving.

FOR EACH SERVING:
156 calories
135 mg sodium
112 mg cholesterol
9 g fat

Halibut with Artichoke Sauce

SERVES 4

EQUIPMENT:	small bowl, 12 × 8- or 13 × 9-inch flat baking dish
COOKING TIME:	10½ to 13½ minutes (Low Wattage ovens 12¼ to 16 minutes)
STANDING TIME:	5 minutes
NUTRITIONAL PROFILE:	low calories, low sodium, low cholesterol

¼ **cup plain yogurt**
3 **scallions, chopped**
1 **14-ounce can artichoke hearts, drained and chopped**
1 **tablespoon fresh lemon juice (see box, page 124)**
½ **teaspoon garlic powder**
4 **¾-inch-thick halibut steaks (about 1½ pounds)**
4 **tablespoons chopped fresh parsley**

In small bowl, blend together yogurt, scallions, artichoke hearts, lemon juice, and garlic powder. Place halibut steaks in baking dish, with the broader ends to the outside of the dish and the smaller ends pointing toward the center. Spread ¼ of the yogurt mixture over each steak and **cover** the dish with wax paper. (If dish is flat-bottomed, **elevate** on an inverted saucer.)

Microwave on 70 percent power or MEDIUM-HIGH for 7 to 9 minutes (LW 8¼ to 10¾ minutes) per pound, **rearranging** fish and **rotating** dish ½ turn every 5 minutes, until fish flakes. Let **stand, covered,** for 5 minutes before serving. Garnish each steak with 1 tablespoon of the parsley.

FOR EACH SERVING:
174 calories
255 mg sodium
112 mg cholesterol
10 g fat

Halibut Italiano

SERVES 4

EQUIPMENT: 6-cup glass measure, custard cup, 12 × 8- or 13 × 9-inch baking dish

COOKING TIME: 16½ to 21½ minutes (Low Wattage ovens 19¾ to 25½ minutes)

STANDING TIME: 5 minutes

NUTRITIONAL PROFILE: low calories, low sodium, low cholesterol

1 **tablespoon minced garlic**
1 **medium onion, diced**
1 **medium green bell pepper, diced**
¼ **cup (about 1 ounce) sliced fresh mushrooms**
1 **15-ounce can low-sodium whole tomatoes, drained and chopped**
½ **teaspoon dried oregano**
½ **teaspoon dried basil**
1 **tablespoon chopped fresh parsley**
dash freshly ground pepper
½ **cup white wine**
1 **tablespoon all-purpose flour**
4 **¾-inch-thick halibut steaks (about 1½ pounds)**

Place garlic, onion, green bell pepper, mushrooms, chopped to-matoes, oregano, basil, parsley, and pepper in glass measure.

In custard cup, **whisk** wine and flour together. Stir wine mixture into vegetables. Microwave, **uncovered,** on HIGH for 6 to 8 minutes (LW 7½ to 9½ minutes) or until vegetables are tender-crisp, **stirring** every 2 minutes.

Place halibut steaks in baking dish with the broader ends to outside of the dish and smaller ends toward the center. Pour the vegetable mixture over steaks and **cover** dish with wax paper. (If dish is flat-bottomed, **elevate** on an inverted saucer.) Microwave on 70 percent power or MEDIUM-HIGH for 7 to 9 minutes (LW 8¼ to 10¾ minutes) per pound, **rearranging** steaks and **rotating** dish ½ turn every 5 minutes, until fish flakes. Let **stand, covered,** for 5 minutes before serving.

For less restricted diets: If you're not watching your salt intake, substitute regular canned tomatoes, which add 173 mg sodium per serving.

FOR EACH SERVING:
198 calories
152 mg sodium
112 mg cholesterol
9 g fat

Lobster Creole

Even though this recipe has a moderate level of cholesterol, not all cholesterol is bad. The kind found in lobster is not a form that clogs the arteries, so don't be concerned about eating lobster.

SERVES 4

EQUIPMENT:	6-cup glass measure, 2-quart round casserole dish
COOKING TIME:	21 to 29 minutes (Low Wattage ovens 25 to 34 minutes)
STANDING TIME:	3 minutes
NUTRITIONAL PROFILE:	low calories, low sodium, moderate cholesterol

2 tablespoons burgundy
1 garlic clove, minced
1 medium onion, chopped
¼ cup (about ¼ large) minced green bell pepper
¼ cup (about 1 large stalk) minced celery
1 28-ounce can low-sodium crushed tomatoes
1 6-ounce can low-sodium tomato paste
½ teaspoon dried oregano
½ teaspoon dried basil
½ teaspoon Parsley Patch All-Purpose herb blend
1 tablespoon snipped fresh parsley
pinch cayenne pepper
pinch dried rosemary
1 pound fresh lobster meat, cubed

Place wine, garlic, onion, green pepper, and celery in glass measure. Microwave, **uncovered,** on HIGH for 4 to 6 minutes (LW 4¾ to 7½ minutes) or until vegetables are tender-crisp, **stirring** every 2 minutes.

In casserole dish, combine crushed tomatoes, tomato paste, oregano, basil, herb blend, parsley, cayenne pepper, and rosemary, stirring to combine. Fold vegetable mixture into tomatoes and **cover** dish with lid or plastic wrap, pulling back one corner to vent the steam. (If dish is flat-bottomed, **elevate** on an inverted saucer.) Place on turntable if available. Microwave on 80 percent power or MEDIUM-HIGH for 12 to 15 minutes (LW 14¼ to 17 minutes) or until bubbly and flavors blend, stirring every 5 minutes. (**Rotate** dish ½ turn when stirring if not using turntable.)

Add lobster, **stir, cover,** and cook on 80 percent power or MEDIUM-HIGH for 5 to 8 minutes (LW 6 to 9½ minutes) or until lobster is firm and opaque, stirring every 5 minutes. (**Rotate** dish ½ turn when stirring if not using turntable.)

Let **stand, covered,** 3 minutes before serving.

Suggestions: Serve each portion over 1 cup cooked eggless linguine or spaghetti, which adds 210 calories per serving.

For less restricted diets: If you're not watching your salt intake, substitute regular crushed tomatoes, which add 313 mg sodium per serving, and regular tomato paste, which adds 24 mg sodium per serving.

FOR EACH SERVING:
191 calories
93 mg sodium
85 mg cholesterol
2 g fat

SALMON

Salmon is an excellent source of high-quality protein. The bones have a considerable amount of calcium, vitamins A and D, iron, zinc, and magnesium. Salmon is a good source of Omega-3, the fat that studies show may prevent the development of heart disease. Even though it contains cholesterol, the fat in this form does not clog the arteries; in fact, it seems to have the opposite effect.

Salmon Cakes

SERVES 4

EQUIPMENT:	meat or bacon rack, medium mixing bowl, 9-inch glass pie plate
COOKING TIME:	18 to 21 minutes (Low Wattage ovens 21½ to 25 minutes)
STANDING TIME:	salmon—2 minutes; cakes—5 minutes
NUTRITIONAL PROFILE:	low calories, low sodium, low cholesterol

1   pound ¾-inch-thick fresh salmon steaks
½   cup (about 1 medium) chopped onion
2   egg whites, well beaten
⅛   teaspoon freshly ground pepper
2   tablespoons skim milk
1   teaspoon fresh lemon juice (see box, page 124)
½   cup plain dry bread crumbs
1   teaspoon snipped fresh parsley

Place salmon on meat rack with **thickest** portions to the outside of the dish. Cook on 70 percent power or MEDIUM-HIGH for 6 to 7 minutes (LW 7¼ to 8¼ minutes) or until fish flakes easily with a fork. Let salmon **stand** for 2 minutes, then flake into mixing bowl, removing skin and bones. Add all remaining ingredients and mix well. Shape into 4 uniformly sized cakes and place in a circle in pie plate. Cover plate with wax paper. (If dish is flat-bottomed, **elevate** on an inverted saucer.) Place on a turntable if available. Cook on 70 percent power or MEDIUM-HIGH for 12 to 14 minutes (LW 14¼ to 16¾ minutes) or until center is firm. (**Rotate** dish ½ turn after 6 minutes if not using turntable.) Let **stand, covered,** for 5 minutes and serve with horseradish sauce (recipe follows).

FOR EACH SERVING:
226 calories
152 mg sodium
40 mg cholesterol
8 g fat

HORSERADISH SAUCE
MAKES 1¼ CUPS, SERVES 6

EQUIPMENT: small bowl
NUTRITIONAL PROFILE: low calories, low sodium, low cholesterol

1 cup plain yogurt
¼ cup well-drained white horseradish
1 tablespoon fresh lemon juice (see box, page 124)
1 tablespoon sugar
1 scallion, chopped

Mix together all ingredients in small bowl. Cover and refrigerate for 1 hour so that flavors can blend. **Stir** well before serving.

PER SERVING:
35 calories
30 mg sodium
3 mg cholesterol
trace fat

Salmon Pie
SERVES 6

EQUIPMENT: meat rack, 1-quart round casserole dish, medium mixing bowl, 9-inch round glass pie plate
COOKING TIME: 25 to 32 minutes (Low Wattage ovens 30 to 37¾ minutes)
STANDING TIME: 7 minutes
NUTRITIONAL PROFILE: low calories, low sodium, low cholesterol

1 pound fresh or frozen salmon steaks
2 tablespoons white wine
1 cup (about 1 large) chopped onion
½ cup (about ½ large) chopped red bell pepper
½ cup (about ½ large) chopped green bell pepper
1 cup (about 4 ounces) sliced fresh mushrooms

½ **cup skim milk**
2 **egg whites, slightly beaten**
1 **cup plain dry bread crumbs**
¼ **teaspoon garlic powder**
⅛ **teaspoon freshly ground pepper**
1 **teaspoon fresh lemon juice (see box, page 124)**
2 **tablespoons snipped fresh parsley**

Place salmon on meat rack, with the **thickest** portions to the outside of the dish, and microwave on 70 percent power or MEDIUM-HIGH for 6 to 7 minutes (LW 7¼ to 8¼ minutes) or until fish flakes easily with a fork. Let **stand** for 2 minutes.

In casserole dish, combine wine, ½ cup of onion, red and green peppers, and mushrooms. **Cover** with lid or plastic wrap, pulling back one corner to vent the steam. (If dish is flat-bottomed, **elevate** on an inverted saucer.) Place on turntable if available. Microwave on HIGH for 5 to 7 minutes (LW 6 to 8 minutes) or until vegetables are tender-crisp, **stirring** once during cooking time. (**Rotate** dish ½ turn when stirring if not using turntable.) Drain and set aside.

Flake salmon into mixing bowl, removing the bones and skin. Blend in milk, egg whites, bread crumbs, remaining ½ cup of onion, garlic powder, pepper, lemon juice, and parsley. Spread ½ of the salmon mixture in the bottom of pie plate and top with ½ of the vegetables. Repeat with a layer of salmon and end with a layer of vegetables. **Cover** with wax paper and microwave on 70 percent power or MEDIUM-HIGH for 14 to 18 minutes (LW 16¾ to 21½ minutes) or until the center is firm. (**Rotate** dish ½ turn every 7 minutes if not using turntable.) Let **stand, covered,** for 5 minutes, then cut into wedges and serve with horseradish sauce (recipe on facing page).

Suggestions: For an attractive presentation, garnish each wedge with a lemon slice and sprinkle with fresh parsley.

FOR EACH SERVING:
205 calories
156 mg sodium
26 mg cholesterol
6 g fat

SCROD

Do you know that fillets cut from small cod fish are called *scrod*? My curiosity got the better of me, and I decided to see just what scrod was and how well it would perform in the microwave. My first mistake was assuming that a fillet meant a piece of fish completely free of bones. Scrod experiment number one produced a lovely-looking dish with great flavor—wonderful, until I cut into the center of the fillet to find a mass of bone. Having had a scary experience with a fish bone as a child, I hate bones in fish.

Fortunately there's a solution. All scrod has one main rib of bone stretching from the broad end of the piece about halfway into the center. To bone the fish, cut along the side of the bone area, which you can feel with your fingers, and remove the entire section, as the bones go through the entire piece. The finished boned piece resembles a horseshoe.

Remember, as with any fish, to place the thicker portions to the outside of the dish and the narrower areas toward the center. The microwave cooks from the outside to the center, giving the thicker portions that sit along the outside edges longer cooking time.

Baked Scrod Leonardo

SERVES 4

EQUIPMENT:	9-inch casserole dish, 4-cup glass measure, custard cup
COOKING TIME:	9 to 11 minutes (Low Wattage ovens 11 to 14¾ minutes)
STANDING TIME:	2 minutes
NUTRITIONAL PROFILE:	low calories, low sodium, low cholesterol

1¼ **pounds scrod or cod fillets, cut into 4 serving size pieces**
½ **teaspoon paprika**
2 **tablespoons corn or soybean oil**
1 **garlic clove, crushed**
½ **teaspoon Parsley Patch Lemon Pepper herb blend**

¾ **teaspoon dried oregano**
1 **teaspoon fresh lemon juice (see box, page 124)**
½ **cup white wine**

TOPPING
1 **tablespoon soft-spread margarine**
¼ **cup plain dry bread crumbs**
1 **tablespoon snipped fresh parsley**
½ **teaspoon Parsley Patch Popcorn herb blend**

Arrange scrod pieces in casserole dish with the **thickest** portions to the outside of the dish and thin ends tucked underneath the piece to prevent overcooking. Sprinkle with paprika and set aside.

Whisk together oil, garlic, Lemon Pepper blend, oregano, lemon juice, and white wine in glass measure. **Cover** with plastic wrap, pulling back one corner to vent the steam. Cook on HIGH for 1½ to 2½ minutes (LW 2 to 3 minutes) or until mixture comes to a boil, whisking once. Pour sauce over fish.

Place margarine in custard cup and microwave, **uncovered,** on HIGH for 30 to 40 seconds (LW 45 to 60 seconds) or until melted. Stir in crumbs, parsley, and herb blend, mixing to combine. Sprinkle over fish. **Cover** dish with wax paper. (If dish is flat-bottomed, **elevate** on an inverted saucer.) Place on a turntable if available. Cook on HIGH for 7 to 9 minutes (LW 8¼ to 10¾ minutes) or until fish flakes easily with a fork. (**Rotate** dish ½ turn every 4 minutes if not using a turntable.) Let **stand, covered,** for 2 minutes before serving.

Troubleshooting: To prevent margarine from spattering, cover custard cup with paper towel or napkin.

FOR EACH SERVING:
204 calories
159 mg sodium
82 mg cholesterol
14 g fat

```
COOKING WITH WINE
```

Cooking with wine is a healthy alternative to using fat in sauces.
The alcohol calories evaporate during cooking, while the flavor
and liquid remain. Wine has fewer calories than fat sources and
no cholesterol.

Spanish Sole

SERVES 4

EQUIPMENT: 9-inch round casserole dish, 4-cup glass measure

COOKING TIME: 18¼ to 23¼ minutes (Low Wattage ovens 21¼ to 28¾ minutes)

STANDING TIME: 1 to 2 minutes

NUTRITIONAL PROFILE: low calories, low sodium, low cholesterol

2   tablespoons white wine
½   cup (about ½ large) chopped red onion
½   cup (about ½ large) chopped green bell pepper
1   large fresh tomato, chopped
1   large garlic clove, minced
1   10-ounce package frozen peas, thawed
1¼   pounds fresh sole or flounder fillets
1   tablespoon soft-spread margarine
1   tablespoon white wine
2   tablespoons all-purpose flour
½   teaspoon Parsley Patch Popcorn herb blend
¼   teaspoon freshly ground pepper
1   cup skim milk
**   paprika**

In casserole dish, combine 2 tablespoons wine, onion, green
pepper, tomato, and garlic. **Cover** dish with lid or plastic wrap,
pulling back one corner to vent the steam. (If dish is flat-bottomed,
elevate on an inverted saucer.) Place on turntable if available.

Microwave on HIGH for 4½ to 5½ minutes (LW 5¼ to 6½ minutes) or until vegetables are tender-crisp, **stirring** after 3 minutes.

Layer peas over the vegetables. Arrange fish fillets over peas, with the broader ends of the fillets to the outside of the dish and the thinner sections toward the center of the dish, **tucking** any pointed ends under the fillet.

Place margarine in glass measure and melt, **uncovered,** on HIGH for 40 to 50 seconds (LW 45 to 60 seconds). **Whisk** in wine, flour, herb blend, and pepper. **Whisk** in milk until completely combined. Microwave, **uncovered,** on HIGH for 4 to 6 minutes (LW 4½ to 7 minutes), whisking every minute, until thickened.

Spoon sauce over fish and sprinkle with paprika. **Cover** again and cook on HIGH for 9 to 11 minutes (LW 10¾ to 14¼ minutes) or until fish flakes. (**Rotate** dish ½ turn every 5 minutes if not using turntable.) Let **stand, covered,** for 1 to 2 minutes before serving.

Troubleshooting: Always use a whisk rather than a fork when making sauces in the microwave to ensure they are lump-free.

If peas are frozen, place paper-covered box on 2 layers of paper towels and microwave on HIGH for 2 to 3 minutes (LW 2¼ to 3¼ minutes) or until thawed.

FOR EACH SERVING:
308 calories
137 mg sodium
31 mg cholesterol
12 g fat

SWORDFISH AND SHARK

Shark steaks are very similar in appearance to swordfish, and many times mako shark is illegally substituted for the more expensive swordfish. The meat of swordfish is pink, tan, or off-white with a maroonish dark meat section. Mako shark very closely resembles swordfish in color, so how does one tell them apart?

One test is to feel the skin. The skin of swordfish will feel smooth, while the grain of shark skin will feel rough, like sandpaper. The light meat of swordfish steaks will have definite eyelike whorls that are not present in shark steaks, and the connective tissue between the meat and skin in shark is thicker.

Although shark and swordfish have a higher fat content than most fish, recent studies have shown this form of fat does not clog the arteries but may in fact help to clear them. If you are watching your cholesterol, shark and swordfish are excellent choices.

Swordfish or Mako Shark Steaks

SERVES 4

EQUIPMENT:	12 × 8- or 13 × 9-inch baking dish
COOKING TIME:	7 to 9 minutes per pound (Low Wattage ovens 8¼ to 10¾ minutes per pound)
STANDING TIME:	3 minutes
NUTRITIONAL PROFILE:	low calories, low sodium, low cholesterol

**4 6-ounce fresh swordfish or shark steaks
juice of 1 small lemon (see box, page 124)**

Place fish steaks in baking dish, with the **thicker** or denser portions to the outside of the dish and the thinner areas to the center. Cover steaks evenly with lemon juice. **Cover** the dish with wax paper. (If dish is flat-bottomed, **elevate** on an inverted saucer.)

Microwave on 70 percent power or MEDIUM-HIGH for 7 to 9 minutes per pound (LW 8¼ to 10¾ minutes per pound), **rearranging** the pieces halfway through cooking time and **rotating** dish ½ turn, until the fish flakes easily with a fork. Let **stand, covered,** for 3 minutes before serving.

Troubleshooting: When rearranging, bring the less cooked areas to the outside of the dish and the areas along the edge of the dish into the center.

FOR EACH SERVING:
173 calories
133 mg sodium
112 mg cholesterol
6 g fat

Shark with Spanish Sauce

SERVES 4

EQUIPMENT:	flat 12 × 8- or 13 × 9-inch baking dish, 6-cup glass measure
COOKING TIME:	14½ to 18½ minutes (Low Wattage ovens 16¾ to 21 minutes)
STANDING TIME:	3 minutes
NUTRITIONAL PROFILE:	low calories, low sodium, low cholesterol

4   **¾-inch-thick 6-ounce shark or swordfish steaks**
3   **tablespoons white wine**
1   **small garlic clove, minced**
2   **scallions, diced**
½   **medium green bell pepper, cut in julienne**
1   **15-ounce can low-sodium whole tomatoes, drained and chopped**
½   **teaspoon dried basil**
    dash Parsley Patch Lemon Pepper herb blend
1   **tablespoon capers**

Place steaks in baking dish, with the **broader** parts to the outside of the dish, and set aside.

Place wine, garlic, scallions, and green bell pepper in glass measure. Microwave, **uncovered,** on HIGH for 4 to 5 minutes (LW 4¾ to 6 minutes) or until green pepper is tender-crisp. Add chopped tomatoes, basil, and herb blend, mixing to combine. Pour tomato mixture over fish steaks and sprinkle with capers. **Cover** with wax paper. (If dish is flat-bottomed, **elevate** on an inverted saucer.)

Microwave on 70 percent power or MEDIUM-HIGH for 7 to 9 minutes per pound (LW 8 to 10 minutes per pound), **rearranging** fish halfway through cooking time and **rotating** dish ½ turn every 5 minutes until fish flakes easily when tested with a fork. Let **stand, covered,** for 3 minutes, before serving.

For less restricted diets: If you're not watching your salt intake, substitute regular tomatoes, which add 172 mg sodium per serving.

FOR EACH SERVING:
201 calories
150 mg sodium
112 mg cholesterol
6 g fat

CANNED TUNA

Tuna is very tasty, whether packed in oil or water. Water-packed tuna has 100 fewer calories than oil-packed. Although canned fish products usually have high levels of salt, tuna packed in springwater has an acceptable level of 70 mg sodium per serving. Check the various brands of tuna for springwater and sodium content before purchasing.

Tuna-Stuffed Mushrooms

Want a quick dinner with a reduced calorie count that not only looks but tastes delicious? You must admit, there is just no comparison between these tasty morsels and a tuna sandwich on thinly sliced bread.

SERVES 4

EQUIPMENT:	paper plate
COOKING TIME:	2 to 3 minutes (Low Wattage ovens 2¼ to 3½ minutes)
STANDING TIME:	1 minute
NUTRITIONAL PROFILE:	low calories, low sodium, low cholesterol

1 6½-ounce can springwater-packed tuna
2 tablespoons (about ½ large stalk) minced celery

1   teaspoon (about ¼ very small) minced onion
2   tablespoons plain yogurt
     freshly ground pepper to taste
¼   teaspoon Parsley Patch Popcorn herb blend
12   large fresh stuffing mushrooms
2   slices Muenster, Cheddar, or Swiss cheese, cut into
     12 squares

Drain, flake, and combine tuna with celery, onion, yogurt, pepper, and herb blend. Carefully remove stems from mushrooms and reserve for another use. Wipe each mushroom cap clean with a damp paper towel. Stuff and mound the tuna salad into the mushroom caps and cover each with a square of cheese.

Place stuffed mushrooms on a paper plate covered with 2 **layers** of paper towels and **elevate** on an inverted saucer. Microwave on HIGH for 2 to 3 minutes (LW 2¼ to 3½ minutes), let **stand** for 1 minute, and serve with sliced tomatoes and lettuce.

Troubleshooting: Mushrooms are like sponges and will absorb water if washed under running water, so just wipe each cap carefully with a damp paper towel.

FOR EACH SERVING:
130 calories
118 mg sodium
40 mg cholesterol
6 g fat

New England Tuna Casserole

SERVES 4

EQUIPMENT:	small and medium bowls, 2-quart round casserole dish
COOKING TIME:	17½ to 22¾ minutes (Low Wattage ovens 21½ to 26½ minutes)
STANDING TIME:	3 minutes
NUTRITIONAL PROFILE:	low calories, low sodium, low cholesterol

1 **cup (4 slices) toasted small cubes whole wheat or white bread, tightly packed**
1 **teaspoon Parsley Patch All-Purpose herb blend**
1 **cup skim milk**
1 **10-ounce paper-covered box frozen peas and carrots**
2 **tablespoons soft-spread margarine**
1 **tablespoon white wine**
½ **cup (about ½ large) chopped green bell pepper**
½ **cup (about ½ large) chopped red onion**
½ **cup (about 2 large stalks) finely chopped celery**
2 **tablespoons snipped fresh parsley**
1 **6½-ounce can springwater-packed tuna**
½ **cup plain yogurt**
¼ **teaspoon freshly ground pepper**

TOPPING
1 **tablespoon soft-spread margarine**
¼ **cup plain dry bread crumbs**
½ **teaspoon paprika**
¼ **teaspoon Parsley Patch Garlicsaltless herb blend**

Place toasted bread cubes in medium bowl. Sprinkle All-Purpose herb blend over bread cubes and cover with milk. Let dish **stand** for 15 minutes or until milk has been absorbed.

Place **paper-covered** box of peas and carrots on 2 layers of paper towels and microwave on HIGH for 6 to 7 minutes (LW 7 to 8 minutes).

Combine 2 tablespoons margarine, wine, green bell pepper, onion, celery, and parsley in small bowl and **cover** with plastic wrap, pulling back one corner to vent the steam. (If dish is flat-bottomed, **elevate** on an inverted saucer.) Cook on HIGH for 5 to 7 minutes (LW 6 to 8 minutes) or until vegetables are tender-crisp, **stirring** after 4 minutes.

In casserole dish, mash tuna with fork. Stir in yogurt, pepper, soaked bread, vegetable mixture, and peas and carrots.

In small bowl, melt 1 tablespoon margarine, **uncovered,** on HIGH for 30 to 45 seconds (LW 60 seconds) or until melted. Stir in bread crumbs, paprika, and Garlicsaltless herb blend. Sprinkle topping over casserole and **cover** with lid or vented plastic wrap. (If dish is flat-bottomed, **elevate** on an inverted saucer.) Place on turntable if available.

Microwave on HIGH for 6 to 8 minutes (LW 7½ to 9½ minutes) or until heated through. (**Rotate** dish ¼ turn every 3 minutes if not using turntable.) Let **stand, covered,** for 3 minutes before serving.

Troubleshooting: Always place paper-covered box or bag of frozen vegetables on 2 layers of paper towels. They will absorb any excess moisture and keep the inks in the wrapper from staining the oven floor.

FOR EACH SERVING:
220 calories
260 mg sodium
25 mg cholesterol
7 g fat

FISH TIPS

One of the most common mistakes made when microwaving fish is overcooking. Fish becomes dry and tough when overdone and should be cooked just until it flakes. Raw fish is relatively firm and will not flake easily when prodded with a fork, but when cooked it flakes with no effort. Unlike red meats, fish contains very little connective tissue and does not require long, slow cooking—it's tender even when it's raw.

Seafood-Stuffed Artichokes

Are you one of those people who love stuffed artichokes, as long as someone else has prepared them? It's a lot easier than you think.

SERVES 4

EQUIPMENT:	round baking dish, 6-cup glass measure, grapefruit spoon
COOKING TIME:	19 to 25 minutes (LW 23¼ to 29¾ minutes)
STANDING TIME:	3 minutes
NUTRITIONAL PROFILE:	low calories, low sodium, low cholesterol

> 4 **artichokes**
> ½ **cup water**
> 2 **tablespoons white wine**
> 1 **cup crab or lobster meat, fresh or frozen (not canned)**
> ¼ **cup (about 1 small) chopped onion**
> ¼ **cup (about 1 ounce) chopped mushrooms**
> ¼ **cup (about 1 large stalk) chopped celery**
> 1 **garlic clove, minced**
> 1 **teaspoon fresh lemon juice (see box, page 124)**
> ¾ **cup plain dry bread crumbs**
> ½ **teaspoon Parsley Patch Garlicsaltless herb blend**

Prepare artichokes according to directions on page 63. Place stem side up in baking dish and add ¼ cup of the water. **Cover** with plastic wrap, pulling back one corner to vent the steam. (If dish is flat-bottomed, **elevate** on an inverted saucer.) Place on a turntable if available. Microwave on HIGH for 6 to 8 minutes (LW 7½ to 9½ minutes) or until just tender. (If not using a turntable, **rotate** dish ½ turn after 3 minutes.) Once tender, remove from baking dish and set aside.

Combine wine, seafood, onion, mushrooms, celery, and garlic in a glass measure. Microwave on HIGH for 6 to 8 minutes (LW 7½ to 9½ minutes) or until vegetables are tender. Add lemon juice, bread crumbs, and herb blend. Open center of each artichoke to form a well. Using a grapefruit spoon, remove the fuzzy center and some of the center leaves to form a hollow for the stuffing. Stuff each artichoke and stand in round baking dish.

Add the remaining ¼ cup of water to dish and **cover** with vented plastic wrap. Place on a turntable if available. Microwave on HIGH for 7 to 9 minutes (LW 8¼ to 10¾ minutes) or until the bottom of the artichoke is tender and the leaves can easily be removed. (If not using a turntable, **rotate** dish ½ turn after 4 minutes.) Let **stand, covered,** for 3 minutes before serving.

FOR EACH SERVING:
185 calories
133 mg sodium
12 mg cholesterol
2 g fat

Seafood-Stuffed Fillets with Dill Sauce

SERVES 6

EQUIPMENT: 9-inch round glass pie plate or casserole dish

COOKING TIME: 5 to 8 minutes (Low Wattage ovens 6 to 9½ minutes)

STANDING TIME: 3 minutes

NUTRITIONAL PROFILE: low calories, low sodium, low cholesterol

- ½ **pound fresh crab or lobster meat, cut into 1-inch chunks**
- 1 **pound fresh fish fillets (flounder or sole works well)**
- ½ **cup plain yogurt**
- ¼ **cup white wine**
- ¼ **teaspoon dried dill**
- 1 **teaspoon Parsley Patch It's A Dilly herb blend**
  juice of ½ fresh lemon (see box, page 124)
  lemon slices

Place several chunks of crab or lobster in center of each fillet. Fold ends of fillet over chunks, turn package over, and place in dish, arranged like the spokes of a wagon wheel. (Secure with round-edged toothpicks if necessary.)

Whisk together yogurt, wine, dill, herb blend, and lemon juice until smooth and spoon evenly over fillets. **Cover** dish with wax paper. (If dish is flat-bottomed, **elevate** on an inverted saucer.) Place on turntable if available. Cook on HIGH for 5 to 8 minutes (LW 6 to 9½ minutes) or until fish flakes easily. (If not using turntable, **rotate** dish ½ turn every 2 minutes.) Let **stand, covered,** for 3 minutes and garnish with lemon slices before serving.

FOR EACH SERVING:
133 calories
48 mg sodium
39 mg cholesterol
5 g fat

Hot Seafood Salad

Except for shrimp, seafood is a low-cholesterol entree choice. The fat found in shrimp is one of those nasty artery cloggers. Shrimp should generally be avoided; if you're crazy about it, reserve it, in small quantities, for special occasions.

SERVES 4

EQUIPMENT:	2-quart round casserole dish, 2 small bowls
COOKING TIME:	14¾ to 20 minutes (Low Wattage ovens 17 to 22 minutes)
STANDING TIME:	3 minutes
NUTRITIONAL PROFILE:	low calories, low sodium, low cholesterol

2 tablespoons white wine
1 cup (about 4 large stalks) thinly sliced celery, cut on the diagonal
½ cup (about ½ large) chopped red onion
¼ pound (about 1 cup) fresh mushrooms, sliced
1 tablespoon chopped pimiento
¼ pound cooked shrimp, cut in half lengthwise
¾ pound fresh crabmeat, cut into 1-inch chunks
1 cup plain yogurt
1 tablespoon fresh lemon juice (see box, page 124)
½ teaspoon Worcestershire sauce
¼ teaspoon freshly ground pepper
½ teaspoon Parsley Patch All-Purpose herb blend

TOPPING
1 tablespoon soft-spread margarine
¼ cup plain dry bread crumbs
½ teaspoon paprika
½ teaspoon onion powder
fresh parsley sprigs

Combine wine, celery, red onion, mushrooms, and pimientos in casserole dish. **Cover** with lid or plastic wrap, pulling back one corner to vent the steam. (If dish is flat-bottomed, **elevate** on an inverted saucer.) Place on turntable if available. Cook on HIGH for

7 to 9 minutes (LW 8 to 10 minutes) or until vegetables are tender-crisp, **stirring** every 3 minutes. Stir in shrimp and crabmeat. In small bowl, blend yogurt, lemon juice, Worcestershire sauce, pepper, and herb blend together. Add to seafood mixture and stir well.

Place margarine in another small bowl and melt, **uncovered,** on HIGH for 45 to 55 seconds (LW 60 seconds). Stir in crumbs, paprika, and onion powder. Sprinkle topping over casserole and **cover** with wax paper. Cook on 80 percent power or MEDIUM-HIGH for 7 to 10 minutes (LW 8 to 11 minutes) or until hot and bubbly. (**Rotate** dish ¼ turn every 3 minutes if not using turntable.) Let **stand, covered,** for 3 minutes and garnish each serving with a sprig of parsley.

Troubleshooting: To prevent margarine from spattering oven, cover dish with a paper towel.

Suggestion: If you are watching your cholesterol, avoid the shrimp and use a full pound of crabmeat instead.

FOR EACH SERVING:
193 calories
203 mg sodium
90 mg cholesterol
4 g fat

Seafood Gumbo

SERVES 6

EQUIPMENT:	deep 3-quart casserole dish
COOKING TIME:	32 to 40 minutes (Low Wattage ovens 38¼ to 48 minutes)
STANDING TIME:	5 minutes
NUTRITIONAL PROFILE:	low calories, low sodium, low cholesterol

1 **pound fresh okra, washed, stemmed, and cut uniformly into ½-inch slices**
1 **medium onion, diced**
¼ **cup (about ¼ large) diced green bell pepper**
1 **garlic clove, minced**
¼ **cup (about 1 large stalk) diced celery**
2 **tablespoons white wine**
1 **28-ounce can low-sodium crushed tomatoes**
½ **pound fish fillets (sole, flounder, or scrod)**
½ **pound fresh crabmeat**
1 **teaspoon Parsley Patch All-Purpose herb blend**
1 **scallion, chopped**

Place okra, onion, green pepper, garlic, celery, and wine in casserole dish. **Cover** with lid or plastic wrap, pulling back one corner to vent the steam. (If dish is flat-bottomed, **elevate** on an inverted saucer.) Place on turntable if available.

Microwave on HIGH for 7 to 10 minutes (LW 8¼ to 12 minutes) or until vegetables are tender-crisp. (If not using turntable, **rotate** dish ½ turn after 4 minutes.)

Add tomatoes, fish fillets, crabmeat, herb blend, and cooked vegetables. **Cover** and microwave on 50 percent power or MEDIUM for 25 to 30 minutes (LW 30 to 36 minutes). (**Rotate** dish ¼ turn every 5 minutes if not using turntable.) Let **stand, covered,** for 5 minutes and garnish with chopped scallions.

Suggestions: Serve each portion over ½ cup cooked long-grain rice and add 70 calories per serving.

For less restricted diets: If you're not watching your salt intake, substitute regular crushed tomatoes, which add 209 mg sodium per serving.

FOR EACH SERVING:
110 calories
75 mg sodium
44 mg cholesterol
3 g fat

Seafood Paella

Many paella recipes call for shrimp, but not this one—too much cholesterol.

SERVES 4

EQUIPMENT:	deep 2- or 3-quart casserole dish
COOKING TIME:	26 to 34 minutes (Low Wattage ovens 31 to 40¾ minutes)
STANDING TIME:	3 minutes
NUTRITIONAL PROFILE:	low calories, low sodium, low cholesterol

1 cup (about 4 ounces) sliced fresh mushrooms
½ cup (about 1 medium) chopped onion
1 garlic clove, crushed
2 tablespoons white wine
1 cup uncooked long-grain rice
1 tablespoon chopped fresh parsley
1 teaspoon Parsley Patch Garlicsaltless herb blend
⅛ teaspoon freshly ground pepper
¼ teaspoon saffron
1¼ cups low-sodium chicken broth or homemade chicken stock (page 44)
½ cup hot water
½ cup low-sodium tomato juice
½ pound fresh bay scallops, rinsed under cold water
½ pound fresh crabmeat
1 10-ounce package frozen peas, partially thawed

In casserole dish, combine mushrooms, onions, garlic, and wine. **Cover** with lid or plastic wrap, pulling back one corner to vent the steam. (If dish is flat-bottomed, **elevate** on an inverted saucer.) Place on turntable if available. Microwave on HIGH for 2 to 4 minutes (LW 2¼ to 4¾ minutes) or until onions are tender. **Stir.**

Add rice, parsley, herb blend, pepper, saffron, broth, hot water, and tomato juice. **Stir** and **cover**. Microwave on HIGH for 5 to 7 minutes (LW 6 to 8¼ minutes) or until bubbly. **Reduce** power to 50 percent or MEDIUM, **cover,** and cook for 15 to 17 minutes (LW 18 to 20¼ minutes) or until rice is tender.

Stir in scallops, crab, and peas. **Cover** and continue cooking on 50 percent power or MEDIUM for 4 to 6 minutes (LW 4¾ to 7½ minutes) or until scallops become opaque and peas are tender. Let **stand, covered,** for 3 minutes before serving.

Troubleshooting: If peas are frozen, place **paper-covered** box (if box is covered with an aluminum foil wrapper, remove it) on 2 layers of paper towels and microwave on HIGH power for 2 to 3 minutes (LW 2¼ to 3½ minutes).

For less restricted diets: If you're not watching your salt intake, substitute regular chicken broth, which adds 281 mg sodium per serving, and regular tomato juice, which adds 107 mg sodium per serving.

FOR EACH SERVING:
236 calories
108 mg sodium
47 mg cholesterol
2 g fat

Seafood Stew

SERVES 6

EQUIPMENT:	deep 3-quart casserole dish, strainer
COOKING TIME:	45 to 54 minutes (Low Wattage ovens 54¼ to 64 minutes)
STANDING TIME:	none required
NUTRITIONAL PROFILE:	low calories, low sodium, low cholesterol

2 **dozen littleneck clams**
¾ **cup plus 2 tablespoons white wine**
½ **teaspoon chopped fresh parsley**
2 **garlic cloves, minced**
1 **celery stalk, minced**
1 **carrot, diced**
1 **teaspoon Parsley Patch All-Purpose herb blend**
1 **15-ounce can low-sodium tomatoes, chopped, with their liquid**

1   **pound red snapper, flounder, sole, or swordfish
      fillets, cut into 1½-inch chunks**
½   **pound fresh sea scallops, cut in half**
1   **pound fresh mussels in their shells
      freshly ground pepper to taste**

Place clams, ½ cup of the white wine, and parsley in casserole dish. **Cover** with lid or plastic wrap, pulling back one corner to vent steam. (If dish is flat-bottomed, **elevate** on an inverted saucer.) Microwave on HIGH for 10 to 12 minutes (LW 12 to 14¼ minutes) or until all clams have begun to open. Remove clams from broth, set aside, and keep warm. **Strain** the broth and set aside.

Place 2 tablespoons of the wine, garlic, celery, carrot, and herb blend in casserole dish and cook, **uncovered,** on HIGH for 6 to 8 minutes (LW 7½ to 9½ minutes), **stirring** and **rotating** dish ½ turn every 4 minutes, until soft. Stir in remaining ¼ cup wine, reserved clam broth, and tomatoes.

Microwave, **uncovered,** on 80 percent power or MEDIUM-HIGH for 10 to 12 minutes (LW 12 to 14 minutes), **stirring** and **rotating** dish ½ turn every 5 minutes.

Add fish and scallops, **cover** again and microwave on 50 percent power or MEDIUM for 10 minutes (LW 12 minutes), carefully **stirring** and **rotating** dish ½ turn every 5 minutes. **Stir,** add mussels, **cover,** and cook for 8 to 10 minutes (LW 9½ to 12 minutes) on 80 percent power or MEDIUM-HIGH. **Stir** carefully, add pepper to taste and clams, **cover,** and cook on HIGH for 1 to 2 minutes (LW 1¼ to 2¼ minutes), until clams are hot and fish flakes easily. **Do not overcook** fish.

Suggestion: Serve this lovely main dish in large deep bowls.

For less restricted diets: If you're not watching your salt intake, substitute regular tomatoes, which add 115 mg sodium per serving.

FOR EACH SERVING:
229 calories
71 mg sodium
62 mg cholesterol
7 g fat

Clam and Scallop Supreme

SERVES 4

EQUIPMENT: custard cup, 1-cup glass measure, 2-quart round casserole dish

COOKING TIME: 12¾ to 18 minutes (Low Wattage ovens 15½ to 19½ minutes)

STANDING TIME: 3 minutes

NUTRITIONAL PROFILE: low calories, low sodium, low cholesterol

CRUMB TOPPING

- **1 tablespoon soft-spread margarine**
- **1 garlic clove, finely minced**
- **¼ cup plain dry bread crumbs**

- **1 tablespoon white wine**
- **4 whole scallions including tops, diced**
- **¼ cup (about 1 large stalk) finely chopped celery**
- **1 pound fresh or frozen shucked chopped clams, drained, with juice reserved**
- **½ pound bay scallops**
- **1 tablespoon all-purpose flour**
- **½ cup skim milk**
- **¼ cup reserved clam juice**
- **1 tablespoon fresh lemon juice (see box, page 124)**
- **¼ teaspoon garlic powder**
- **¼ teaspoon cayenne pepper**

Place margarine and garlic in custard cup, **cover** with a paper towel, and microwave on HIGH for 45 to 55 seconds (LW 60 seconds) or until melted. Stir in bread crumbs and set aside.

In glass measure, combine wine, scallions, and celery. Microwave, **uncovered,** on HIGH for 2 to 4 minutes (LW 2½ to 4½ minutes), stirring once, until soft.

Arrange a layer of clams in casserole dish and cover with a layer of scallops. Top fish with scallion and celery mixture. **Whisk** together flour, milk, clam juice (add water to make ¼ cup if necessary), lemon juice, garlic powder, and cayenne pepper; spoon over fish. **Cover** dish with lid or plastic wrap, pulling back one corner to vent the steam. (If dish is flat-bottomed, **elevate** on an inverted saucer.) Place on a turntable if available.

Microwave on 70 percent power or MEDIUM-HIGH for 10 to 13 minutes (LW 12 to 14 minutes) or until clams and scallops are opaque. (If not using turntable, **rotate** dish ½ turn every 5 minutes.) **Uncover** dish during last minute of cooking and add crumb topping. Let **stand** for 3 minutes before serving.

Troubleshooting: Forgetting to whisk sauce may cause it to be lumpy.

FOR EACH SERVING:
187 calories
182 mg sodium
64 mg cholesterol
3 g fat

COOKING WITH CLAMS

Be careful not to substitute canned clams for fresh or frozen ones if salt is a concern for you. Canned clams require a large amount of salt to preserve them; they'll add an extra 1,000 mg salt to the recipe.

If fresh shucked clams aren't available, scrub about 24 to 30 unshucked fresh cherrystone clams. Place them in a circle around the edge of a large flat plate and cover with plastic wrap, pulling back one corner to vent the steam. **Elevate** on inverted saucer.

Microwave on HIGH for 3 to 5 minutes (LW 3½ to 6 minutes) or until shells pop open. Repeat process until all clams are cooked, discarding any that don't open. Empty liquid and clams into a strainer, chopping clams and reserving juice for recipe.

Breads and Desserts

Kernel Corn Bread

SERVES 8

EQUIPMENT:	2-quart glass ring mold, medium and large mixing bowls
COOKING TIME:	8 to 10 minutes (Low Wattage ovens 9¾ to 12¼ minutes)
STANDING TIME:	10 minutes
NUTRITIONAL PROFILE:	moderate calories, low sodium, low cholesterol

- 1 **cup all-purpose flour**
- 1 **cup yellow cornmeal**
- 4 **tablespoons sugar**
- 2 **teaspoons baking powder**
- ½ **teaspoon baking soda**
- 3 **egg whites, well beaten**
- ¼ **cup corn or soybean oil**
- ½ **cup plain yogurt**
- 1 **8½-ounce can low-salt creamed corn**

Grease ring mold with solid shortening and set aside. Combine flour, cornmeal, sugar, baking powder, and baking soda in large bowl, stirring to blend well. In medium bowl, combine egg whites, oil, yogurt, and creamed corn. **Whisk** until well blended. Add to dry ingredients and stir until mixture is well moistened. Spoon into prepared dish.

Microwave on 50 percent power or MEDIUM for 6 minutes (LW 7½ minutes), **rotating** dish ½ turn every 3 minutes. **Increase** power to HIGH and cook for 2 to 4 minutes (LW 2¼ to 4¾ minutes) or until toothpick inserted in the center comes out clean, **rotating** dish ½ turn every 2 minutes. Let **stand** on hard heatproof surface for 10 minutes before inverting onto serving platter.

For less restricted diets: If you're not watching your salt intake, substitute regular creamed corn, which adds 73 mg sodium per serving.

FOR EACH SERVING:
248 calories
160 mg sodium
1 mg cholesterol
6 g fat

Orange Grove Muffins

You may not have the time to perk your coffee on your stove top and for those busy mornings a microwave perk coffeepot really comes in handy. They are hard to find, but you can order one directly from Nordic Ware by calling toll-free 1-800-328-4310 extension 584.

On those mornings when a cup of coffee just doesn't seem to be enough, try whipping up a batch of these zesty muffins to accompany it.

MAKES 10 MUFFINS

EQUIPMENT:	large bowl, plastic muffin pan or 6 custard cups, wire cooling rack
COOKING TIME:	3 to 4 minutes (Low Wattage ovens 3½ to 4¾ minutes)
STANDING TIME:	none required
NUTRITIONAL PROFILE:	moderate calories, low sodium, trace cholesterol

  ½ **cup soft-spread margarine**
  ¾ **cup sugar**
  3 **egg whites**
  ½ **cup plain yogurt**
  2 **tablespoons grated orange zest**
  ½ **cup orange juice**
  1 **teaspoon baking powder**
  ½ **teaspoon baking soda**
1¾ **cups all-purpose flour**

In large bowl, **cream** together margarine and sugar until fluffy. **Beat** in egg whites. Add yogurt, orange zest, orange juice, baking powder, and baking soda. Gradually blend in flour. **Line** muffin pan or 6 custard cups with **2** cupcake papers (see box, page 249). Fill papers ⅔ full. Place muffin pan on turntable if available. If using custard cups, place in a circle. Microwave on HIGH for 3 to 4 minutes (LW 3½ to 4¾ minutes) or until a toothpick inserted in the center comes out clean. (**Rotate** pan ¼ turn after 2 minutes if not using a turntable. If using custard cups, **rearrange** them after 2 minutes.) Remove muffins from their containers and immediately discard the outer paper baking cup. **Cool** on wire rack.

Troubleshooting: Failing to use 2 cupcake papers will produce hard, tough muffins, as they absorb the moisture that the second paper should have taken care of.

Suggestions: Freeze the unused muffins for later use. Remove frozen muffin from freezer, completely wrap in a paper towel, and microwave on 30 percent power or LOW for 1 minute to defrost. Increase power to HIGH for 20 to 25 seconds, just until warm.

FOR EACH SERVING:
203 calories
146 mg sodium
trace cholesterol
6 g fat

Orange Cranberry Nut Bread

Cranberries are selected for their quality before they are picked,
and the bags you buy should hold firm, plump berries that are red
to reddish black in color. Avoid fresh berries that are sticky, soft,
or shriveled up. Cranberries freeze beautifully in their bags, so
you can enjoy them any time of year.

SERVES 8

EQUIPMENT:	9 × 5-inch glass loaf pan, medium mixing bowl, pastry blender or 2 table knives
COOKING TIME:	11 to 14 minutes (Low Wattage ovens 13 to 17 minutes)
STANDING TIME:	10 minutes
NUTRITIONAL PROFILE:	moderate calories, low sodium, no cholesterol

1¾ **cups all-purpose flour**
¾ **cup sugar**
1½ **teaspoons baking powder**
½ **teaspoon baking soda**
¼ **cup soft-spread margarine**
1 **tablespoon grated orange zest**
¾ **cup orange juice**
3 **egg whites, well beaten**
½ **cup chopped unsalted nuts**
1 **cup finely chopped fresh cranberries**

Line bottom *only* of loaf pan with wax paper and set aside. **Sift** together flour, sugar, baking powder, and baking soda. In mixing bowl, **cut** margarine into dry ingredients, using pastry blender or 2 table knives, until mixture resembles coarse cornmeal. Combine orange zest and juice with the egg whites. Pour orange juice mixture into the dry ingredients, mixing just enough to dampen. Carefully fold in nuts and cranberries and spoon into prepared dish.

If your oven manufacturer allows the use of small, completely **flat** pieces of aluminum foil, carefully **shield** the ends of the pan with 1-inch-wide strips of foil. **Cover** the end of the dish and mold the overlapping ends to the dish so that the foil is not crimped, folded, or touching itself. (If dish is flat-bottomed, **elevate** on an inverted saucer.) Place on turntable if available. Microwave on 50 percent power or MEDIUM for 8 minutes (LW 9½ minutes). (**Rotate** dish ¼ turn every 3 minutes if not using turntable.)

Remove foil shields, if used, and **increase** power to HIGH. Microwave for 3 to 6 minutes (LW 3½ to 7½ minutes) or until when you look through the bottom of the dish no unbaked batter appears in the center. Let **stand** on hard heatproof surface for 10 minutes. **Loosen** edges and turn out onto a cooling rack. Remove wax paper and cool completely before cutting. Wrap any leftover bread in aluminum foil and keep in refrigerator.

SHIELDING
SQUARE-CORNERED DISHES

Microwaves are attracted to, and overcook, whatever they find in square corners. To prevent this problem when baking in a loaf pan, shield the square corners with small, flat pieces of aluminum foil, if your oven manufacturer allows its use. Be sure the foil is not folded, crimped, or touching itself in any way, or it will arc. How will you know if it arcs? As soon as you turn on the microwave it will look like a Fourth of July fireworks extravaganza in your oven. Should this happen, immediately shut off the oven and open the door. Readjust the foil so that it is completely flat and try again. When using aluminum foil, be sure to observe the cooking container for several seconds after the oven is turned on, to be sure it isn't arcing.

FOR EACH SERVING:
310 calories
159 mg sodium
0 mg cholesterol
8 g fat

Pineapple Nut Bread

SERVES 8

EQUIPMENT:	9-inch glass ring mold or bundt pan, custard cup or small bowl, large mixing bowl, wire cooling rack
COOKING TIME:	8¾ to 13 minutes (Low Wattage ovens 10½ to 15¼ minutes)
STANDING TIME:	5 to 10 minutes
NUTRITIONAL PROFILE:	moderate calories, low sodium, low cholesterol

¼ **cup chopped walnuts, 1 tablespoon reserved and finely chopped for dusting pan**
¼ **cup soft-spread margarine**
1 **8¼-ounce can unsweetened crushed pineapple**
1 **teaspoon pineapple extract**
¾ **cup plain yogurt**
2 **egg whites, slightly beaten**
2 **cups all-purpose flour**
¾ **cup sugar**
1½ **teaspoons baking powder**
½ **teaspoon baking soda**

Lightly **grease** ring mold with solid shortening and dust with 1 tablespoon finely crushed walnuts. Place margarine in custard cup or small bowl and microwave, **uncovered,** on HIGH for 45 to 55 seconds (LW 50 to 60 seconds) or until melted.

In large bowl, combine melted margarine, pineapple with juice, pineapple extract, yogurt, egg whites, and remaining walnuts. Combine flour, sugar, baking powder, and baking soda. Stir into pineapple mixture but **do not overmix.** Spread into prepared dish and cook on 70 percent power or MEDIUM-HIGH for 8 to 12 minutes (LW 9½ to 14¼ minutes) or until toothpick inserted comes out clean, **rotating** dish ¼ turn every 3 minutes. Let **stand** on hard heatproof surface for 5 to 10 minutes before removing from dish to cooling rack.

Troubleshooting: To keep melting margarine from spattering oven, cover top of custard cup with paper towel or napkin.

Suggestions: To heat slices for breakfast, wrap completely in a paper towel and microwave for 15 to 25 seconds on HIGH until just warm.

FOR EACH SERVING:
279 calories
168 mg sodium
2 mg cholesterol
6 g fat

APPLES

An apple a day keeps the doctor away. What is the magic power in the apple? Nutritionally, nothing special, but it is a source of carbohydrate providing B vitamins, potassium, vitamin A, a little vitamin C, and calcium. It provides some fiber, but less than you will find in a pear.

McIntosh apples are great for eating but split if you try to bake them. These delicious eating apples don't stand up well in long-cooking recipes, but the microwave cooks so quickly that I feel they do better in a microwaved pie than they would in a conventional one. A mix of McIntosh and almost any other apple except Red Delicious will produce a tasty applesauce. Cortland apples seem to be the best for all-around baking and cooking. The flesh of a Cortland stays white longer than other apples when you slice it for a fresh fruit or Waldorf salad. Cortlands hold their shape very well for baked apples and in slices for a pie.

Macoun and Red Delicious apples are excellent eating apples, while Red Delicious are also good cut up in salads. Neither of these 2 varieties is recommended for pies, while Golden Delicious are good all-around pie and eating apples.

Stayman apples are good firm cooking apples that hold their shape when cut into slices for cakes. Rome apples are also good to cook with and hold their shape in cakes, while Greenings are too tart for eating apples and are best in pies. But these are just general guidelines; your taste buds are your best guide.

Old Fashioned Betty Browns

SERVES 6

EQUIPMENT:	large mixing bowl, 8-inch round baking dish
COOKING TIME:	10 to 12 minutes (Low Wattage ovens 12 to 14 minutes)
STANDING TIME:	10 minutes
NUTRITIONAL PROFILE:	moderate calories, low sodium, no cholesterol

½ **cup soft-spread margarine**
½ **cup light brown sugar**
2 **egg whites, slightly beaten**
1 **cup all-purpose flour**
½ **teaspoon baking soda**
½ **teaspoon baking powder**
1 **teaspoon ground cinnamon**
2 **cups peeled and chopped apples**

GLAZE
¼ **cup sifted powdered sugar**
2 **teaspoons skim milk**
dash vanilla extract

In bowl, combine all ingredients except apples and glaze ingredients and mix until well blended. Carefully stir in apples. Spread batter evenly in baking dish. (If dish is flat-bottomed, **elevate** on an inverted saucer.) Place on turntable if available.

Microwave on 70 percent power or MEDIUM-HIGH for 10 to 12 minutes (LW 12 to 14 minutes) or until top springs back when lightly pressed with a finger and cake starts to come away from the sides of the dish. (**Rotate** dish ¼ turn every 3 minutes if not using turntable.) Let **stand** for 10 minutes on a hard heatproof surface. Combine all glaze ingredients and mix well. Drizzle glaze over dish after standing time and serve warm.

FOR EACH SERVING:
280 calories
191 mg sodium
0 mg cholesterol
9 g fat

Honeyed Apple Crisp

SERVES 8

EQUIPMENT:	deep 8-inch baking dish, 2-cup glass measure, medium bowl, pastry blender or 2 table knives
COOKING TIME:	13 to 16 minutes (Low Wattage ovens 15¼ to 18¼ minutes)
STANDING TIME:	none required
NUTRITIONAL PROFILE:	low calories, low sodium, no cholesterol

4 cups (4 or 5) cored, peeled, and uniformly sliced apples
¼ cup honey
1 teaspoon grated lemon zest
1 tablespoon fresh lemon juice (see box, page 124)
½ teaspoon ground cinnamon
¼ teaspoon freshly grated nutmeg

TOPPING
½ cup whole wheat flour
¼ cup light brown sugar
1 tablespoon ground cinnamon
¼ cup chopped unsalted nuts
¼ cup soft-spread margarine

Arrange apple slices in baking dish. In glass measure, stir together honey, lemon zest, lemon juice, cinnamon, and nutmeg. Microwave, **uncovered,** on HIGH for 1 minute (LW 1¼ minutes), **stir,** and pour over apples.

Combine topping ingredients in bowl. Cut in margarine with pastry blender or 2 table knives until mixture resembles cornmeal. Sprinkle evenly over apples. (If dish is flat-bottomed, **elevate** on an inverted saucer.) Place on turntable if available. Microwave on HIGH for 12 to 15 minutes (LW 14 to 17 minutes) or until apples are tender. (**Rotate** dish ½ turn every 6 minutes if not using turntable.) Serve hot or very warm.

Suggestions: For a pretty presentation, place each serving in a footed dessert dish or Champagne glass.

FOR EACH SERVING:
190 calories
84 mg sodium
0 mg cholesterol
6 g fat

USING HONEY IN PLACE OF SUGAR

Honey is a form of sugar, and it has the same nutritional breakdown. Honey has its own unique flavor and can be substituted in equal amounts for sugar when you want that special flavor only honey can give.

Apple Noodle Pudding

Kugel, the Yiddish name for this dish, or noodle pudding, can be baked in the microwave ahead of time, frozen, defrosted, and reheated in the microwave beautifully. When baked in a conventional oven, noodle pudding becomes very brown, crusty, and dry on the top. When microwaving, the top of the dish will not brown but will be soft and moist. Be careful not to overcook trying to get a crusty dry top, or you will ruin the recipe.

SERVES 6

EQUIPMENT: medium and large mixing bowls, 2-quart casserole dish
COOKING TIME: 21 to 26½ minutes (Low Wattage ovens 25¼ to 31¾ minutes)
STANDING TIME: 5 minutes
NUTRITIONAL PROFILE: moderate calories, low sodium, trace cholesterol

¼ **pound soft-spread margarine**
½ **pound hot cooked medium eggless noodles, drained**
6 **egg whites**
8 **ounces low-fat cottage cheese**
1 **cup plain yogurt**
½ **cup sugar**
1 **teaspoon ground cinnamon**
1 **teaspoon vanilla extract**
4 **tablespoons plain dry bread crumbs**
½ **cup raisins**
1 **apple, peeled and diced**
ground cinnamon

Place margarine in medium bowl and microwave, **uncovered,** on HIGH for 1 to 1½ minutes (LW 1¼ to 1¾ minutes) or until melted. Mix hot cooked noodles with melted margarine and set aside.

In large bowl, **beat** egg whites and cottage cheese together until smooth. Stir in yogurt, sugar, 1 teaspoon cinnamon, vanilla, bread crumbs, raisins, and apple pieces. Add noodles and mix gently. Pour noodle mixture into casserole dish and sprinkle with cinnamon. (If dish is flat-bottomed, **elevate** on an inverted saucer.) Place on turntable if available. Microwave, **uncovered,** on HIGH for 20 to 25 minutes (LW 24 to 30 minutes) or until just set. (**Rotate** dish ¼ turn every 5 minutes if not using turntable.) Let **stand** on a hard heatproof surface for 5 minutes. Cut into squares and serve warm.

Troubleshooting: You will not be able to beat all of the curd out of the cottage cheese, but beat until it appears smooth.

FOR EACH SERVING:
319 calories
175 mg sodium
trace cholesterol
5 g fat

CREAM CHEESE SUBSTITUTE

Cream cheese has very concentrated calories and high fat. Substituting low-fat cottage cheese that is whipped in a food processor or blender or with an electric mixer gives you a healthier product that contains more protein, while being lower in cholesterol and saving 88 calories per tablespoon over cream cheese. Keep in mind, no matter how much you whip the cottage cheese and how smooth it appears, you won't actually be able to whip out all of the curd—some tiny bits of curd will remain.

Bananas Amaretto

SERVES 4

EQUIPMENT:	1-quart round casserole dish, small bowl
COOKING TIME:	2½ to 3 minutes (Low Wattage ovens 2¾ to 3¼ minutes)
STANDING TIME:	none required
NUTRITIONAL PROFILE:	low calories, low sodium, no cholesterol

4 bananas
2 tablespoons soft-spread margarine
1 teaspoon fresh lemon juice (see box, page 124)
2 tablespoons light brown sugar
1 tablespoon Amaretto

Peel and slice bananas into **uniformly** sized coins and place in casserole dish. Melt margarine in small, **uncovered,** bowl on HIGH for 45 to 55 seconds (LW 50 to 60 seconds). Stir in lemon juice, brown sugar, and Amaretto.

Microwave, **uncovered,** on HIGH for 40 to 50 seconds (LW 45 to 55 seconds) or until hot. Stir and pour over bananas, tossing gently. Microwave, **uncovered,** on HIGH for 1 minute (LW 1¼ minutes), until hot. Divide into individual serving dishes and drizzle with sauce.

Troubleshooting: Do not overheat in final step or bananas will turn mushy.

FOR EACH SERVING:
199 calories
30 mg sodium
0 mg cholesterol
4 g fat

PEARS

Pears develop their best flavor when picked still hard and ripen best at room temperature. Pears ripen from the inside to the surface, so be sure to select ones that are still a bit firm to the touch, yet starting to soften near the stem. Always remove the fruit from plastic bags and gently place in a bowl on the kitchen counter to ripen. Once the pears have ripened, store, uncovered, in the refrigerator or use them for cooking. One medium pear has 120 calories, is an excellent source of fiber, and provides some potassium, phosphorus, and B vitamins.

Pear Chutney

MAKES 3 CUPS

EQUIPMENT: deep 3-quart casserole dish
COOKING TIME: 40 to 45 minutes (Low Wattage ovens 46 to 52 minutes)
STANDING TIME: none required
NUTRITIONAL PROFILE: low calories, low sodium, no cholesterol

6 peeled, cored, and diced fresh pears
1 medium onion, chopped
⅔ cup cider vinegar
⅓ cup water
⅓ cup golden raisins
1 garlic clove, finely minced

¼ **cup firmly packed light brown sugar**
½ **teaspoon ground ginger**
¼ **teaspoon ground cloves**
   dash freshly ground pepper
¼ **teaspoon ground cinnamon**

Place pears in casserole dish. Add all remaining ingredients, **stirring** well to combine. (If dish is flat-bottomed, **elevate** on an inverted saucer.) Place on turntable if available. Microwave, **uncovered,** on HIGH for 40 to 45 minutes (LW 46 to 52 minutes) or until thickened, stirring mixture every 8 minutes. (**Rotate** dish ¼ turn when stirring if not using turntable.) Let **cool** and refrigerate in tightly sealed container.

Suggestions: To can and preserve the mixture for use all year, pour hot mixture into hot sterilized canning jars, adjust caps, and process for 15 minutes in water bath canner.

FOR EACH TABLESPOON:
69 calories
3 mg sodium
0 mg cholesterol
0 g fat

Raspberry-Sauced Pears

SERVES 6

EQUIPMENT:	9-inch round casserole dish, 6-cup glass measure, small bowl
COOKING TIME:	11¾ to 18 minutes (Low Wattage ovens 14 to 21¾ minutes)
STANDING TIME:	none required
NUTRITIONAL PROFILE:	moderate calories, low sodium, no cholesterol

  1 **cup water**
  3 **tablespoons fresh lemon juice (see box, page 124)**
  6 **medium-size firm, ripe fresh pears**
  1 **cup dry white wine**
  ½ **cup water**
  ¼ **cup sugar**
  1 **cinnamon stick**
  4 **whole cloves**
  ¼ **cup low-sugar raspberry preserves**
  2½ **tablespoons raspberry liqueur**

Combine 1 cup water and lemon juice; set aside. Peel pears, leaving stem in place. Cut a slice from the bottom so pears will stand up. Dip pears in lemon-water, coating well. Place dipped pears in casserole dish; set aside.

Place wine, ½ cup water, sugar, cinnamon stick, and cloves in glass measure. **Cover** with lid or plastic wrap, pulling back one corner to vent the steam. Microwave on HIGH for 4 to 6 minutes (LW 4¾ to 7½ minutes) or until mixture comes to a boil. Pour hot wine mixture over pears and microwave, **uncovered,** on HIGH for 7 to 11 minutes (LW 8¼ to 13¼ minutes) or until pears are fork-tender but still hold their shape. Let **stand** in wine mixture to cool while making topping.

In small bowl, combine preserves with liqueur and micro-wave, **uncovered,** on HIGH for 40 to 50 seconds (LW 60 seconds) or until preserves melt and sauce is warm. Transfer pears to individual serving dishes and drizzle with raspberry sauce.

FOR EACH SERVING:
205 calories
3 mg sodium
0 mg cholesterol
0 g fat

Nutty Pears

SERVES 6

EQUIPMENT: round or 12 × 8-inch casserole dish, 4-cup
             glass measure, small bowl

COOKING TIME: 7 to 12 minutes (Low Wattage ovens 8¼ to 14¼ minutes)

STANDING TIME: 5 minutes

NUTRITIONAL PROFILE: low calories, low sodium, no cholesterol

3 medium-size ripe fresh pears, peeled, halved, and cored
½ cup unsweetened pineapple juice
2 tablespoons orange liqueur
1 teaspoon cornstarch
⅓ cup chopped unsalted pecans
¼ cup firmly packed dark brown sugar
½ teaspoon vanilla extract
¼ cup honey
4 maraschino cherries, cut in half

Place pears, cut side up, in casserole dish in a circle like the spokes of a wagon wheel. **Whisk** pineapple juice, orange liqueur, and cornstarch together in glass measure. Microwave, **uncovered,** on HIGH for 2 to 3 minutes (LW 2¼ to 3½ minutes), until glaze begins to thicken, **whisking** every minute. Pour over pears.

In a small bowl, mix together pecans, brown sugar, and vanilla. Fill pear cavity with pecan mixture and **cover** dish with wax paper. (If dish is flat-bottomed, **elevate** on an inverted saucer.) Place on turntable if available.

Microwave on HIGH for 5 to 9 minutes (LW 6 to 10¾ minutes), until pears are tender, **basting** with glaze after 4 minutes of cooking time. (**Rotate** dish ½ turn when basting if not using turntable.) Let **stand, covered,** for 5 minutes before placing in individual dessert dishes and topping with a tablespoon of glaze and a maraschino cherry half for garnish. Serve warm.

Troubleshooting: If sauce is lumpy, you forgot to whisk.

FOR EACH SERVING:
193 calories
8 mg sodium
0 mg cholesterol
4 g fat

SELECTING FROZEN OR CANNED FRUITS

Be sure to read labels when purchasing frozen or canned fruit and juices. There are 3 different kinds of syrups, containing different amounts of sugar. Fruits packed in a heavy syrup are high in sugar and calories, versus light or natural juices with none or just a small amount of sugar added. To save calories, purchase only those in natural juices or unsweetened. Of course, the *best* selection for fruit is fresh.

Hot Fruit Compote

SERVES 6

EQUIPMENT:	deep 3-quart round casserole dish
COOKING TIME:	8 to 13 minutes (Low Wattage ovens 9½ to 15½ minutes)
STANDING TIME:	none required
NUTRITIONAL PROFILE:	moderate calories, low sodium, no cholesterol

1¾ **cups water**
1 **16-ounce can unsweetened pineapple chunks, drained and ¼ cup juice reserved**
2 **tablespoons cornstarch**
½ **cup dark brown sugar**
½ **cup sherry**
2 **apples, peeled, cored, and quartered**
2 **peaches, peeled, pitted, and quartered**
2 **pears, peeled, cored, and quartered**
3 **plums, pitted and quartered**
1 **cup fresh strawberries, hulled**

In casserole dish, combine water and reserved pineapple juice. **Whisk** cornstarch into liquid until combined. **Whisk** in brown sugar and sherry. (If dish is flat-bottomed, **elevate** on an inverted saucer.) Place on turntable if available. Microwave, **uncovered,** on HIGH for 3 to 5 minutes (LW 3½ to 6 minutes) or until thickened, **whisking** every minute.

Add apples, peaches, pears, and plums, **stirring** to combine. Microwave, **uncovered,** on 80 percent power or MEDIUM-HIGH for 5 to 8 minutes (LW 6 to 9½ minutes) or until fruit is soft, carefully **stirring** every 3 minutes. (**Rotate** dish ½ turn when stirring if not using turntable.) Fold pineapple into hot mixture and allow to **cool**. If serving hot, layer strawberries over top of fruit mixture. If serving cold, allow dish to cool, then fold in strawberries and chill.

Troubleshooting: Failing to whisk sauce ingredients may cause it to be lumpy.

Suggestion: For an attractive presentation, serve each portion in a footed dessert or Champagne glass.

FOR EACH SERVING:
235 calories
28 mg sodium
0 mg cholesterol
trace fat

Cherry Cobbler

SERVES 4

EQUIPMENT:	9- or 10-inch round baking dish, pastry blender or 2 table knives, small mixing bowl
COOKING TIME:	7 to 10 minutes (Low Wattage ovens 8¼ to 12 minutes)
STANDING TIME:	5 minutes
NUTRITIONAL PROFILE:	moderate calories, low sodium, no cholesterol

  1 21-ounce can cherry pie filling
 ¾ cup all-purpose flour
  2 tablespoons sugar
  1 teaspoon baking powder
  2 tablespoons soft-spread margarine
  2 tablespoons skim milk
  2 egg whites
    ground cinnamon

BAKING IN THE MICROWAVE

Preparing baking pans for the microwave is a bit different from conventional baking. If you plan to remove the baked item from the pan for frosting or glazing, you must grease and *sugar,* not flour, your pan. If you are going to serve it right from the container it was baked in, no greasing is necessary. Do not use spray shortenings or, like the flour, they will stick to the outside of the cake. Instead of flour you can use granulated or brown sugar, graham cracker crumbs, cocoa, or chopped nuts to dust the greased pan.

A general rule to use for determining doneness: the cake will pull away from the sides of the pan and there will be no raw batter spots left on top of the cake. Testing with a toothpick is not always accurate, especially if the cake has a fruit filling underneath it.

Standing time in baking is another important step that must not be eliminated. The last part of the cake to cook is the bottom, and some of this is done during standing time. Once the baking process is finished, remove the cake to a hard heatproof surface—not a wire rack—because you want to trap as much heat as possible in the bottom of the pan. Let the cake stand for 10 minutes to ensure that the bottom is completely baked. If, after the 10-minute standing period is finished, when you invert the cake onto a serving plate there is still raw batter on the bottom, put the cake back in the pan and microwave for another 2 minutes and allow to stand again.

Spread pie filling evenly over the bottom of baking dish. In mixing bowl, combine flour, sugar, and baking powder. **Cut** margarine into mixture with pastry blender or 2 table knives until mixture resembles coarse crumbs. Mix milk with egg whites and add to dry ingredients, **stirring** until moistened.

Spoon batter over pie filling in baking dish and sprinkle with cinnamon. (If dish is flat-bottomed, **elevate** on an inverted saucer.) Place on turntable if available. Microwave, **uncovered,** on 50 percent power or MEDIUM for 5 minutes (LW 6 minutes). (**Rotate** dish ½ turn if not using turntable.) Microwave on HIGH for 2 to 5 minutes (LW 2¼ to 6 minutes) or until **no** moist batter spots are visible. (**Rotate** dish ½ turn every 2 minutes if not using turntable.) Let **stand** on hard heatproof surface for 5 minutes. Serve warm.

FOR EACH SERVING:
325 calories
165 mg sodium
0 mg cholesterol
4 g fat

Hot Applesauce Cake

Don't become alarmed when you add the baking soda to the hot applesauce and find that the applesauce becomes foamy. Grandma believed that this method made the texture of the applesauce very light and easier to mix with the dry ingredients. She also added cocoa to deepen the spice flavor and to enhance the rich color of this delicious cake.

SERVES 8

EQUIPMENT: 9-inch glass ring mold or bundt pan, large mixing bowl, 2-cup glass measure, wire cooling rack

COOKING TIME: 14 to 16½ minutes (Low Wattage ovens 16½ to 19½ minutes)

STANDING TIME: 10 minutes

NUTRITIONAL PROFILE: moderate calories, low sodium, no cholesterol

- ½ **cup soft-spread margarine**
- 1 **cup sugar**
- 3 **egg whites, slightly beaten**
- 1 **cup unsweetened applesauce**
- ½ **teaspoon baking soda**
- 2 **cups all-purpose flour**
- 1 **teaspoon cocoa**
- 1 **teaspoon ground cinnamon**
- ½ **teaspoon freshly grated nutmeg**
- ¼ **teaspoon ground cloves**
- ½ **cup raisins or chopped dates**

Grease mold or bundt pan with solid shortening and set aside. In large mixing bowl, cream margarine and sugar together. Add egg whites, mixing well. Place applesauce in glass measure and microwave, **uncovered,** on HIGH for 2 to 2½ minutes (LW 2¼ to 2¾ minutes) or until hot, **stirring** once.

Stir in baking soda and add the applesauce to margarine mixture. **Sift** together flour, cocoa, cinnamon, nutmeg, and cloves. Add to applesauce mixture, **stirring** well. Stir in raisins and spoon batter into prepared dish. Microwave, **uncovered,** on 30 percent power or LOW for 5 minutes (LW 6 minutes).

Increase power to HIGH and cook for 7 to 9 minutes (LW 8¼ to 10¾ minutes) or until cake pulls away from the sides of the dish and there are no moist spots, **rotating** dish ¼ turn every 3 minutes. Let **stand** on a hard heatproof surface for 10 minutes before removing from dish. Place on rack to cool.

Troubleshooting: Forgetting to rotate dish may cause cake top to rise unevenly.

FOR EACH SERVING:
317 calories
133 mg sodium
0 mg cholesterol
7 g fat

Rice Pudding

SERVES 4

EQUIPMENT:	4-cup glass measure, 2-quart round casserole dish
COOKING TIME:	16 to 22 minutes (Low Wattage ovens 18¾ to 26 minutes)
STANDING TIME:	5 to 10 minutes
NUTRITIONAL PROFILE:	moderate calories, low sodium, no cholesterol

1¼   **cups skim milk**
  1   **teaspoon soft-spread margarine**
  3   **egg whites, lightly beaten**
½   **cup sugar**
½   **teaspoon vanilla extract**

¼ **teaspoon almond extract**
¼ **teaspoon ground cinnamon**
½ **cup raisins**
2 **cups cooked long-grain rice**
freshly grated nutmeg for garnish

Place milk and margarine in glass measure. Microwave, **uncovered,** on HIGH power for 2 minutes (LW 2¼ minutes). Stir and microwave, **uncovered,** on HIGH for 2 to 3 minutes (LW 2¼ to 3½ minutes) or until milk is very hot but **not** boiling.

In casserole dish, blend together egg whites, sugar, vanilla, almond extract, and cinnamon. **Slowly** stir in hot milk. Fold raisins and rice into milk mixture, stirring to combine. (If dish is flat-bottomed, **elevate** on an inverted saucer.) Place on turntable if available.

Microwave, **uncovered,** on HIGH power for 3 minutes (LW 3½ minutes); stir well. (**Rotate** dish ½ turn if not using turntable.) **Reduce** power to 50 percent or MEDIUM and microwave for 9 to 14 minutes (LW 10¾ to 16¾ minutes) or until mixture thickens, **stirring** every 3 minutes. (**Rotate** dish ¼ turn when stirring if not using turntable.) Sprinkle top with nutmeg and let **stand** on a hard heatproof surface for 5 to 10 minutes until set. Serve warm.

Troubleshooting: If you have only HIGH power on your microwave, place a glass of water next to the casserole dish when the recipe calls for a lower power setting. Stir more frequently and reduce the final cooking time by 2 to 3 minutes.

FOR EACH SERVING:
274 calories
93 mg sodium
0 mg cholesterol
1 g fat

Splurges

SPLURGES

Regardless of how diligent you are, there are always times when you need to treat yourself to something special. If you're following a strict low-cholesterol, low-sodium diet, you must never deviate from those guidelines. However, for a special occasion you can add a few calories by topping off your meal with one of my splurge desserts, which will add from 18 to 111 extra calories (more than the desserts in the last chapter) to your day's tally—not bad for a big treat.

These desserts follow the criteria for sodium and cholesterol but are high in empty sugar calories and should be served only for holidays, birthdays, or very special occasions—unless you're a skinny minnie.

Granny's Baked Apples

SERVES 4

EQUIPMENT:	9-inch round baking dish, small bowl
COOKING TIME:	11 to 12 minutes (Low Wattage ovens 13½ to 14¼ minutes)

STANDING TIME: 2 to 3 minutes
NUTRITIONAL PROFILE: high calories, low sodium, no cholesterol

4 Granny Smith or other apples
½ cup raisins
½ teaspoon ground cinnamon
½ cup light corn syrup
½ cup packed light brown sugar
2 tablespoons soft-spread margarine

Wash apples and remove a 1-inch strip of skin from the top of each apple to vent the steam and keep the apple from splitting. Core apples, being careful not to cut all the way through to the bottom. Arrange apples, cored side up, in baking dish, leaving the center of the dish open. Mix raisins and cinnamon together and fill apple cavities.

In small bowl, combine corn syrup, brown sugar, and margarine. Microwave, **uncovered,** on HIGH for 5 minutes (LW 6 minutes) or until boiling, **stirring** halfway through cooking time to dissolve brown sugar. Pour syrup over and around apples. **Cover** dish with lid or plastic wrap, pulling back one corner to vent the steam. (If dish is flat-bottomed, **elevate** on an inverted saucer.) Place on turntable if available.

Microwave on HIGH for 6 to 7 minutes (LW 7½ to 8¼ minutes) or until apples are almost tender. **Baste** with sauce every 3 minutes. (**Rotate** dish ½ turn when basting if not using turntable.) Let **stand, covered,** on a hard heatproof surface for 2 to 3 minutes before serving.

Suggestions: For an attractive presentation, serve each apple topped with sauce in a footed dessert or Champagne glass.

FOR EACH SERVING:
356 calories
66 mg sodium
0 mg cholesterol
4 g fat

Deep-Dish Blueberry Cake

SERVES 8

EQUIPMENT:	deep 10-inch baking dish, medium mixing bowl, sifter
COOKING TIME:	13 to 15 minutes (Low Wattage ovens 15¾ to 18¼ minutes)
STANDING TIME:	10 minutes
NUTRITIONAL PROFILE:	high calories, low sodium, no cholesterol

1	**21-ounce can blueberry pie filling**
½	**cup miniature marshmallows**
¼	**cup soft-spread margarine**
1	**cup sugar**
2	**egg whites**
2	**cups all-purpose flour**
2	**teaspoons baking powder**
¾	**cup skim milk**
½	**teaspoon vanilla extract**

TOPPING

1	**tablespoon sugar**
½	**teaspoon ground cinnamon**

Place pie filling in deep baking dish and sprinkle with marshmallows; set aside.

In mixing bowl, cream together margarine and sugar until light and fluffy. Blend in egg whites. Sift the flour and baking powder together. Add alternately with the milk to creamed mixture. Add vanilla and mix well.

Spoon batter very carefully over blueberry filling. Combine topping ingredients and sprinkle over batter. (If dish is flat-bottomed, **elevate** on an inverted saucer.) Microwave on 50 percent power or MEDIUM for 6 minutes (LW 7½ minutes), **rotating** dish ¼ turn every 3 minutes.

Increase power to HIGH and microwave for 7 to 9 minutes (LW 8¼ to 10¾ minutes) or until top appears almost dry and cake begins to pull away from the sides of the dish, **rotating** dish ¼ turn every 3 minutes. Let **stand** on a hard heatproof surface for 10 minutes.

FOR EACH SERVING:
344 calories
145 mg sodium
0 mg cholesterol
2 g fat

Blue Ribbon Carrot Cake

SERVES 10

EQUIPMENT:	10- or 12-cup bundt pan or tube pan, large mixing bowl
COOKING TIME:	14 to 16 minutes (Low Wattage ovens 17 to 19½ minutes)
STANDING TIME:	10 minutes
NUTRITIONAL PROFILE:	high calories, low sodium, low cholesterol

1½	**cups sugar**
6	**egg whites**
¾	**cup corn or soybean oil**
2	**teaspoons vanilla extract**
2	**cups all-purpose flour, sifted**
1	**tablespoon pumpkin pie spice**
1	**teaspoon baking soda**
1	**6-ounce container vanilla yogurt**
2	**cups (about 8 whole carrots) finely shredded carrots**

Grease bundt pan or tube pan with solid shortening and lightly dust with sugar. Set aside. Mix sugar, egg whites, oil, and vanilla together in large mixing bowl and beat until well blended. Combine flour, pie spice, and baking soda. **Alternately** beat flour mixture and yogurt into sugar mixture. Stir in carrots and pour into prepared dish. (If dish is flat-bottomed, **elevate** on an inverted saucer.) Place on turntable if available. Microwave, **uncovered,** on 50 percent power or MEDIUM for 6 minutes (LW 7½ minutes). (**Rotate** dish ¼ turn every 3 minutes if not using turntable.)

Increase power to HIGH and cook for 8 to 10 minutes (LW 9½ to 12 minutes) or until top appears almost dry. (**Rotate** dish ¼ turn every 3 minutes if not using turntable.) Let **stand** on hard heatproof surface for 10 minutes, then invert onto serving plate. Once cool, frost with pineapple icing (recipe follows).

FOR EACH SERVING:
356 calories
133 mg sodium
1 mg cholesterol
13 g fat

PINEAPPLE ICING

YIELDS ENOUGH TO FROST A 10-SERVING CAKE

EQUIPMENT: medium bowl
NUTRITIONAL PROFILE: low calories, low sodium, no cholesterol

1 tablespoon soft-spread margarine
2 tablespoons unsweetened pineapple juice
¼ teaspoon pineapple extract
1 cup powdered sugar

In medium mixing bowl, blend together margarine, pineapple juice, and extract. Add the sugar and beat until well blended. Spread on cooled cake.

FOR EACH SERVING:
83 calories
11 mg sodium
0 mg cholesterol
1 g fat

Chocolate Pound Cake

SERVES 10

EQUIPMENT: 2-quart glass ring mold, small and large mixing bowls, electric mixer

COOKING TIME: 13 to 15 minutes (Low Wattage ovens 15¾ to 17¾ minutes)

STANDING TIME: 10 minutes

NUTRITIONAL PROFILE: high calories, moderate sodium, low cholesterol

¾ **cup cocoa**
2 **tablespoons corn or soybean oil**
8 **ounces low-fat cottage cheese**
¾ **cup soft-spread margarine**
1 **cup sugar**
6 **egg whites**
1 **teaspoon vanilla extract**
1¾ **cups all-purpose flour**
1¼ **teaspoons baking powder**
1 **21-ounce can cherry pie filling**

Grease with solid shortening and lightly sugar ring mold; set aside. Mix cocoa and oil together in small bowl; set aside.

Whip cottage cheese in blender or with electric mixer until smooth. Place whipped cottage cheese, margarine, and sugar in large bowl. With an electric mixer, beat until light and fluffy. **Beat** in egg whites one at a time. Blend in vanilla and cocoa mixture.

Add flour and baking powder, mixing well. Spoon batter into prepared dish and microwave on 30 percent or LOW power for 7 minutes (LW 8¼ minutes). **Raise** power to HIGH and microwave for 6 to 8 minutes (LW 7½ to 9½ minutes) or until there are no moist spots on top and cake begins to come away from the sides of the dish, **rotating** dish ½ turn every 3 minutes. Let **stand** on a hard heatproof surface for 10 minutes. After standing, **invert** onto a serving dish. Once cool, slice and serve each portion topped with cherry pie filling.

Troubleshooting: Be aware that you will not be able to whip all of the curd out of the cottage cheese; just whip until as smooth as possible.

Suggestions: For an attractive presentation, slice each portion into thirds and alternately layer the cake and pie filling in footed dessert or Champagne glasses.

Wrap any leftover cake tightly in plastic wrap to keep it from drying out.

FOR EACH SERVING:
380 calories
251 mg sodium
3 mg cholesterol
13 g fat

CHOCOLATE

Recent studies have shown chocolate products are not harmful to our health as was once thought—they're not even bad for your skin. The fat source in chocolate does not clog the arteries, so you may enjoy your chocolate and still eat healthfully. There are several liquid chocolate baking products on the market that are great for convenience but are high in sodium and calories. By substituting cocoa powder and adding polyunsaturated oil you can produce the same chocolate, only healthier.

Fruitcake Ring

This very moist cake needs no icing.

SERVES 10

EQUIPMENT: 2-quart glass ring mold, small and large mixing bowls, custard cup
COOKING TIME: 15½ to 19 minutes (Low Wattage ovens 19 to 23 minutes)
STANDING TIME: 10 minutes
NUTRITIONAL PROFILE: high calories, low sodium, no cholesterol

½ **cup chopped unsalted nuts, 1 tablespoon reserved and finely chopped**
½ **cup soft-spread margarine**
1 **cup dark brown sugar**

> 3   egg whites
> 1   tablespoon grated orange or lemon zest
> 1   teaspoon vanilla extract
> 3   tablespoons orange or lemon juice
> 2   cups all-purpose flour
> ½   teaspoon baking soda
> ½   cup golden raisins
> ½   cup maraschino cherries, each cherry cut into thirds
> 1   cup chopped dates
> 1   cup skim milk

GLAZE
> ⅓   cup sugar
> 6   tablespoons orange juice

Grease ring mold with solid shortening and sprinkle with finely chopped nuts. In large mixing bowl, **cream** together margarine and brown sugar. Beat in egg whites and add orange zest, vanilla, and 3 tablespoons orange juice. **Sift** flour and baking soda together. Place raisins, cherries, and dates in small bowl and add 3 tablespoons of the flour mixture, tossing until well coated.

Add the remaining flour mixture to the creamed mixture, alternately with the milk. Stir in fruits and nuts and spoon into prepared mold. (If mold is flat-bottomed, **elevate** on an inverted saucer.) Microwave on 50 percent power or MEDIUM for 9 minutes (LW 10¾ minutes), **rotating** mold ¼ turn every 3 minutes. **Increase** power to HIGH and cook for 6 to 9 minutes (LW 7½ to 10¾ minutes) or until cake pulls away from the sides of the mold and there are no visible moist spots on top, rotating mold ¼ turn every 3 minutes. Let **stand** on a hard heatproof surface for 10 minutes. Invert to serving plate.

Pierce top of cake all over (while still warm) with a long wooden pick or meat fork. In custard cup, combine sugar and 6 tablespoons orange juice. Microwave, **uncovered,** on HIGH for 30 to 60 seconds (LW 45 to 90 seconds) or until very warm, **stirring** until sugar is dissolved. Drizzle over cake, allowing glaze to drip down into the holes. When cake is completely cool, cover tightly and let **stand overnight**.

FOR EACH SERVING:
409 calories
128 mg sodium
0 mg cholesterol
9 g fat

Pumpkin Bread

SERVES 8

EQUIPMENT:	9-inch glass ring mold, large mixing bowl, wire cooling rack
COOKING TIME:	13 to 16 minutes (Low Wattage ovens 15½ to 19 minutes)
STANDING TIME:	5 to 10 minutes
NUTRITIONAL PROFILE:	high calories, low sodium, no cholesterol

⅓ **cup soft-spread margarine**
1 **cup sugar**
¼ **cup dark brown sugar**
3 **egg whites**
1 **cup canned pumpkin**
2 **tablespoons orange juice**
2 **cups all-purpose flour**
½ **teaspoon baking powder**
1 **teaspoon baking soda**
½ **teaspoon freshly grated nutmeg**
1 **teaspoon ground cinnamon**
1 **cup raisins**
½ **cup chopped unsalted walnuts**

Grease ring mold with solid shortening and set aside. In large mixing bowl, **cream** together margarine, sugar, and brown sugar. Beat in egg whites, add pumpkin, and orange juice. **Sift** together flour, baking powder, baking soda, nutmeg, and cinnamon and blend into pumpkin mixture. Stir in raisins and nuts.

Spoon batter into prepared dish and microwave on 50 percent power or MEDIUM for 9 minutes (LW 10¾ minutes). **Increase** power to HIGH and microwave for 4 to 7 minutes (LW 4¾ to 8¼ minutes) or until a toothpick inserted comes out clean, **rotating** dish ¼ turn every 3 minutes. Let **stand** on hard heatproof surface for 5 to 10 minutes before removing from mold to cooling rack.

FOR EACH SERVING:
437 calories
180 mg sodium
0 mg cholesterol
9 g fat

Index .